Love Time & Butter

THE BROILING,
ROASTING,
BAKING,
DEEP-FAT FRYING,
SAUTÉING
BRAISING,
AND BOILING

COOK BOOK

JOE HYDE

♈

RICHARD W. BARON
NEW YORK
1971

This book is for
those people who have helped me to be where I am:

Virginia Gandy and Dr. Robert Bartlett Haas
of the U.C.L.A. Extension,
Kent and Molly Leavitt, Eric and Anne Giegler,
all of my students,
and last but not least,
my family:
Gail, Barry, Philip and Annie

First published in 1971 by the Richard W. Baron
Publishing Co., Inc.
Library of Congress Catalog Card Number: 77-88495
Printed in the United States of America
SBN 0-87777-011-5

Illustrated by
Robert Strimban

Contents

Preface   1

Introduction   11

General Information   17

Hints from the Author   21

The Kitchen   23

Chapter One: Stocks, Soups and Sauces   29

Chapter Two: Broiling   53

Chapter Three: Roasting   63

Chapter Four: Baking   87

Chapter Five: Deep-fat Frying   101

Chapter Six: Sautéing   109

Chapter Seven: Braising   129

Chapter Eight: Boiling   145

Chapter Nine: Salads   177

Index   183

Preface

I SUPPOSE I should say a little about why I cook. Well, first of all I love to eat, and always have. When I was eight years old I remember returning home for lunch, feeling very bilious from my first encounter with a cigarette. Mama had cooked my favorite meal for us (we were four children)— flounder pan-fried in butter with exquisite fresh peas and a platter of large slices of vine-ripened tomatoes literally covered with chopped parsley, a little garlic, and, I would imagine, some salt. We were at our home on Martha's Vineyard. The water surrounds us there and is very close to the house on the seaside. The sea was so calm, the sun so warm and comforting. It was one of those days that lift you away from reality. It makes you feel so good, unless, of course, you have just smoked an entire cigarette and feel like throwing up. I missed a greal meal.

The only other meal cooked by my mother that I missed (I think she was a great cook as well as a most precious person) was a macaroni and cheese affair. This time it was her fault. Because she had an inventive mind, and because we had to cart the drinking and cooking water in jugs from town, she had decided to boil the macaroni in sea water. I guess she figured that if it worked for lobsters, corn, and poached fish, then why not for macaroni? It was awful—so salty it was inedible.

The main event during the summer months was her jam and jelly business. One summer she made $750; not bad for the Thirties. Blueberry jam was first. We all helped pick the berries, with small pails hanging from our necks to free our hands for picking. She always put some lemon into the blueberry jam. Then came the wild cherries for jelly. To pick these, she pulled her old Ford up under the tree and put a sheet over the car, with the center on the roof and the four corners held high by long poles. We all climbed up on the sheet-covered car roof and pulled the bunches of cherries down on top of us. In no time we had picked twenty or thirty pounds of cherries. We were streaked with dark purple, and so was the car, which stayed that way (fading just in time for the next season). A wild-cherry picker's car would look that way, I supposed. It was fun!

The beach plums came in September. It wasn't hard to find and pick as many as we wanted. But it wasn't much fun either, because they didn't taste very good (unless you came across a great big deep purple one) and the bushes were scratchy. To prepare the beach-plum jam, my mother sat on the porch in the sun for hours, removing the pits from the fruit. She always made more beach-plum jam and jelly than anything else, so it was a long job. But she loved it, at least when she was sitting right there on the planks of the porch in the warm sun, surrounded by the busy sound of the breaking waves and the comforting voices of her children playing in the sand dunes—clothed in a long red sarong with big white flowers or totally naked with only the privacy that her long black hair and the large wood salad bowls filled with beach plums afforded her. She was a warm and infectiously delightful person. Her jams, jellies, all of her cooking—everything she did was a reflection of her. I don't think it matters what you do, say, or cook; it will be good if you put your heart and soul into it.

We were sad when summer was over. For us it meant school; for Mama, it meant the end of the warm summer days at the Vineyard camp by the sea and a long wait for the blueberrying in June. She had a bad heart, and after the beach plums one autumn, when we all had gone away to school, she died. I felt very sad, and I still do, but I feel very close to her because I am cooking, and I love to cook, and she would like that.

If I wasn't in love with my mother, at least I adored her and was crushed when she died. The transition from those warm Vineyard days with naked Mama and her wonderful beach plums to the flimsy values of a rich boys' boarding school was hectic and cruel. My marks were terrible, but not because I was dumb; I just didn't care. What was so important about *puer, pueris,* etc.? That is, compared to a good batch of beach-plum jam. I

played football so hard (it was the only thing that made any sense to me, and the rich boys didn't play well) that I made the varsity in my third-form year at the age of fourteen and was captain in my last year. Then, at a college where relatively dumb boys go, I took a number of courses in French and found a terrific French professor who gave me private lessons in conversational French. I enjoyed the friendship of the drama coach and his wife, and did some acting, topped off by what the local paper and I thought was an excellent job as the lead in *A Bell for Adano.* I wanted to be an actor. My coach friend and his wife said it was a bad life and dissuaded me from doing the only thing I really wanted to do.

In the spring of 1950 I was in my senior year and didn't know what work I wanted to do. I liked entertaining people, so it occurred to me that the hotel business might be a possibility—not making beds, because I hate to make beds, but somewhere there might be a place for me. Mr. Kurt Schifeler, manager of the Hotel Raleigh in Washington, D. C., hired me as an on-the-job trainee for $20 a week. I was to work in all parts of the hotel, beginning in the kitchen and winding up, I presumed, in his chair. He enjoyed himself, eating too much and lavishly entertaining all the greats in the world of Grand Opera. He sang bass, very, very bass. I'll never forget the morning all twelve cooks in the hotel kitchen stopped work to listen to him sing over the local radio station (it must have been Wagner). Lord, what a noise he made! Even the copper pots trembled.

My first assignment was the roast section. A big, wonderful white-haired Italian presided over that part of the kitchen. He liked me, and we had a great time together, especially when Welsh rarebit was on the menu (almost every day). Every waiter giving an order had to deliver a glass of beer. If the order was for more than one Welsh rarebit and the waiter brought only one beer, Alfonso would get very angry. Now when a cook gets angry, there's a standard procedure. He grabs the nearest, biggest pot by the handle, lifts it into the air, and brings it crashing down on the stove. If the pot has some sauce in it, there's quite a mess. But usually the chef chooses an empty pot, because he knows he'll just have to remake the sauce or whatever it was that flew up into the air.

So we drank beer all the time. Once (I guess as a joke) Alfonso actually put some beer into the Welsh rarebit. He laughed like a demon, for the beer curdled the potful of rarebit. Still laughing, Alfonso threw it away. He must have dreamed up the business of putting beer into rarebit. What a genius, what a racket! Speaking of rackets, we played the numbers. (You had to or they'd think you were an informer.) In addition to the Welsh rarebit, we made all the omelettes as well as large frying pans full of home-fried potatoes, which Alfonso would turn by heaving the whole panful high into the air like a twenty- or thirty-pound pancake. The potatoes would turn beautifully in the air and fall back perfectly into the pan, brown side up. That was something to watch! Alfonso let me try it once. The solid mass of potatoes went up in the air, but only a small part found the pan on the return flight; the rest made a big *woosh* as it hit the floor. Alfonso laughed and said something incredibly dirty in Italian. Kitchen language is not just a

little off-color; it's totally foul. There's a competition to see who can say the worst thing.

Mr. Jean Mores, the chef, stayed in his glass-enclosed office, working on menus and ordering; a really fine man. At the other end of the kitchen was the pastry shop (*patisserie*) and his exalted highness, the pastry chef, who was the kind of man who has manicures. His mustache was waxed and pointed, his chef's hat beautifully pleated. His long white apron almost touched the tops of his brilliant shoes. I worked in the pastry shop for two weeks. All I did was make Melba toast. The chef was too fussy to let me touch anything else. When he was working on a huge wedding cake, I couldn't make a noise. The pastry chef didn't talk to the cooks, and they didn't talk to him. He was much too fancy. I didn't get to the sauce section or the butcher shop because the Korean War began and I was drafted.

I went to Fort Devens in Massachusetts and then to Camp Cook in California. It is near Santa Barbara, where my father and two sisters live with their families. I guess I had put something on paper about my cooking at the Raleigh, because the company warrant officer in charge of the mess asked if I would be a cook. I said yes, if he would let me cook with wine. Then I got a pass, went to Santa Monica, and bought a copy of Betty Crocker's cookbook. The next day at 6:00 A.M. I was in the mess kitchen when the warrant officer arrived with three gallons of wine. After the breakfast for 170 men of the Heavy Mortar Company, the mess sergeant told me to cook the chicken for lunch. He was pretty impressed with the wine business, so he let me alone. I cut the fifty chickens into quarters and threw them into large roasting pans and then into the oven at who-knows-what temperature—if only Alfonso had been there.

Eventually the chickens were all brown (parched might be a better word). Betty Crocker's chicken recipes had given me a few ideas, I used a few of my own, and, of course, I had my eye on the wine. I had no idea when to use it, but there didn't seem to be any big hurry. But I did have to surround the chicken with some kind of liquid. I mixed lots of flour in with the chicken, then quantities of catsup (four gallons, I think), a handful of bay leaves, and a bottle of Frank's Hot Sauce. All this began to simmer, and since lunch time was near, I decided to use the sherry. It took most of a gallon to thin the sauce. Boy, what an aroma! The taste was incredible. The point is that those soldiers ate it. I was amazed.

During the time at Camp Cook I was able to visit my family. My father was bulldozing a lake on top of a mountain. The local zoning board had refused his application to build on the property. He had quite a hassle with it until he thought of making a lake with a houseboat on it, which he did with much fanfare and hoopla in the Santa Barbara press. I think even the Coast Guard got into it. It was terrific. My father is something. He's built innumerable houses, he knows all about spiders and minerals, he makes jewelry out of strange rocks, and he has written many novels and short stories. He drills horizontally into the sides of cliffs for water, and he's an expert player of the game "Go," having outgrown chess, at which he was a master.

From California we were sent to Japan. It was terrific; so many different sounds, smells, and sights. Our company spent nine months at Camp Schimmelpfennig in Sendai. There we had a battalion mess, which meant feeding five hundred men. It's hard to say much about the food. It was awful! My most unnerving experience in Sendai was cutting up a whole cow for stew. I had no idea how to dice a cow, and Betty Crocker was not much help. Our team of cooks worked two days a week, which left plenty of time for traveling, and this, of course, involved eating Japanese foods. I was flabbergasted by the beauty of the platter of beef and vegetables that went into the sukiyaki. The dish has fair taste, but after seeing those huge platters with the perfectly cut vegetables, the taste was forgotten.

In Korea we cooked in a field kitchen and took the chow in insulated cans to the boys in their bunkers. There I did help the army a bit. While hamburgers and steak may keep warm in a steaming can, they certainly do get tough. When the menu said steak, I always made stew. I made a casserole dish with the hamburger meat. I browned the meat, poured off the fat, added garlic, bay leaf, onion, and tomato purée, and simmered the meat sauce for two hours. Then I put layers of cooked elbow macaroni, sauce, and sliced American cheese into deep pans until they were full. The whole affair was baked for an hour; one pan went out to each platoon. The boys liked it. They called it "Holy Mattress." Korea is a beautiful country. We spent nine months there, then took another month to get home. I worked in the officers' mess aboard the ship that brought us home, slept on the floor and ate great quantities of vanilla ice cream topped with sliced frozen strawberries.

A civilian again, I took a job as a room clerk at the Hotel Statler, opposite Pennsylvania Station in New York. After six months of selling rooms, I asked for a job in the banquet department. They said I could have a job when I knew more about food. (Of course, the menus of most large hotels are French.) "You mean I should go to France and learn fancy cooking?" I asked. I had spent six weeks in the summer of 1947 bicycling through France and putting in the usual two hours at mealtime, eating and drinking wine. French food is good. They really know how to do it. They care.

So there I was in Paris with about $600, staying in an awful hotel on a street with a perfectly beautiful name, *Passage de la Petite Boucherie* (Little Butcher Shop Alley). I was offered a job in a small restaurant on the Left Bank. The proprietor explained that I must be a member of the union before he could hire me. At the union they said I could not become a member until I had the job. In France that is when everyone throws their arms up in the air; it's called a *cul de sac* (dead end). Through UNESCO I got a job in a Lyonnaise restaurant by way of a system in which the French Hotel Association exchanges hotel apprentices with forty nations. It was complicated, because the United States does not take part in these exchanges, which is too bad for us.

I had gotten a job at the Raleigh for Gilles Savin, and he in turn got me a job at the Restaurant Chez Nandron in Lyons. The arrangements had taken three months. When I arrived at the station in Lyons I had two thousand francs left (that was about $6). Gilles' father was to meet me, so I looked around for someone looking for a stranger and finally homed in on a man who advanced with arm outstretched. I told him that Gilles had sent his love, and we shook hands for the longest time. (The French love to shake hands.) It was *not* M. Savin. Finally *he* found me, and I spent the next day, with M. Savin as my guide, getting identity cards, work permits, and finally some white cook's jackets and a few hats, called *toques*. Mme. Savin starched and ironed the toques for my debut in Nandron's kitchen at 8:00 A.M. I was pretty excited about the job. There was so much I wanted to learn about the French kitchen. During the previous three months I had been eating in very inexpensive cafés, where workmen came at midday and lots of people sat at the same tables together, sharing the wine, bread, and conversation. The food was always superb. One ingredient was always present—it must have been love. The French have an expression—If you eat well and love well, your work will take care of itself.

I was late to work the first morning. I changed into my white cook's outfit and hurried to the kitchen. It was full of activity. The cooks were chopping vegetables, cleaning fish, and stirring the contents of huge copper pots on a big black stove standing in the center of the room. There were work tables along the walls. One by one, all of the twelve men stopped working and looked in my direction. Soon the kitchen was silent, with all eyes fixed on what was later called *L'Amerlo* (a mixture of "the American" and a bad word in French.) I had no idea what to say, so I proceeded to announce in a loud voice, *"Bonjour, je m'appelle Joe."* I'm sure such a stark introduction crippled their sensitive Gallic regard for etiquette. The silence continued, the pots bubbled, the chef (the man with the tallest hat) whispered to a boy next to him. The young man left the kitchen, returning with a large bushel of what looked like dead sparrows. He put it next to the drainboard, where a big bearded man stripped to the waist had been washing pots. The chef took one of the birds and, beckoning to me, proceeded to pluck the feathers from it. I followed suit. He left me with the birds, and the activity resumed. Occasionally water splashed over the drainboard onto the birds and me, but I felt the worst had passed. The pot washer spoke to me. He was Italian and had been a prizefighter by the name of Dino Tempesti. He had fought in the United States and loved to talk about America and his days of glory. He later showed me all his newspaper clippings. After I had plucked a few of the birds, which turned out to be larks, one of the cooks came over and grabbed one and started to pluck it. Then another cook joined him, and soon all of them were standing around the bushel. They asked me where I lived, if I were rich, and was it really true that Americans eat jelly with meat. Do they eat complete dinners from tin cans? We talked about Indians, cowboys, and Marcel Cerdan, the great French middleweight. One of the young apprentice cooks (he was about thirteen years old—I was also an apprentice—age twenty-five!) brought a bottle of cool, dry, white wine, which we drank while we worked on the larks. Although I was an apprentice, the first cooks let me eat with them because of my age. Fried tripe was the first meal; we often ate pigs' heads and feet or Coq au Vin made with just the peeled chicken gizzards. Each chef

had his own bottle of Beaujolais. Vast quantities of bread were consumed with each meal. The pastry chef brought parts of tortes and cakes from the previous evening and a large platter of bits and pieces of the many French cheeses. Twice the chef asked me to contribute to the help's dinner, so once I baked beans and another time prepared platters of bacon, lettuce, and tomato sandwiches. The sandwiches were a big hit; the beans were not.

During the two hours of mealtime, the only word that describes the kitchen is "mayhem." The chef screamed the orders written on slips handed to him by the waiters. Two moules marinière, one escargots, one chateaubriand, and one civet de lièvre. The fish cook's apprentice grabbed a copper pot and raced to the walk-in icebox. But he couldn't find the mussels as he frantically pushed crocks of sauce to one side and uncovered other crocks. He came upon one and called to the apprentice sauce cook, "Hey, Michel, here's the lièvre." Michel pushed in and dug his big spoon into the crock of wild hare engulfed in an almost black red wine sauce. He filled his small pot and pushed his way out of the crowded icebox. The roast cook had already unhooked the long fillet or tenderloin from which the chateaubriand was to be cut. The apprentice *poissonier* (fish cook) yelled in despair, *"Hey, Chef, où sont les moules?"* ("Where are the mussels?") They were already cooking on the stove. The chef had gotten them out of a bag in the fish drawer, where fish were kept packed in ice.

There were so many different kinds of fish. All colors, shapes, and sizes. On bouillabaisse days, a bushel of all kinds of little fish arrived from the

6

Mediterranean, some no larger than your thumb. One day when we returned from the afternoon break, there on the workbench was a sturgeon that weighed three hundred pounds. What a big fish! We all worked on it. After skinning, it was filleted and cut into thin slices. I expected to see a whale in the kitchen one day. Another time there were eight deer hanging from the kitchen ceiling by their feet. We butchered and cleaned them. All the meat was put into crocks with celery, carrots, onions, garlic (whole heads cut in half), bay leaves, peppercorns, and thyme, and all this was covered with Beaujolais red wine. The meat lasted for months.

Two afternoons a week the other apprentices and I went to a cooking school run by the town. As we passed restaurants, other apprentices joined us. They were all about thirteen or younger. As I wandered along to the school, my brood ever-increasing, I felt like the Pied Piper. They enjoyed me as I enjoyed them. Once, when the old retired chef was trying to explain the variations of Sauce Béarnaise, they raised hell, and we all had to turn around and face the wall for five minutes.

At Nandron's there were two things I tasted that really impressed me. One was the Béarnaise sauce and the other was the white wine sauce for fish. How good they were! I didn't learn how to make the Béarnaise until I got to Chez Point. M. Savin had arranged for me to do a tour of duty in Lyons at the Restaurant de la Pyramid Chez M. Fernand Point, through the restaurant's chef, M. Paul Mercies. They say about Lyons that there are three rivers—the Rhône, the Saône, and the Beaujolais. This last one really did appeal to me. (M. Savin once came to see me at the Nandron to tell me he had heard I was drinking too much Beaujolais.)

At Chez Point the kitchen was large, with a huge stove in the middle. There were no big grates or chimneys above the broad iron surface of the coal-burning stove. Instead, it had a chimney that went under the floor to the wall, and then up. Besides being beautiful, it was practical, because the cooks could work all around it. There were doors to the ovens on either side. The walls of the kitchen were white tile with a continuous row of copper pots circling the whole room. The floor was dark red tile. The menu was very small with specialties of the hour recurring often. The dishes were carefully prepared—each was a little jewel AND NOT COMPLICATED!

The terrace outside the restaurant was canopied by large trees and overlooked a beautiful rose garden with paths of freshly raked red sand. M. Point was huge and fussy. One day I wandered out of the kitchen while I was smoking a cigarette. He saw me and I thought I felt an earthquake. "How dare you smoke in the kitchen!" He was also a joker. I had changed my clothes and was about to leave for the afternoon. I put my jacket on a table and was washing my hands when he came in. *"Petit, cherche-moi une bouteille."* (He drank great quantities of only the very best champagnes.) I went to get him some. When I had returned with the bottle and poured him a glass, he asked for a large glass bowl. "Pour the rest of the bottle in there and drink it." I began to drink, and he proceeded to tease me about drinking from a bowl. The French are too much.

He left; I finished my bowl of bubbles and put

on my jacket. When I reached the gate of the restaurant, M. Point stepped from behind a tree and ordered, *"Arrêtez*—stop!" He said he was checking all the help to make sure they weren't stealing from him. He looked in the pockets of my jacket and proceeded to pull out handfuls of watercress, which he had obviously planted while I was getting his champagne. He pretended to be furious. "Most cooks steal meat or something worthwhile. It takes an American to want to steal watercress!" He was delighted with his joke. What a character!

There was nothing funny about M. Point's restaurant. There were almost as many help as customers. They often served as few as thirty for a given meal. At mealtime, no one was allowed to talk in the kitchen but the chef, who announced the waiters' orders and later commanded them when the waiters returned to pick them up. That chef's job was not easy. A meal at Chez Point consisted of nine parts. Counting two announcements for each dish and almost twenty announcements for each client, an average of forty customers per meal required almost eight hundred announcements. I worked with the *poissonier* for two months. His name was Claude, and he hated Americans. But he was not unkind to me. Occasionally he booted me in the rear when I made a mistake. Once I kicked him back, much to the pleasure of the chef, who liked me and hated Claude. There are recipes from Point's Restaurant de la Pyramid in this book. Some I did not include because I can't find the same ingredients we used at Chez Point.

Too soon I was back in the States and working as chef in the Jupiter Island Golf Club Restaurant in Hobe Sound, Florida. I was under the chef who handled the big restaurant. I got ingredients and much-needed advice from him. One wild recipe I decided to try on my clients was chicken poached inside a pig's bladder. I had brought the dried bladders with me from France. First the trussed chicken is put into the presoaked bladder, then vegetables (celery, carrots, onions), chicken stock, and some Madeira. The bag is tied tightly and put into the stockpot, where it soon blows up like a balloon. One hour later this balloon is delivered to the guest on a platter. The bladder is cut and the juicy chicken carved and served. Among the famous recipients of this delicious but seemingly outlandish dish were Mr. Marshall Field and the poet Sir Osbert Sitwell.

I went on to be chef at the Misqamicut Club in Watch Hill, Rhode Island, the following summer, and that was my last chef's job for a bit. I felt I had to work under someone and learn a great deal more. I worked for six months at the Waldorf-Astoria kitchen in New York and one year at the Brussels, also in New York, as assistant sauce cook. I worked as chef at the Holiday House in Malibu, California, and then as second cook at the Chalet Froscati in Santa Monica, California, where we fed more than three hundred at each meal. Cooking in such quantities becomes terrible drudgery, so I decided to try to teach cooking. I went to the extension office of the University of California at Los Angeles and told them they should have a class in cooking. They agreed, and set up three sections for the next semester. The teaching was fun, and I learned as much as the students. Within a year I was teaching six sessions a week, each with thirty students. Then the house in Palisade, New York, left me by my mother, became vacant. It was a huge house with a large kitchen. I decided to teach cooking there.

During my Waldorf-Astoria days I had married and had two children. Since I needed more money, I began doing some catering. It's a lucrative business, and I began doing more and more of it. I had brought a big fish poacher back from France. Large poached fish became my specialty. Roast saddle of lamb, my mother's peas, endive meunière, and M. Point's potatoes were my main course specialties. For dessert, I concocted an orange mousse and whipped-cream meringue flavored with Kirsch and Grand Marnier. Of course, I always use freshly squeezed oranges.

Now I have given up teaching and just cater, but I did learn something that I have tried to pass on to you in this book: a way of understanding cooking, to see it as a subject with a structure rather than as a series of recipes. There are methods of cooking which you must understand first. Then the dishes and recipes themselves will be easy.

Introduction

Grouping recipes according to the methods of cooking and devoting one chapter to each method seems to me to be an orderly way of teaching and understanding cooking. Once you have learned the method, the recipes will be easy.

So what's cooking? Cooking is applying heat to raw food to make it taste good. Cooking is also dealing with raw meats and vegetables—using your hands, a knife, a rolling pin, or peeler to make them ready to eat. Some foods are eaten raw, but others must be subjected to heat. What kind of heat? Where does it come from? How much heat and for how long? With what result? The methods of applying heat to food are called Boiling, Sautéing, Braising, Roasting, Baking, Broiling, and Deep-Fat Frying. These methods, described in detail and with demonstrating recipes, form the main sections of this book.

You never roast a minnow, deep-fat fry ribs of beef, or poach calves' liver. Tiny minnows, called "shiners" by fishermen and known to gourmets as whitebait, take so little time to cook that they must be fried in deep fat. Deep-fat frying is the quickest way of cooking. What do you roast? Large pieces of meat. Where? In the oven. Why? The hot air surrounding the meat browns it on all sides and the heat slowly directs itself toward the cold center of the roast. For how long? That depends on the thickness of the meat. Use the time schedule that follows each recipe in the chapter about roasting. To achieve an evenly pink rib roast is a sure thing and not a hit-or-miss proposition. A slice of liver a ½ inch thick must be brown on both sides and on the table within 10 minutes. The best way to do this is on top of the stove with a little butter in a preheated frying pan. This is called sautéing. The brown cover is important to seal in the juices, and for its good taste, texture, and appearance. The same thin slice of liver roasted in the oven would be dry and inedible by the time it had achieved any color. However, a leg of lamb cannot be sautéed because it would get too brown before it was cooked through. Also, one browned side would get cold while the other side was browning. In the oven, all sides of the lamb get equal heat.

There are obvious and simple answers as to why you do what you do in cooking. The water for poached fish must barely simmer. Why? Because if the water boils, the fish, which is quite fragile, will break. Why does beef have to go into a very hot preheated oven to roast? It has to get a brown crust right away to seal in the juice. Why seal in the juice? Because the juice is a lubrication that makes the meat easy to swallow. To sauté stew meat, the meat must be put into a hot pan that contains a little hot butter or fat. Again, the meat must brown right away to seal in the juice. If the pan is cold, the cubes of stew meat will boil, since meat is composed of more than 50 percent water. If it boils, the juice will come out of the meat and the meat will be dry and stringy. No amount of simmering in an accompanying sauce will put the juice back into the meat. The brown cover on meat imparts taste and color to the sauce. If may be important not to undercook anything, but it is more important not to overcook it. Given the choice, I'd choose to undercook. I have sometimes served roast chicken that was still pink next to the joint and thighbone. In France, where chicken roasted to order is a specialty, a little pink at this joint is proof that the chicken has been roasted to perfection.

There is an important message in this book other than the description of methods of cooking. It is that when meats and vegetables are exposed to heat, they will *continue to cook* when separated from the heat. This cooking away from heat, or *reposing,* must be considered part of the cooking time. A steak will continue to cook through after it has been removed from the heat, but without suffering the drying effect that continued exposure to heat would have on it.

There is so much that can be said about cooking. What follows here will be brief and, I hope, useful. Here are a few of my feelings about cooking, cookbooks, and you. If there is a single word to use as a byword to cooking and to understanding what all cooking involves, that word is *simplicity.*

The menu must be simple. Too many dishes full of too many ingredients and conflicting tastes compete with each other and confuse the diners. The dishes on a menu should complement one another. Cook what you feel like cooking and eating. Don't just cook what you think your guests would enjoy. It's been said that it's impossible for someone who doesn't drink coffee to make a pot of good coffee. What would be a simple recipe for an experienced cook might be too hard for a beginner. Choose a menu using recipes you really understand. Don't show off. Serve no more than three courses, not counting salad. Salad is unnecessary in a dinner menu where two or more vegetables are served because it just makes too much to eat. How do you compose a menu? You have to begin somewhere, by deciding on a dessert you feel like eating and something you feel like cooking. How about fresh peas? Perhaps a roast of veal. Then choose another vegetable, a potato dish, and a dessert. A good rule is no more than one thick sauce per meal.

Color is important in making a menu. A meal beginning with vichyssoise, followed by veal in a cream sauce, mashed potatoes, cauliflower, endive salad, and seedless grapes in sour cream with brown sugar tastes good, but everything is white. Begin a meal with tomato salad, followed by rare beef, beets, carrots, then strawberries for dessert and you have the same problem in red. The colors must be different.

Shapes, too, must vary. Thin slices of smoked salmon followed by a sliced meat and then orange slices result in too many flat shapes. If you serve little cherry tomatoes, do not make little round potato balls. You could slice the potatoes or cut them into cubes. There are all shapes: carrots, string beans, and asparagus are long, peas and tomatoes are round, while branches of cauliflower have an interesting and individual shape. Potatoes, squash, and eggplant can all be cut into various shapes to lend contrast.

Taste, too, may vary in a menu. A highly spiced meat course should be accompanied by a bland vegetable. Suppose you choose to add shrimps or bay scallops to ratatouille. The obvious accompaniment is boiled rice. Ratatouille is highly seasoned and very rich. Rice is its exact opposite. However, this rule does not follow in all cases. If you chose to serve poached halibut, you could not serve a highly seasoned vegetable like mustard greens and garlic because the big taste would dominate and destroy the effectiveness of the delicate poached fish. The halibut is the star, and cannot be upstaged, either by an accompanying vegetable or by anything in the entire menu. Pick a vegetable that will give a subtle contrast in taste. String beans, for instance. What sauce? Hollandaise—perfect with poached fish.

There is still another consideration other than color, shape, and taste. That is consistency. Many meats, fruits, and vegetables owe their popularity to distinctive consistency. Avocado has a tiny taste but immeasurably delicate consistency. Calves' brains are practically tasteless, but are very soft. Tripe is chewy. So, in a menu everything cannot be soft. Something soft, like mashed potatoes or creamed spinach, could be served with something

crunchy, like an endive salad, and something chewy—meat.

Eating is fun. The French love to start a meal with something diverting and entertaining. Snails, artichokes, or frogs' legs. People forget their worries to laugh and enjoy their meals. So when you are planning a menu, think of contrasting colors, shapes, tastes, consistencies, and fun.

Cooking can be a great art. It appeals to all the senses. You look at food that is tastefully decorated, steaming, or even on fire. There is the delicious odor of meat roasting in the oven. You can even hear it softly sizzling its way to perfection. You bite into a tender steak or strip the soft kernels of corn from the cob. Which is the more important sense to satisfy? It's hard to pick between appearance and taste. I think appearance is the more important. That is the first impression, and it establishes a mood for what follows. Taste. If the presentation of a dish is dull or even ugly, a delicious taste can hardly make up for it. Happily, it's not difficult to make food look attractive, since often there is little time for decoration when what you have cooked must get to the table hot.

Platters and vegetable bowls of plain white china or silver are best for showing off what is served in or on them. Designs and color just compete with the looks of what you are serving and confuse the impression. Wooden platters and bowls are perfect for certain things—bread, salad, cold meats. A handsome plain glass bowl is ideal for serving cold soups, salads, and fruit desserts.

In the classic French kitchen there are a myriad of different garnishes to dress up a platter. The most important are parsley and watercress. Cress for meat and parsley for fish. A large roast on a platter surrounded by a small amount of brown sauce needs only a bouquet of watercress at one end. A handful of parsley sprigs suffices as decoration for a platter of fish meunière. When a meat, fowl, or fish is practically swimming in a sauce, there are other decorations employed. Sliced or chopped truffles, sliced olives, pieces of tomato, capers, chopped chives, sliced or quartered hard-boiled egg, anchovy fillets, onion rings, and chopped pickles are just a few decorative items for hot and cold dishes.

Orderliness is imperative in the arrangement of meat, fish, chicken, or vegetables on a platter. For example, carrots should be peeled, cooked, and served whole if possible. They should be neatly arranged in a shallow oval bowl or on a small platter. Melted butter should make them glisten. A sprinkling of parsley comes as a decorative finishing touch and should not be administered to camouflage careless cutting, cooking, or arrangement on the platter.

No decoration is better than too much. Cooked fresh spinach lightly sautéed in olive oil and butter is superb. A mound of it on a platter does not, cannot, and should not look too pretty. It just has to look like spinach. That's what it is—floppy, green, delicious spinach. Any decoration would be distracting and superfluous. (I hate sliced hard-boiled egg on spinach.)

What you serve should look its natural best. Of what you cook, you are the best judge of excellence. Be critical; don't consider just superficial beauty. Your work, to really be beautiful, should show the excellence of materials used and the un-

compromised quality of workmanship. Keep it simple. Understate when you season, plan menus, and decorate.

Originality is important. People love to see and eat something different. Be generous—large, handsome roasts, a big turkey. Amount is important, but individual helpings must be small. If you served a gigantic portion to someone with a modest appetite, it would seem vulgar and surely embarrass the guest if he had to leave unfinished half of what he was served. It is better to offer seconds and thirds.

Food must taste like what it is. Anything added must enhance this taste, not change or camouflage it. If the dish is chicken sautéed with tarragon, both the sauce and the chicken must still taste like chicken. The tarragon taste and the wine taste complement the chicken taste without dominating it. Added ingredients should assist in bringing out the taste of the food they accompany.

To achieve good cooking, you must use the best ingredients. Do not compromise. Always use heavy cream in soups and sauces when the recipe calls for it, never light cream. A small amount of heavy cream will whiten and enrich a sauce, whereas it would take more light cream to do the same job, with the disastrous result of further diluting the taste. It's hard enough to get good taste. Keep it at all costs.

My book tries to teach you cooking methods —a different method in each chapter. Each is introduced by a detailed description, the reasons for following one method instead of another, and what results to anticipate. I've tried hard to avoid omissions, especially those too often found in recipes—

those that may mean the difference between total success and total disaster.

In addition to the chapters on each method, there are chapters on stocks, soups, sauces, and salads, and also a chapter of general information on meats, fish, vegetables, and fresh fruits—and hints from the author. Not thousands of recipes, just my favorites and those that best show the method of cooking. In this book I want to share my adventures with you, to recount to you all of my experience and knowledge of each method of cooking and each recipe.

General Information

You SHOULD BUY the very best ingredients—heavy cream, pink veal, white firm mushrooms—never skimp or compromise on quality.

Meats

The quality of meat is very hard to judge. Find a good butcher, trust him, and pay his price without complaining. Carcasses are inspected by impartial government inspectors, graded and stamped according to their excellence. Just because a steak has a thick covering of very white fat does not mean it will be tender. I have had delicious and tender steaks with a thin, scrawny covering of yellow fat. Flecks of fat in beef, known as marbling, often indicate good quality. On the other hand, some very tender beef has no marbling whatsoever. Beef should be slightly pinker than deep red and must never be wet with blood or bleeding. The secret of good meat is aging, which breaks down tissue and tenderizes the meat. Good beef should age about two weeks, lamb for ten days. Pork and veal must be a very pale pink. Chickens must be plump with a full breast, not skinny. I prefer a chicken of 2½ pounds or smaller even for roasting. You get more of that delicious brown skin per bite than you do with a large, meaty roasting chicken. Pigeons, too, should be plump and no more than one pound each. Freezing is less harmful to ducks than to other meats and poultry. The fat seems to protect the meat and acts almost like an automatic baster as the duck roasts.

If you have to use a frozen steak, chop, slice of meat, or fish that is no more than one inch thick, I would suggest that the meat or fish be only partially defrosted. Remove the meat from the freezer and put it into the refrigerator for 8 hours instead of leaving it out at room temperature for 8 hours. Then fry or broil it in a soft-frozen stage. The brown exterior will then hold the juice in the meat. Otherwise most of the all-important juice will leak into the package the meat was defrosted in.

Fish

Fish must be very fresh. Very fresh fish has almost no odor at all. You can take it from there.

Vegetables

Most often small vegetables are better than large ones. Vegetables, like fish, should be fresh

to be at their best. Lettuce and cauliflower should be crisp; mushrooms very white; carrots, beans, broccoli, and asparagus firm and not rubbery.

Fruit

Whenever it's a problem of what to serve for dessert, fruit is the answer—fruit in its purest, simplest form. Like vegetables and fish, there is a tremendous variety to select from. Even in the winter there is a huge variety of fresh fruit on the market. The juice of the fruit is its best sauce. To make sauce for strawberries, strain a few of the smaller or bruised berries, add sugar and a bit of Kirschwasser. Sprinkle sliced peaches with lemon juice and sugar. More bizarre and not as pure would be to sprinkle a bowl of freshly cut up fruit with sugar, a little lemon juice, Cognac, Kirschwasser, Grand Marnier, and dark rum. Roman Beauty apples are good baked; Golden Delicious are good eating apples.

Finding the perfect-tasting ripe melon is always the experience of a lifetime. It should be slightly soft to the touch at the stem end, and should have a good smell that goes only with a ripe melon.

There's nothing I can't think of that lemon wouldn't improve except shredded wheat. Don't forget the skin; it gives great taste.

Used in moderation, Kirschwasser, along with vanilla bean, is the best friend of fruit desserts.

Hints from the Author

Keep salt in a bowl. Use Kosher salt—it's pure and feels better in your hand (which you should use instead of pouring salt from the spout of a box). Your fingers are a far better judge of quantity than a spout. Salt tends to draw the juice from meat, so you put it on just before cooking. Salting at the table is very unsatisfactory. Everything—all soups, vegetables, and meats—should have salt from the beginning to the end of their cooking. Time and experience will make your fingers a good judge of how much salt to use.

Pepper should be freshly ground, from a pepper grinder. It is almost impossible to get one that works well, but there are a few on the market that are dependable.

Sugar should be kept in a 5-pound glass container with vanilla beans. How many? As many as you can afford. They are expensive.

Egg yolks alone as thickening are risky. It is better to use them combined with flour. The same is true when you cook with sour cream. Flour will prevent curdling.

Wine used in cooking should always be dry wine, except in desserts.

Melted butter is the perfect sauce and the only ingredient that by itself constitutes a sauce. Don't worry about the repetition of butter; it can be used everywhere in the meal to great advantage.

In general, fresh herbs are so delicious that it's depressing even to consider the little bottles of dried ones.

Some of the great French restaurants feature simple dishes. The chefs of these restaurants are certainly capable of preparing more ornate specialties, but they know that in staying with simple dishes, perfection is nearer.

Work on one project at a time. Don't clutter up your work table or counter with ingredients for several dishes. Each project should be kept in a separate area of the counter.

Wash pots and utensils as you go along. Mealtime will arrive with a kitchen neat and ready to receive the dirty dishes from the dinner table.

Relax! Be calm! Have fun! If you drop the chicken on the floor, don't let it upset you; just wash it off. If the phone rings, don't answer it. If you break a plate, get it into the wastebasket as quickly as possible. If the sauce begins to burn on the bottom of the pot, change pots. If the roast beef turns out well done, don't be upset. If you lack an ingredient for a recipe, omit it; most recipes have too many ingredients anyway. No music, cats, dogs, bills pinned to the wall, children, or canaries should be present in the kitchen to distract you while you are creating.

Be temperamental! It's expected of a good cook. Even if you have not achieved that reputation, you can at least be in character. Have a glass of wine. It's a perfect kitchen drink. Have three glasses of wine if it pleases you. Laugh or at least smile. Don't you suppose that the French chefs chuckle a little each time they put something into a *bain-Marie* (Mary's bathtub, better known as a double-boiler)?

The Kitchen

YOU WILL CERTAINLY need a stove, sink, and refrigerator—also a table or counter where you can work. These four monstrous necessities to a kitchen must be positioned properly. The door of the refrigerator should open the right way so you don't find yourself pinned in the corner while you are holding a bowl of cold soup with both hands. Going clockwise, there should first be a counter, then a sink counter, a stove counter, and finally the refrigerator with door opening to the right as you face it. All this can be in line or on two adjacent walls. Parallel to the sink should be a table with a heavy, laminated wood top about 5 feet by 3 feet. The height of this table should suit your height and the length of your arms. As you stand next to the table with arms straight down, your palms should just lie flat on the table. Invariably this makes the table a bit high for dining, but it is a real blessing for your posture and ease in food preparation. There will be traffic around the table, so the corners should be slightly rounded against hip bruises. I find it difficult to work with overhead cabinets almost hitting me in the head unless the counter is very broad. Often-used pots and utensils, anything that can hang, could be kept on a pegboard nearby (or if the ceiling is high enough,

from an iron rack above the work table). Surely the pots and pans outside of a cabinet will get dusty, but I always rinse out a pan I'm about to use. The kitchen must be well lit. It should also be kept neat. Canisters of flour, sugar, tea, and so forth are clutter. If you must have them, they do not belong on the counters. A blender, toaster, and electric beater are necessary. The kind of beater you hold in your hand does very well. It is compact and can be kept in a drawer. It is best to keep counters absolutely free.

Formica makes a good surface for counter tops. The floor should be of some tough vari-colored material that will not show dirt. A double sink is preferable, with one sink for washing and one for rinsing. A built-in, sloping drainboard is ideal. I am not very enthusiastic about disposals. They break down, they won't dispose of certain garbage, and they chew up silverware. I prefer a stove with two ovens. Before mealtime one oven can be used for warming plates and keeping things warm, while the other oven can be used for whatever is still roasting, baking, or broiling. An electric broiler on the roof of the oven is easier to use than a gas broiler underneath. You need at least four gas burners or electric units on top of the

stove. There should be a hood with exhaust fan above the stove.

UTENSILS AND GADGETS: There are so many of these drawer-jammers that all your attention and care are demanded to keep from stuffing the drawer with nonessentials. Among the essentials are: two stainless-steel kitchen spoons about a foot long, and a slotted spoon. I love wooden spoons for stirring soups and sauces or for folding stiffly beaten egg white or whipped cream into some mixture. A sturdy two-pronged fork that won't bend when you pick up a roast. (You won't find all of these suggested utensils in any old hardware store. You may have to go to a department store or restaurant-supply store.) Large and small rubber scrapers for getting that last bit out of a pot or mixing bowl. A dipper with a little more than a half-cup capacity.

The following can all be of the cheapest dime-store variety: a potato peeler, apple corer, grapefruit-sectioning knife, a scoop for making potato, carrot, or melon balls. Tongs or a spatula to turn meat. A fine strainer. A 9-inch whisk with at least sixteen wires and a handle at least an inch in diameter. A food mill, sieve, colander, and grater. Measuring cups, and measuring spoons.

You will also need a good-quality pastry brush, rolling pin, corkscrew, and can opener. A set of stainless-steel mixing bowls is very expensive but won't break. The bread knife and grapefruit knife can be made of stainless, but the other knives should be of carbon steel. This stains easily, but sharpens better than stainless. Other than the bread and grapefruit knives, the only other knives you really need are a Sabatier-type French chef's knife, which is tapered from top to edge and from heel to point (12 inches long), a paring knife of the same form (about 5 inches long, including the handle), and a carving or slicing knife, with a blade that is thin and flexible and tapered to a point (about 12 inches long).

How about POTS and PANS? The different kinds all have their advantages and disadvantages. Tin-lined thick copper pots are the best, but are expensive and hard to clean. I would eliminate stainless-steel pots. Soups and sauces attach and burn in them (for the price they should be faultless.) Thin, cheap pots are fine for boiling vegetables and spaghetti, but are not for simmering a thickened soup or sauce. (It would burn in a jiffy.) Food should always fit the utensil in which it is cooked. You will need a large 4-gallon pot for boiling lobsters, artichokes, corn, a smoked tongue, or for making stock. The pot need not be expensive. Then an inexpensive set of four enamel pots, with capacities ranging from two quarts to one pint, and a double-boiler. For sautéing liver, sole meunière, and potatoes, a 12-inch cast-iron frying pan is ideal. Just wipe it out or rinse it whenever possible. If you wash it in soap and water, the fat collected in the surface of the iron will be lost. It is this fat that keep things from sticking.

You will also need a thick aluminum sauté pan about 2½ inches high and 12 inches in diameter. A large enamel-coated iron casserole is ideal for stews, roasting chicken, and thickened sauces and soups. Roasting pans should have borders about 4 inches high, to cut down the spattering on the oven walls. They can be of a cheap thin stuff, since the heat surrounds a roast anyway. For poaching whole fish, you need a fish poacher with rack. For deep-fat frying, a one-gallon French-fryer with basket insert. For broiling over coals, a hibachi stove and a hinged wire grill with long handles for turning meat or for lifting it away from the coals if rendering fat is making the fire too hot.

Finally, custard cups, small baking dishes or ramekins will be necessary. Also some baking pans of assorted sizes and a 1½-quart ring mold. You will find that, if you use care and apply thought in the purchase of your kitchen tools, you will be a much happier cook.

CHAPTER ONE

Stocks, Soups and Sauces

Sᴛᴏᴄᴋ is the very heart and soul of good cooking. The liquid strained from simmering bones is directly responsible for the excellence of the famous French sauces. No kitchen in a French restaurant is without its large copper pot of *fond* (stock). *Fond* means base, and that's what the big *marmites* (pots) contain—the very base or platform on which the whole structure of French cuisine is built. Anyone can sauté a very thin slice of veal. But can they coat it with a glistening brown sauce that is full of depth and character? Such a sauce is not thickened with flour or starch, but with the concentration of gelatin from the veal bones, achieved by reducing one gallon of brown veal stock to one cup. It seems like such an obvious and natural procedure that the bones of the meat be used to make a stock, which is then used to make the sauce to accompany that same meat. Fish sauce from fish bones, sauce for chicken from chicken bones, for venison from deer bones.

There are two kinds of stock—brown and white. Brown stock is used to make brown gravies; white stock is for light-colored sauces and soups. A brown stock is made from bones and vegetables that are browned in the oven before being put in a pot to simmer. A small amount of tomato is always used in a brown stock to help the brown color. Brown stock is always more highly seasoned to give a robust flavor in keeping with the dark color of the stock. For a white stock, the bones are not browned, they are just simmered in water. Very little seasoning is added to white sauce, since it will be used in soups and light-colored sauces which demand a more delicate taste.

So stock is made by simmering bones (browned or not) in water with a combination of roughly cut celery, carrot, and onion. (Never too much or the stock and ultimate sauce or soup will be too sweet.) A few branches of parsley are good in any stock. The green leaves of leeks and scallions can also be used, but very sparingly, in white stock (the green leaves tend to make it gray). A vegetable such as a green bell pepper should not be used except in a very strong brown stock—the taste is too overpowering.

As a stock reduces, "boils away," or evaporates through simmering, all the important qualities remain and become more concentrated. Flavor increases, brown stock gets browner, and the gelatin content increases. The gelatin that boils out of the bones is a very important part of the liquid. It gives richness, body, and character to a soup or sauce.

Stock must be salted, but very lightly. As the volume of stock reduces, the saltiness will increase. Do not cover a stockpot with a lid unless you feel it has reduced enough. Use a ladle to skim any foam or fat from the top as soon as the stock comes to a boil, and from time to time while the bones simmer. This is particularly important in white stocks. The stock will be cloudy if too much fat simmers with it. Do not stir the stock. Stirring just mixes into it what should be skimmed from the top.

How long do you simmer the bones? It depends on their gelatin content. Beef and deer bones take at least 10 hours. Veal bones require 8 hours; lamb bones, 4 hours; chicken bones, 2 hours; fish bones, 45 minutes.

Once a stock has cooked its prescribed length of time, it should be strained, cooled to room temperature, and then refrigerated as soon as possible. Do not be careless about this, because stock may "sour," and you will have to throw it away. (Sour is a kitchen term; what actually happens is that the stock begins to ferment. It will bubble just like a barrel of grape mash.) The bowl or pot of strained stock will cool quickly in a basin or sink full of cold water, but for goodness' sake, take care that it doesn't tip over.

Any stock will keep for at least a week in the refrigerator. Do not freeze it. When frozen, stock loses its gelatinous quality and also seems to lose flavor. At the end of a week the stock can be boiled, cooled, and refrigerated. Then it will last for another week. In restaurant kitchens the old remaining stock is brought to a boil; then the new bones, vegetables, and additional water are added to make a new stock.

Sauces so often lack depth and character. They are made simply from the juice the meat or fowl has cooked in or from the drippings of the roast pan. If sauces with insufficient taste are combined with a reduction of a stock made from the bones, the resulting sauce will have a far more complete and satisfying taste. Stocks are perhaps difficult and messy, but you have to remember that it is fairly easy to make something good, but much, much more difficult to achieve excellence. A stock cooking slowly on the kitchen stove will fill the whole house with a warm and friendly odor.

FISH STOCK

YIELD: 2 TO 3 QUARTS

This may seem ill-advised, but if the bones are a little smelly, the stock will taste better.

3 pounds fish bones (halibut, sole, flounder, fluke, bass, or snapper; any heads and bones except those from oily fish like blue and mackerel)
2 medium-sized leeks, washed, drained, and roughly cut
1 teaspoon thyme leaves (not *powder*)
3 onions, peeled and roughly cut
1 stalk celery, roughly cut
1 teaspoon peppercorns
1 teaspoon salt
Juice of 1 lemon
2 cups dry white wine
Water

Rinse the bones in cold water. Drain. Put into a 2-gallon pot. Add the rest of the ingredients, including the juice of the lemon and half of its skin. Half-cover with cold water. Bring to a boil over medium-high heat, stirring occasionally so the bones touching the bottom of the pot will not attach and burn. Simmer for ¾ hour, strain, cool, and refrigerate. The stock will keep for one week.

A small amount of water is used because as soon as it comes to a boil, the fish bones will liquefy (except for the inner bone).

LOBSTER STOCK

YIELD: 2 TO 3 QUARTS

The point is that, when you throw a lobster dinner, rinse off the shells and keep them for stock.

½ stick butter
Shells of 1–6 lobsters (including the claws)
2 carrots, peeled and roughly chopped
2 stalks celery, peeled and roughly chopped
4 onions, peeled and roughly chopped
½ cup flour
2 bay leaves
2 cups dry white wine
1 quart tomato purée
Water
Salt and pepper

Heat a 2-gallon stockpot over high heat. Add the butter and heat until it begins to turn brown. Put in the shells. Let them sizzle in the butter, turning them occasionally, for 12 minutes. (If the butter begins to blacken, reduce the heat slightly.) Add the vegetables. Let them sizzle for another 12 minutes. Add and thoroughly mix in the flour. Add the rest of the ingredients and enough water to cover the shells. Simmer for 2 hours, or until the volume of liquid has reduced by half. Strain, cool, and refrigerate the stock (covered).

WHITE STOCK

YIELD: 2 TO 3 QUARTS

5 pounds chicken bones or 5 pounds veal bones, sawed in 3-inch pieces
3 medium onions, peeled and quartered
1 stalk celery
1 bay leaf
6 branches parsley
1 teaspoon salt
Water

Rinse the bones well in water. Drain. Put them into a stockpot of 2-gallon capacity. Add the rest of the ingredients and barely cover them with cold water. Bring to a boil. Scum or foam forms on the top of the simmering stock. Skim it off with a ladle or kitchen spoon. Simmer veal bones for 8 hours; chicken bones, 4 hours. Strain, cool, and refrigerate the stock.

Cool strained stock as quickly as possible in a sink half full of cold water or in a cool place. It is likely to sour if it takes too long to cool before going into the refrigerator.

BROWN STOCK

YIELD: 3 TO 4 QUARTS

Brown stock is made with browned bones. If you have some white stock in the refrigerator, use it instead of, or in addition to, water for covering the browned bones. It will give you a far better brown stock, with more gelatin and better taste. In French kitchens the remnants of old stock are always used to wet down the new.

Like white stock, brown stock has a slight and noncommittal taste. But it will acquire flavor when simmered with the drippings and vegetables from a roast leg or saddle of lamb, leg of veal, or roast of beef, and it will, in turn, enrich the *jus* (juice) or sauce. You may use water with the drippings to make a sauce (and no stock), but then you will not get as much sauce. All that water will dilute the taste, while the same amount of stock will reinforce the taste.

⅓ cup peanut oil
5 pounds sawed veal bone pieces (shin or knuckle preferred)
3 onions, peeled and roughly cut
2 carrots, peeled and roughly cut
1 tablespoon tomato paste
2 bay leaves
⅓ teaspoon thyme
Water

Preheat oven to 400°. Put the oil into a roasting pan and heat it in the oven for 10 minutes. Add the bones. After about ½ hour, when the bones are partially brown, add the onions and carrots. Stir the bones at 15-minute intervals until they are quite brown, but *not* burned—burned bones will give the stock a bad taste. Remove to stockpot and add remaining ingredients. Rinse out the roasting pan with water, and add that water to the contents of the pot. Cover the ingredients with water and simmer very slowly for at least 12 hours. Skim the top occasionally as the stock cooks. Strain, cool, and refrigerate the stock.

DEMI-GLAZE

Prepare the brown stock according to the preceding recipe, strain, and reduce by rapid boiling to about three cups. Remember to skim the foam from the stock as it reduces.

MEAT GLAZE

This is trouble to prepare, but so worthwhile. It really gives depth and character to a brown sauce.

Prepare a brown stock according to the preceding recipe. Strain this stock into another pot. Let it boil over high heat until it is reduced to about $\frac{1}{20}$ its original volume, or until what is left is quite syrupy. The thicker it is, the better, but pay close attention to the last stages of boiling. This reduced stock or meat glaze is gelatinous and burns easily.

This glaze will keep for months in the refrigerator. Keep a film of oil over the top and the container covered tightly. The glaze is used to enrich brown sauces and to coat cold roasted meats, tenderloin, or strip loin of beef, loin of pork, duck, veal, etc. You will need 1½ cups for a small roast and 3 cups for a larger roast. After you have cooked, cooled and refrigerated your meat, place the roast on a wire rack over a shallow pan. Melt glaze over medium heat. Put the pot containing warm glaze into a larger bowl and surround it with ice and water. Stir constantly until it is cool and thicker than heavy cream. Pour the glaze directly from the pot right over the top of the roast. If it all runs off, recover the glaze from the pan underneath, return it to the pot surrounded by ice and water. Let the glaze get thicker this time before it is poured over the roast.

Soups

Whether it's called a broth, bouillon, or consommé, chowder, bisque, or potage, whether it's hot or cold, a good soup served with hot French bread can be a meal in itself. Some soups are thin and clear, others are thick and creamy. Some are made with vegetables and others with meat, chicken, fish, or even eggs. In some soups the liquid used is water; others require a good strong stock of fish bones, lobster shells, chicken, veal, or beef bones.

Broth or bouillon is simply the liquid strained from the stockpot and salted to taste. Of course, the stock must be well reduced to have a good flavor. Consommé is clarified beef stock. It becomes very clear by being cooked with a mixture known as a *clarification*. A few egg whites are mixed with lean hamburger, finely minced celery, onions, leek, a few roughly chopped tomatoes, salt, pepper, and herbs. This clarification should be refrigerated for 6 hours before being added to the cool beef stock. Then the mixture is brought slowly to a boil and simmered for one hour. After it has been strained, what was a cloudy broth will be crystal clear, with its taste and color reinforced by the ingredients in the clarification.

Thickened soups using stock as the liquid base are known as *velouté* (like velvet). The veal, chicken, or fish stock is thickened with a mixture of flour and butter. Cooked asparagus and cream are added to a veal velouté for cream of asparagus soup, mushrooms and cream for cream of mushroom soup. Diced chicken and cream are added to chicken velouté for cream of chicken soup, fish or shellfish and cream to a fish velouté, and so on.

Not all soups are thickened with flour. Greek egg and lemon soup is made from lamb stock thickened with rice and eggs. I must mention here that cornstarch as a thickening agent has certain advantages over flour. It's faster to use. Mix a little cornstarch with cold or room temperature water or wine and simply stir it into the simmering soup to be thickened. Flour seems to slightly alter the taste of what is thickened by it. Cornstarch or arrowroot will not change the taste at all. One disadvantage of cornstarch is that when it's used to thicken a soup or sauce, the thickened liquid remains translucent. The same liquid thickened with flour would be opaque.

The taste message in a soup must be a simple one. Asparagus soup must taste of asparagus, lobster bisque of lobster. Since cold soups tend to desensitize the palate as much as ice cream does, the taste must be especially distinct. Hot leek and potato soup is made with water. The same soup cold —vichyssoise—must be made with chicken stock. The stock reinforces the taste.

Soups must look attractive—display a pleasing texture and color. The garnish, whether pieces of lobster, chicken, or the vegetables in a cold gazpacho, must be neatly cut. The tureen, dipper, soup plates, bowls, or cups must be a color that contrasts sympathetically with the appearance of the soup. If you have a choice, I recommend plain white china.

A luncheon menu could feature soup, perhaps followed by a simple green salad, a mature Brie cheese at room temperature, lots of French bread, dry white wine, and a few cookies or pastries with coffee.

LOBSTER BISQUE
10 TO 12 CUPS

This is also the basis for such famous fish soups as bouillabaisse. Simply add Pernod, saffron, perhaps fresh fish and lots of various little fishes and shellfish poached in it, and there you are.

1 recipe fish or lobster stock (see page 31)
1½ pints light cream
¼ cup imported Cognac
½ cup diced lobster meat (optional)
Salt and pepper

Bring the stock to a boil. Add the cream, Cognac, and lobster. Add salt and pepper to taste and serve. With the addition of more thickening (cornstarch mixed with Cognac) this would be a fine sauce in which to mix lobster meat, cooked scallops, fish, or shrimp to be served as a casserole dish with rice. Poach and drain any raw seafood before adding it to the sauce.

CONSOMMÉ BELLEVUE
SERVES 6

Vite et bien! (Quick and good!) is the French cook's formula for success in this day and age of can openers, scarcity of trained chefs, and the ever-increasing number of people who "eat out."

3 cups bottled clam juice
3 cups chicken broth
⅓ cup heavy cream
Parsley, chopped

Combine the clam and chicken broths in a pot. Whip the cream. Chop a few sprigs of parsley and combine them with the whipped cream. Heat the broths and keep them over a low flame until ready to serve. Don't let the soup boil away. Heat the soup cups slightly in warm oven. Place a ladleful of broth in each cup, garnish with a spoonful of the whipped cream and parsley, and serve.

BAY SCALLOP CHOWDER

SERVES 10 TO 12

Fish sometimes taste alike, but this fantastic bivalve has a unique and superb taste.

⅓ stick butter
2 leeks
1 stalk celery, diced
2 onions, diced
1½ pounds boiling potatoes, peeled, washed, and diced
1 tablespoon salt
1 quart water
1 pound bay scallops
1 pint heavy cream
1 tablespoon parsley, chopped

Melt the butter in a pot. Cut most of the green leaves off the leeks and save them for your stockpot. Cut the leeks lengthways into fourths or eighths, keeping the root ends intact. Plunge the leeks into cold water several times to remove sand and dirt. Drain them. Dice the leeks and discard the root ends. Sauté the leeks, celery, and onions slowly in butter over medium-low heat until the onion is transparent. Do *not* brown. Add the potatoes, salt, and water to the vegetables. Bring to a

boil and simmer for 30 minutes.

This can be done hours in advance, even a day or so before serving. Twenty minutes before the chowder is to be served, bring it to a boil, add the scallops and their juice, if any. Bring back to a boil. Heat the cream to boiling point in a separate pan. Stir it into the chowder with parsley and a little salt, if needed. Heat (do not boil) before serving.

CLAM CHOWDER

SERVES 12

This is different from the classic New England variety, but is much better.

18 cherrystone clams
⅔ stick butter
4 leeks
2 stalks celery, chopped
3 onions, chopped
4 large boiling potatoes, peeled, washed, and diced
1 teaspoon salt
1½ quarts water
1 pint heavy cream

Preheat oven to 400°. Scrub the clams with a stiff brush under cold running water. Place them in a deep roasting pan and put in the oven for 20 to 25 minutes, or until all the clams open. Remove them from the oven. Melt the butter in a pot. Cut off and discard half of the top green leaves from the leeks. Cut the leeks lengthways into fourths or eighths, keeping the roots intact. Plunge the leeks into cold water several times to remove the sand and dirt. Drain them. Dice the leeks, using the green as well as the white part, and discard the root ends. Sauté the leeks, celery, and onions in the butter over medium-low heat until they are wilted. Add the potatoes, salt, and water to the vegetables. Bring to a boil and simmer for 40 minutes.

Remove the clams from their shells. Pour the juice from the clams into a bowl. Rinse the clams in the juice to remove any sand—simply stir them around in the juice and remove to a strainer. Let the sand settle to the bottom of the bowl of juice and carefully pour off the juice. When you get close to the sand, stop pouring and discard the rest. Then firmly chop the clams or give them 5 seconds in the blender at high speed. If you use the blender, do the clams in two lots, using half the juice each time. Add the juice and the clams to the vegetables. In a separate pan, heat the cream to boiling point and add it to the soup. Heat (do not boil) before serving.

OYSTER STEW

SERVES 6

Try to get some extra juice from the fish man. The taste is good, but subtle, so do not salt this very much.

1 pint oysters with juice (about 18 oysters)
1 quart half and half (half milk and half light cream)
Salt and pepper
½ stick butter
¼ cup parsley, chopped

Put the oysters into a pot and pour in the juice,

avoiding the very last bit at the bottom of the container. This may have some sand or shell fragments in it. Bring the oysters and juice to a boil and skim any residue from the top with a spoon. Bring the half and half to a boil in a separate pot. Combine it with the oysters and add barely enough salt and some freshly ground pepper. Keep the soup warm in the top of a double-boiler or in a pot over an asbestos-covered low flame. Do not let the soup boil. Add the butter just before serving, with a sprinkling of parsley on top.

COLD CAULIFLOWER SOUP

SERVES 12 TO 15

Do not brown the vegetables. This would ruin the taste of the soup. Just let them wilt in the butter.

6 medium-large leeks
2 medium onions, diced
1 stalk celery, diced
½ pound butter
2 medium-sized cauliflowers, cut into pieces
Salt
2 quarts water
1 pint heavy cream

Cut the roots off the leeks. Cut off the greens at a point where they begin to pale. Too much of the green will give the soup a gray color. Stick a paring knife through the center of the leek ½ inch from the base. Holding the ½ inch of the base between your thumb and index finger, cut straight to the top of the leek. Then make a similar cut at right angles to the first. Swish the leeks around in lots of cold water. A very large leek would need one or two more cuts. This way of slicing them from the bottom to the top releases the dirt and sand. It also keeps them together so that you can easily put them side by side on a board and cut them into small pieces.

Put the leeks, celery, and onions into a pot over medium heat with half of the butter. Let them stew this way, stirring occasionally, until they are translucent and give off a pleasant odor (about 12 minutes). Add the cauliflower and the salt. Pour the water over all and simmer, covered, for 50 minutes.

Never oversalt. Understatement is more desirable. Put the soup through a sieve or food mill. Cool and refrigerate covered. Add the cream just before serving.

GAZPACHO

SERVES 8 TO 10

¼ cup red wine vinegar
¼ cup olive oil
Salt and pepper to taste
2 tablespoons sugar
3 cups chicken broth
3 cups tomato juice
5 medium tomatoes, peeled and diced
8 scallions
1 cucumber
2 inner stalks celery, finely diced
6 radishes, washed and finely diced
½ bell pepper, diced into ⅛-inch squares
½ bunch watercress
1 pint sour cream (optional)

Mix the vinegar, oil, salt and pepper, and sugar together in a soup tureen or glass bowl. Add the broth, tomato juice, and tomatoes. Remove most of the green of the scallions and one layer of outer leaves. Cut the remaining scallions crossways into slices about ¼ inch thick. Peel the cucumber and cut into quarters lengthways. Cut away and discard the seeds. Cut the quarters into cubes ¼ inch square. Add all the vegetables except the bell pepper and watercress to the soup.

The soup should be refrigerated for at least 3 hours before serving. It can be made 24 hours in advance. Add the bell pepper just before serving. Garnish with leaves of watercress. Serve the sour cream separately.

Serve with hot French bread.

LEEK AND POTATO SOUP

SERVES 8 TO 10

This is the most popular of all French soups. It is the ideal vehicle for the delightful taste of leeks. My very favorite soup.

6 medium-large leeks (diameter of a nickel)
1 stalk celery, diced
2 medium onions, diced
1 stick butter
1½ pounds boiling potatoes, peeled, washed, and diced
Salt to taste
1½ quarts water
1 pint heavy cream

Cut off the green part of the leeks at the point where they begin to pale. Too much of the green will give the soup a gray color. Cut the leeks length-ways into fourths or eighths, depending on their size, keeping the roots intact. Swish them around in lots of cold water to release the dirt and sand. Cut off the root ends and discard. Dice the leeks. Put the leeks, celery, and onions into a pot over medium heat with half of the butter. Stirring occasionally, let them stew this way until they are translucent and give off a pleasant odor (about 12 minutes). Do not brown the vegetables. This would ruin the taste of the soup. Just let them wilt in the butter. Add the potatoes and the salt. Add the water and simmer, covered, for 50 minutes.

Heat the cream in a separate pan. Stir it into the soup with a little salt if needed. Fleck the rest of the butter over the top and serve. The French pinch butter over all of their finished hot cream soups. The soup can be made hours in advance. However, the hot cream should be added just before serving.

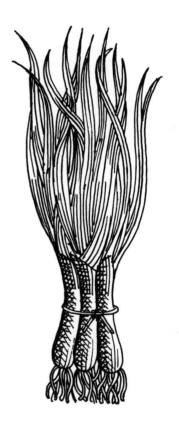

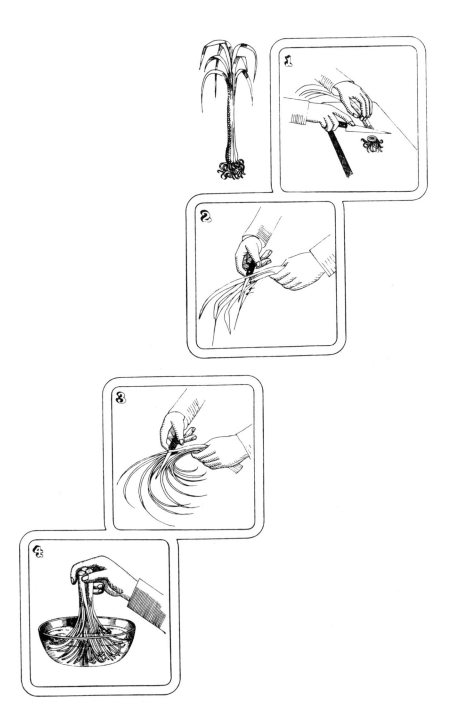

VICHYSSOISE

SERVES 8 TO 10

This soup, unlike the Leek and Potato Soup (see page 37), must be made with chicken stock. Since it is served cold, it must have a stronger taste.

6 medium-large leeks
2 medium onions
1 stalk celery
½ stick butter
1 pound boiling potatoes, peeled, washed, and
*   diced*
1½ quarts chicken stock (Top-quality canned
*   chicken stock is available—watch the salt if you*
*   use it. It's salty, so don't add any more.)*
2 teaspoons salt
Dash of Worcestershire Sauce
⅓ cup chives, chopped
1½ pints light cream

The procedure for this cold soup is exactly the same as for Leek and Potato Soup. The vegetables can be more roughly cut, since as soon as the soup is cooked it must be passed through a fine food mill or sieve. When the soup has been sieved and is cool, stir in most of the chives, cover, and refrigerate for at least 6 hours. Before serving, stir in the cream. Add a little salt if needed. Serve in cold soup cups or plates with the rest of the chopped chives sprinkled over the top. Put the chives into the soup before refrigerating to allow ample time for them to give their good taste to the Vichyssoise.

A summer soup, it could precede a platter of cold meat (*assiette Anglaise*), salads, cheeses, and pickles.

PEA SOUP SAINT GERMAIN

SERVES 8 TO 10

I would say to use dried split peas (and you can if you want), but there is a distinct and beautiful taste that the fresh peas have that the dried ones don't have. Fresh peas also make a greener soup.

2 ham hocks
2 quarts water
2 carrots, roughly cut
2 stalks celery, roughly cut
3 medium onions, roughly cut
2 cups water
1 teaspoon salt
5 pounds fresh peas, shelled
1 teaspoon baking soda
1 cup light cream

Place the ham hocks in a pot with the 2 quarts of water and the celery, carrots, and onions. Cover and simmer over a very low heat, until the ham hocks are tender (about 2 hours). The ham hocks have a good odor of smoke, which is also an important flavor in pea soup. In another pot bring the 2 cups of water with the salt to a boil. Add the peas and baking soda, and cook, covered, until the peas get soft (about 15 minutes). Drain.

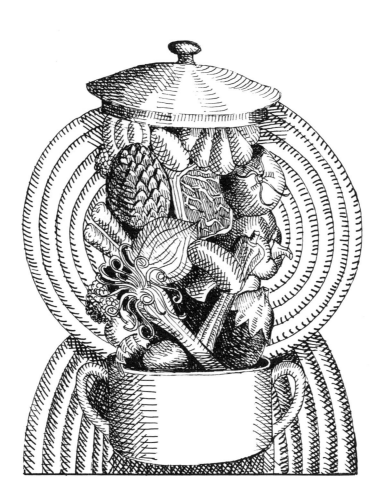

Remove the ham hocks from the pot. Strain the stock, vegetables, and peas through a sieve or food mill. Put into the pot and thin with heated light cream. Season with salt and pepper as needed. The meat of the ham hocks can be diced and used as a garnish for the soup. Serve with croutons separate. This soup is apt to burn, so be careful. Reheat or keep warm in the top of a double-boiler over water.

CROUTONS

4 slices white bread
1 stick butter

Remove the crusts from the bread. Cut the slices into ¼-inch cubes. Fry them in hot butter over medium-high heat. There must be a slight excess of butter in the pan while they are browning. One stick of butter should be ample, but if it is not, add more. As the cubes fry turn them constantly with a fork or small spatula so they brown uniformly. Drain them as you would bacon, on several thicknesses of paper towel.

Sauces

Sauce—poured or spooned over the top, served apart or mixed with the meat it accompanies—must complement that meat. It must not be so full of flavor that it dominates the meat. Nor can it be too bland. Its texture and color must be appealing to the eye. As in other kinds of cooking, the key to successful sauce-making is simplicity, hard work, and the best ingredients money can buy: heavy cream, shallots, good wine, lemons, and real butter.

The most important sauces begin with a stock. Brown stock for brown gravies is made from the roasted bones of the meat the sauce is to accompany. How does the stock become sauce? Sometimes it is mixed with the juices rendered from the cooked meat, sometimes thickened with flour, arrowroot, or cornstarch. Salt and pepper are added to taste, and that's a sauce. For example, after a roast leg of lamb has been removed to a platter to repose (after roasting and before serving), brown veal stock is added to the roasting pan. There it must simmer for 10 minutes, to take on the taste of the ever-present browned celery, carrots, and onions, and the crusty residue that clings to the sides and bottom of the roasting pan. Then the mixture is strained, salt and pepper added to taste, and the sauce for the roast is ready—and it's a good one. Water could be added to the pan instead of stock, but the sauce would not be as rich or as plentiful.

A sauce made from white stock is thickened first with flour or cornstarch or egg yolk. (Egg yolk is sometimes used to further thicken a sauce, and cream is usually added to whiten it.) For example, in the recipe for Fillets of Sole Bonne Femme (see page 155), the final sauce is reduced, thickened first with flour, and, just before serving, with a cup of Hollandaise. Both the Blanquette de Veau (see page 157) and the Chicken à la Crème Tarragon (see page 131) produce their own white stock, strong enough to make exquisite sauce. In both cases the stock is thickened with flour, creamed, and then further thickened with egg yolk.

Sauces, white and brown, may be garnished with seedless white grapes, pearl white onions, sliced mushrooms, truffles, chopped parsley, chives, capers, chopped pickles, and so on. Every time a garnish is added to a sauce, it gets a new name, so a cookbook may contain a hundred sauce recipes when actually there are no more than a half-dozen basic recipes. Some sauces are hot, some cold, some are thickened, some unthickened.

There are brown sauces and white sauces. There are sauces pink from adding paprika, red sauces of lobster shells and tomatoes, green sauces of finely chopped herbs mixed with mayonnaise or whipped cream. When a white creamed sauce is whisked into several egg yolks, it will have a beautiful yellow color. Many sauces require no stock.

Now this is important: If a sauce, either light-colored or brown, lacks depth of flavor, you'll wonder what can be done, what could be added. Add nothing! The trick is to reduce the sauce by boiling it. As it reduces in volume, it will gain in flavor. If the flavor is vague at first, it will become stronger as the volume of the sauce reduces, so don't alter the flavor by dumping in a myriad of spices and dribbles of prepared bottled sauces. The flavor is there, but is indistinct. Reduce the quantity by boiling the sauce until the flavor pleases you. There are only three ingredients that I might add to a brown sauce if, after reduction, it still lacks depth: salt, freshly ground pepper, and if that doesn't do it, a little finely chopped garlic or even a shot of Cognac. If reduction doesn't do the trick for a white sauce, add lemon juice and a tiny amount of Cognac. (Here Cognac helps even more than with brown sauce.) In reduction, sauces gain deeper color and thickness in addition to taste.

The most famous sauce, other than those made with stock, is Hollandaise Sauce. Hot butter is beaten into warm egg yolk. The bubbles of the cooked egg yolk hold the hot butter. The only seasoning is a small pinch of cayenne pepper and a squirt of lemon juice. The resulting sauce is pale yellow and has a smooth superb texture, perfect for poached fish and vegetables. Hollandaise is used in the French kitchen to thicken and enrich creamed sauces. There are several variations of Hollandaise. The best known is Béarnaise (my favorite), which is used with broiled fish, broiled chicken, and best of all with roast beef.

In connection with Hollandaise, which is 80 percent butter, you have to consider the other butter sauces and the importance of butter in cooking. No French kitchen could function without butter. It would simply have to close down. One of the best and most widely used sauces is plain melted butter. It is used for lobster, poached fish, steamed clams, and boiled vegetables. With or without lemon juice, melted butter is a sauce in itself and a very, *very* good sauce it is. Chopped shallots, lemon juice, chopped parsley can be added to melted butter to make what is called Beurre Maître d'Hôtel for broiled fish or meats. Browned butter for *meunière* is superb, and has an entirely different taste from melted butter. Then there's black butter, which is usually combined with capers and red wine vinegar as a sauce for fried eggs and calves' brains. Anchovy Butter, in the recipe for Broiled Blue Fish, is again a different sort of butter sauce. It is what the French call *beurre travaillé* (worked butter). Butter is pushed around and mixed with the fingers or a spoon until it is soft; then chopped anchovies and chopped shallots are mixed with it.

Returning to the different types of hot sauces, you could get a very clear idea of them by visiting the work table of a French sauce cook just before the noon rush hour. On the table, in various sized crocks, are the following basic sauce components for his frantic, 2-hour struggle: solid butter and melted butter, a thickened fish stock, a thickened white stock that is called *velouté* (like velvet), a cream sauce called Bechamel, which is flour and butter mixed and thickened with hot milk, well-reduced brown stock called demi-glaze, a crock of Hollandaise. Seven in all. It's hard to think of a hot sauce that could not be made using one or more of them as the base, remembering, of course, that they would be mixed with the juices of the cooked meat or fish they are to accompany.

The important basic cold sauces are mayonnaise and vinaigrette. Mayonnaise is a sauce similar in many ways to Hollandaise. One difference is that it is a cold sauce; another difference is that oil is used instead of hot butter. Egg yolk is the thickening agent or "liaison" that holds the oil. Lemon juice (or wine vinegar), mustard, and cayenne pepper season it. A variety of cold sauces can be made using mayonnaise as a base, such as Russian dressing and tartar sauce. One variation of vinaigrette is thickened with egg white.

Here's one fact you must know. Just because a meat has a beautiful, smooth sauce served with it, that is not an excuse to do a bad job in cooking the meat. No amount of good sauce will compensate for a dry piece of meat or fish. Sauce is an accom-paniment. It must be carefully made, but remember that its role is secondary, and season it accordingly. Its taste must not overwhelm what it is to accompany.

BEURRE MANIÉ

YIELD: ½ CUP

This is easier to make and as good as *Roux,* in which the butter and flour are cooked together.

½ stick butter
½ cup flour

Put butter and flour into a medium-sized bowl. Using one hand, thoroughly combine the two ingredients. Use as needed to thicken sauces or soups by adding small amounts at a time, and whisking it into the simmering sauce until the desired thickness is achieved. Be careful. If the sauce gets too thick, it will have to be thinned, which will dilute the taste. Store in refrigerator.

SHALLOT SAUCE FOR BEEF

SERVES 6

This sauce is to be spooned over slices of roast beef or steak. It's so simple, and honestly, I cannot think of a better sauce for slices of rare beef or steak.

1 stick butter
½ cup shallots, chopped

Brown the butter in a deep 2-quart saucepan over medium-high heat. When the butter is brown and has a nutty odor, turn off the heat and put in the shallots. The butter will foam a great deal as soon as the shallots are added. This is why I've suggested a deep 2-quart pot. The shallots will brown in the hot butter. Transfer the mixture to a sauce bowl. When serving the sauce, go to the bottom for each spoonful, since the shallots will remain there.

SAUCE AMANDINE
SERVES 6 TO 8

The beauty of this recipe is that the almonds will be crisp, not soggy.

⅔ stick butter
2 ounces almonds, sliced

Brown the butter. Shut off the heat and add the almonds. If you put the almonds into the butter before it is brown, the almonds will be brown before the butter is. The brown butter taste is very important. In French, brown butter is called *beurre noisette* (nut). It does have a nutty taste. The brown almonds add to this taste. The combination is delicious. This is a last-minute procedure, but it's a simple one.

Serve Sauce Amandine for fish meunière, broiled fish, cauliflower, string beans, and so on.

BEURRE MÂITRE D'HÔTEL
SERVES 6 TO 8

This is a very great sauce, and is such an addition of simple and complementary tastes to broiled meats and fish.

1 stick butter
2 tablespoons shallots, chopped
2 tablespoons lemon juice
Salt and pepper
¼ cup parsley, chopped

The butter should be melted and warm, not hot. Add the chopped shallots, lemon juice, salt, and pepper. This mixture can stand as long as an hour in a warm place. Stir in the parsley before serving. Adjust the seasoning according to your taste—more lemon juice or salt, etc.

BEURRE BLANC #1
SERVES 8 TO 10

This sauce goes as well with hot poached fish as Hollandaise, and is much easier to prepare.

⅓ cup shallots, chopped
⅓ cup white vinegar
¼ cup water
1 pound butter
Salt and pepper
⅓ cup parsley, chopped

Do not pack down the chopped shallots in the cup when measuring them. Slowly simmer the shallots with the vinegar in a saucepan over medium heat until all the vinegar has boiled away (about 4 minutes). Be careful. If the shallots burn or even get brown, the taste of the sauce will not be good. Add the water and bring to a boil over high heat. Quickly whisk in the butter, piece by piece. All the butter should be incorporated, and the sauce boiling again within 2 minutes. Add salt and freshly ground pepper to taste. Stir in parsley just before serving.

Do not try to keep the sauce warm or to reheat it. It will not matter if it is barely warm or almost cool, since the fish will be hot and the plates warm.

BEURRE BLANC #2
SERVES 6 TO 8

Do not let the chopped shallots burn or even brown. It ruins the taste of the sauce.

½ cup white distilled vinegar or red wine vinegar
2 tablespoons shallots, chopped
4 egg yolks
1 pound butter
Ground pepper or a pinch of cayenne pepper

Slowly simmer the vinegar and shallots in a saucepan over medium heat until all the vinegar has boiled away (about four minutes). Do not burn the shallots. Add the egg yolks to the pan as soon as it is cool and proceed with directions as for Hollandaise (see below). Omit the lemon juice. This is good with poached fish.

HOLLANDAISE SAUCE
SERVES 6 TO 8

Contrary to popular thought, Hollandaise can be made *hours* in advance. It does not need to be reheated.

4 egg yolks
2 tablespoons water
1 pound butter
Juice of 1 lemon
Cayenne pepper
Salt

Remember, do not use an aluminum double-boiler. It will turn the sauce green. Before combining butter and yolks, both should be at a comfortable bathtub temperature, more than warm, almost hot.

Whisk or beat the egg yolks and 2 tablespoons of water continuously in the top of a double-boiler. The water in the bottom pot should be just simmering. Remove from the heat as soon as the yolks thicken. Empty the simmering water and replace the bottom of the double-boiler under the top to help keep it in place. Add the butter very slowly, whisking as it melts. As you whisk it in, the mixture thickens. Add a little lemon juice. Hollandaise should be a bit thinner than mayonnaise; it should just run or move when stirred with a spoon.

After whisking in the butter, whisk in a tiny pinch of cayenne, then lemon juice, and salt to taste. If the sauce is very thick, it can be thinned with additional lemon juice. If it has enough lemon taste, it can be thinned with a little warm water. If you are not serving it right away, do not keep it over or near a constant heat source. Put it on a shelf above the stove or wherever there is a little warmth. If the sauce curdles, heat it over medium heat until it is warm. Then whisk it spoonful by spoonful into 2 tablespoons of cold water in a medium-sized bowl. As the mixture thickens, you can add the curdled Hollandaise in larger quantities.

SAUCE MOUSSELINE

SERVES 8

This is a more delicate version of Hollandaise Sauce.

2 cups Hollandaise Sauce (page 46)
½ cup heavy cream, whipped
Sprig parsley

Place the Hollandaise in a bowl. Before serving, put the whipped cream in a tuft on the Hollandaise. Stand a sprig of parsley in the center of the tuft. Mix the whipped cream into the Hollandaise as you serve it.

This sauce goes well with hot poached fish or with asparagus.

BÉARNAISE SAUCE

SERVES 8 TO 10

This sauce certainly deserves its growing popularity. Once Hollandaise Sauce has been mastered, this variation will not seem at all difficult. It is good with all broiled meats and is best when served with hot roast beef.

¼ cup peppercorns
⅓ cup red wine vinegar
¼ cup water
3 tablespoons shallots, finely chopped
⅓ cup fresh tarragon, chopped, or ¼ cup dried tarragon
4 egg yolks

1 pound butter
Salt
2 tablespoons parsley, chopped, or 3 tablespoons fresh or dried tarragon leaves

Crack the peppercorns on a hard board under the heel of a French knife or with a heavy pot or casserole. Combine with vinegar, water, finely chopped shallots, fresh or dried tarragon, and simmer this mixture over direct medium heat until the liquid has evaporated. Do not let it burn. In the top of a double-boiler whisk the yolks with the shallot mixture. After all the butter is incorporated, the mixture must be strained through 4 thicknesses of cheesecloth. Allow it to cool slightly so you don't burn yourself. Lay the cloth over a bowl. Pour the Béarnaise into the cloth, using a rubber spatula to scrape out the pot. Gather together the corners and sides of the cloth and tuck them between your thumb and index finger. Squeeze the sauce through with your other hand. Add the finely chopped tarragon or parsley to speckle the sauce green. Salt to taste. This sauce can be made in advance. Treat it the same way you would the Hollandaise (see page 46).

MAYONNAISE

SERVES 6 TO 8

3 egg yolks
1½ tablespoons Dijon-style mustard (Mr. Mustard has my vote.)
1 tablespoon wine vinegar
1 teaspoon salt
⅛ teaspoon cayenne pepper
1½ cups peanut or olive oil

47

Beat or whisk the egg yolks for a few seconds. Whisk in the mustard, vinegar, salt, and cayenne pepper. Add the oil very slowly, beating constantly. Add salt if needed.

HORSERADISH SAUCE (COLD)

SERVES 6 TO 8

This sauce is excellent for cold roast beef.

½ pint heavy cream
Horseradish to taste
Salt

Whip the cream. Mix in the horseradish and salt to taste.

GREEN SAUCE
FOR COLD POACHED FISH

SERVES 4 TO 6

This whipped cream sauce is a welcome relief from the usual mayonnaise with cold poached fish, and it's good, too.

½ pint heavy cream
Juice of 2 limes
½ cup parsley, chopped
¼ cup fresh tarragon, chopped

Whip the cream. Fold in the lime juice, chopped parsley, and finely chopped tarragon. Chill and serve with the fish.

CREOLE SAUCE

SERVES 8 TO 10

It is shameful to admit, but two bottles of chili sauce can be substituted for the last six ingredients.

4 medium onions, peeled
4 bell peppers
1 pound mushrooms
¼ cup olive oil
3 tablespoons sugar
1 bay leaf
1 teaspoon allspice
¼ cup wine vinegar
1 quart Italian tomatoes
Cayenne pepper and salt to taste

Slice the onions into thin strips. Cut the bell peppers in half lengthways, remove the seeds, and cut the halves in strips, the same size as the onions. Slice the mushrooms from top to bottom, stems attached, about ⅛ inch thick. In a saucepan, wilt these vegetables in the olive oil over medium heat until they begin to give off a pleasant aroma. They should not fry or brown. The French word for this wilting over a modest heat is *tomber*. Add the rest of the ingredients and simmer them slowly for 2 hours (or add chili sauce and simmer for 20 minutes). Stir and squash the tomatoes occasionally. The sauce will get quite thick. If you are serving this with boiled smoked beef tongue, thin it once or twice with the tongue broth. This will lend additional good flavor to the sauce.

VINAIGRETTE #1

ENOUGH FOR A SALAD FOR 2

This is the classic, unbeatable vinaigrette for all green salads. Imported wine vinegars tend to be very strong. I really prefer our domestic brands.

1 teaspoon coarse salt
¼ teaspoon black pepper, freshly ground
2 tablespoons red wine vinegar
2 tablespoons olive or peanut oil

First the salt is sprinkled on the lettuce, then the pepper. The red wine vinegar is poured over the top and then the oil. Toss the salad. Just because this sauce is so simple doesn't mean that it can't be the very best—because it is.

VINAIGRETTE #2

SERVES 8

This thickened vinaigrette will adhere to, and not slip off of, a piece of broccoli or an asparagus spear *en voyage* from plate to mouth.

1 egg white
2 tablespoons Dijon-style mustard
¼ cup red wine vinegar
1 teaspoon salt
¼ teaspoon pepper
1¼ cup peanut oil
1 teaspoon garlic, chopped (optional)

Whisk or beat together the egg white, mustard, vinegar, salt, and pepper in a bowl. When thoroughly mixed, add the oil very slowly, beating constantly. Add more salt and pepper if needed. If the sauce is too strong or too thin, add more oil. This can be made well in advance of serving. If it curdles or separates, give it a vigorous beating.

This sauce goes well with cold broccoli, asparagus or artichokes.

VINAIGRETTE FOR ARTICHOKES

SERVES 12

The vinaigrette can be kept for a long time if the egg and parsley are not added until just before serving. Do not refrigerate.

2 tablespoons shallots, chopped
1 teaspoon garlic, chopped
1 tablespoon dry mustard
⅓ cup red wine vinegar
½ cup peanut oil
Salt and pepper
1 hard-boiled egg
¼ cup parsley, chopped

Mix the shallots with the garlic. Add the mustard and a small amount of vinegar. Mix; add the oil, vinegar, salt and pepper.

Shortly before serving, put the hard-boiled egg through a sieve and add to the vinaigrette along with the chopped parsley. Save some of the parsley for a garnish.

NEWBURG SAUCE

SERVES 6

This can be used as a sauce, or mixed with about 2 pounds of boiled shrimp, scallops, or lobster in a casserole dish to be served with boiled rice and a fresh green vegetable. It is good for large groups.

¼ stick butter
1½ teaspoons paprika
1½ tablespoons flour
1 cup light cream
¼ cup sherry
Salt to taste (about ½ teaspoon)

Melt the butter in a saucepan over medium-low heat. Whisk in the paprika and let simmer for a moment. Whisk in the flour and let it cook for several seconds. Slowly whisk in the cream, bringing the sauce to the simmering point as you do so. While the sauce is still quite thick, whisk it vigorously to eliminate any lumps. Put some of the sherry over the top of the sauce after all of the cream is mixed in and the heat shut off. It will keep a scum from forming. Add the rest of the sherry just before serving.

ROQUEFORT DRESSING

SERVES 6 TO 12

Watch your calories!

¼ pound Roquefort or bleu cheese
1 pint sour cream
1 cup mayonnaise
3 tablespoons red wine vinegar
2 tablespoons onion, finely chopped
Salt and pepper to taste

Put the cheese into a bowl and mash it with a fork. Blend in the sour cream, then the other ingredients.

RUSSIAN DRESSING

SERVES 6 TO 12

Put in some salmon roe just before serving if you want to doll this up.

2½ cups mayonnaise
½ cup bell peppers, finely chopped
½ cup onions, finely chopped
¼ cup chili sauce
2 tablespoons red wine vinegar
Salt and pepper to taste

Mix all the ingredients and refrigerate for at least two days before serving, so that the ingredients will marinate. The sauce will be inferior if it is used earlier.

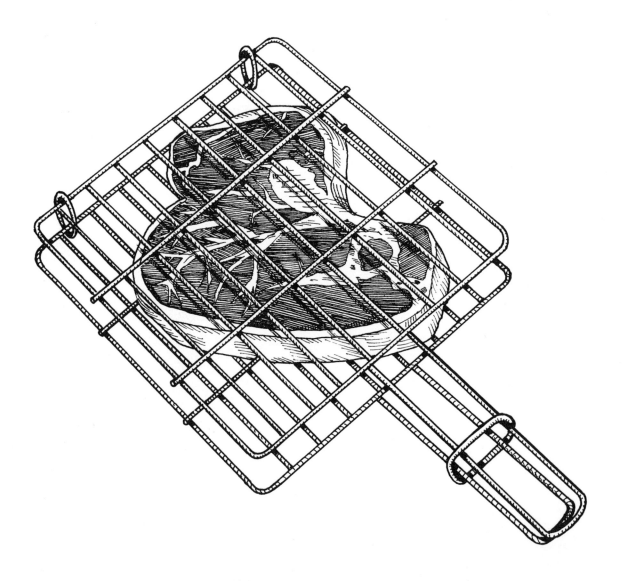

CHAPTER TWO

Broiling

WHATEVER IS BROILED comes in direct contact with the heat. There's no pan or boiling water in between what is to be cooked and the flames of a gas broiler, the red-hot unit of an electric broiler, or glowing charcoals. Toasters are small broilers. There was a restaurant in New York where a blowtorch was used to char and cook the steak right at a diner's table. At Gage and Tollner's restaurant in Brooklyn, New York, big chunks of anthracite coal are used in the broiler. The heat from the coals is so intense that thick cuts of steak and the restaurant's famous double mutton chops are seared and cooked in just a few minutes.

It's hard to judge the cooking time for broiling. When the intensity of the heat has been considered, along with the distance of the meat from the source of heat, and finally the thickness of the piece of meat, then the cooking time can be calculated.

Anything being broiled must be seared on the outside. This charred, crusty exterior has a pleasant, smoky taste and—more important—seals in the juice. The distance between what is being broiled and the heat can then be increased for the remainder of the cooking time so that the food doesn't get too burned on the outside. In the recipes

for very thick cuts of swordfish and rack of lamb, I have suggested that the meat spend a certain amount of time in a moderate oven after it has been browned on both sides over a charcoal fire. Some meats can't be cooked on a charcoal grill; they must be cooked in the stove broiler. Some, such as steak and kidneys and chicken, are better done over charcoal. This information appears with the recipes themselves.

Stove broilers are unpopular. The main complaint is that they don't get hot enough. The fault may be ours rather than the fault of the broilers. Home stove broilers, whether gas or electric, must be preheated for at least 12 minutes, with the unoccupied broiler pan in position below the heat, so that, when the meat goes onto the pan, it will get maximum heat. The meat must begin to brown immediately to seal in the juice. Raw steaks, less than an inch thick, should be broiled over hot coals. They cannot be broiled in the stove broiler, because it just doesn't get hot enough. By the time the meat is brown on both sides it will be too well done. Pork chops and chicken, however, can be cooked in the stove broiler because the meat should be well done. The broiler pan should be positioned as close as possible to the heat source, allowing enough clearance for the piece of meat. If the meat is extremely thick (requiring a long time to cook), the rack can be lowered, but only after both sides of the meat are good and brown. Broiled meats should be turned twice. After the first side is brown, the meat must be turned over to brown the other side. When that side is brown, the meat is turned again so that the first side is toward the heat. This is done because the juice that the seared exterior is attempting to hold in the meat will tend to moisten this crusty exterior when it is away from the heat. Returning this side to face the heat will, in effect, re-sear it.

Broiling foods outdoors or in the fireplace can be lots of fun. The hibachi type of broiler does well in either place. Or simply put a wire rack (like those used in the oven) on the irons that extend from the andirons to the back of the fireplace. A hinged wire grill with long handles is useful for turning the meat or for lifting it away from the coals if rendering fat is making the fire too hot. Most of the exterior fat should be trimmed from meats that are to be broiled over charcoal. A little fat and a few flames help to brown the meat, but things can get out of hand if the blaze engulfs the meat. All charcoal grills should be constructed so that it is possible to raise and lower the grill. Be sure the wires of the grill are spaced no more than an inch apart so that small pieces of meat such as lamb chops can't fall through into the coals. The bone of a lamb chop should be wrapped in foil for broiling or it may burn and fall off.

Most fish must be cooked in the stove broiler. Fish will stick to a grill. Also, fish gets fragile as it cooks and is very hard to turn over. In the stove broiler, it browns on only one side, but it cooks through because there is more surrounding heat in the broiling compartment. Swordfish, finnan haddie, and, of course, lobster can be cooked on a charcoal grill.

The Time Chart for Sautéing Steak (on page 118) can also be used to calculate broiling time.

I have suggested Beurre Maître d'Hôtel in many of the following recipes. It is really good with broiled meats.

54

BROILED LOBSTER

SERVES 3

Lobster can be cooked in the stove broiler or over coals. When over coals, the lobster is broiled with the shell toward the coals and the split side up. Of course, the meat does not get browned as it does under a stove broiler, where the heat comes from above. If a lobster cooked over charcoal is turned over, it will lose too much juice and the meat will be dry and hard to chew. Then why cook a lobster over coals? Because the shell imparts a delicious taste to the meat as it gets hot over the coals. Under a stove broiler, the meat does not get as much of this taste, because the shell is not in direct contact with the heat. But the meat gets browned, and that's good. Which method is better? I think it's a toss-up.

3 lobsters (1–1¼ pounds each)
Salt and pepper
⅔ cup bread crumbs (when cooked in the stove
*   broiler only)*
2 sticks butter

Preheat broiler. Split (or have your fish man split) the lobsters so that there are two separate halves. There will be, at the head of each, a small half-sack containing sand, which should be removed. There is also a varicolored tube which runs through the center of the tail meat to the end of the tail. If you can see it, take it out. If you can't see it, forget it.

For stove broilers, arrange the halves with cut sides up on the broiler pan. Sprinkle them with salt and pepper. Sprinkle bread crumbs over the stomachs. (The stuff in the stomach, called coral, is delicious.) Distribute flecks of one stick of butter over the stomachs and tails of the halved lobsters. Place the broiler pan in center position and broil the halves for 25 minutes. The tops of the lobsters should be about 5 to 7 inches from the heat. The rest of the butter should be melted and served separately.

For a charcoal broiler, distribute flecks of butter over the cut halves of lobster. Salt and pepper. Place them with cut sides up on the grill. They will be done when the meat is no longer translucent, but white (about 25 to 40 minutes).

BROILED BLUEFISH WITH ANCHOVY BUTTER

SERVES 6

This must be cooked in a stove broiler. Do not use the slotted tray insert in the broiler pan, just the pan itself. The fish broils and browns only on the top. Use the butter and lemon juice to baste the browned tops of the fillets.

Aluminum foil
3   2-pound bluefish (6 fillets)
1½ lemons
Salt and pepper
Paprika
½ stick butter

Preheat broiler and broiler pan. Cover the surface of the pan with aluminum foil. Put the fillets on the pan, with skin sides down. Squeeze the juice of ½ lemon over them. Sprinkle them with salt, pepper, and paprika. Thinly slice the other lemon and distribute the slices over the fish. Distribute the butter in flecks over the fish. This part of the preparation (except the salt) can be done hours before, and the pan with the fish can be kept in the refrigerator until it is time to cook dinner. Broil for no more than 25 minutes. The fillets must not be overcooked. They broil on one side only and need not be turned over. Using a spatula, arrange them on a platter. Pour the juice left in the pan over the fish.

Anchovy Butter

1½ tablespoons anchovy paste, or 4 or 5 finely
  chopped fillets
⅓ cup parsley, chopped
2 medium shallots, finely chopped
½ stick sweet butter

The anchovy butter can be prepared long before mealtime. Simply mix the anchovy paste (or chopped fillets), chopped parsley, and chopped shallots with the butter. Keep at room temperature. The anchovy butter should have the consistency of mayonnaise. Do not put it into the refrigerator because it will get too hard. It's a good sauce for all broiled fish.

Serve the bluefish with mashed potatoes, broccoli, or Brussels sprouts, followed by sliced oranges for dessert.

BROILED SHAD ROE WITH BACON
SERVES 6

This dish is not for charcoal broiling because of the bacon that is wrapped around the roe. There would be so much fat dripping into the coals that the resulting flames would get out of hand.

6 slices of bacon
3 pair shad roe
Unsalted water
Salt and pepper
1 lemon
2 shad fillets (optional)

Remove the bacon from the refrigerator 20 minutes before using so that it will become soft enough for the slices to be separated. Preheat broiler and the slotted tray of the broiler pan. Place the shad roe in unsalted cold water. Bring to the simmering point, lower the heat, and poach the roe for one minute. Do not allow the water to boil, or the roe will split. Put the pan under gently running cold water until the roe are completely cool. Take the pairs of roe out of the water and drain. Separate them by removing the membrane between the two, and pat dry with paper towels. Pinch the end of a slice of bacon against the tip of the roe and, stretching the bacon slightly, wrap it around in a spiral to the other end of the roe. Arrange the roe on the preheated tray of the broiler pan. Slide the broiler pan into the broiler at center position. When the bacon is good and brown (no more than 15 minutes), the roe will be cooked and ready to serve. It will not be necessary to turn the roe, because the bottom will have browned slightly on the preheated broiler tray. Roe is very fragile, so turning it might break it, and would also disturb the folds of the bacon. The shad roe must not be dry, so they must be served no more than 5 minutes after removal from the broiler and while they are still pink in the center. Serve with lemon wedges.

This seasonal dish is elegant, but slightly expensive. Begin the meal with clam chowder and serve the shad with boiled new potatoes and asparagus. Follow it with grapefruit sections with honey or a ripe melon.

Note: The poaching process is necessary because it seals the outer portion of the roe and inhibits its tendency to explode. If the broiler isn't preheated, the bacon will not get brown fast enough. The exposure to the gradually increasing heat will make the roe too well done by the time the bacon gets brown. The slotted tray that fits on top of the broiler pan is necessary so that the fat rendered from the bacon will drain away from direct contact with the heat. The danger here again is fire. Also, if the roe were stewing in this fat, the bacon would not get crisp and the undersides would probably be soggy.

BROILED SHAD

If you wish to serve broiled, boned shad with the shad roe, follow the recipe for Broiled Bluefish (see page 55). The shad should be broiled before the roe in a separate shallow pan. The substitution of one thinly sliced small onion distributed over the top of the shad in place of the shallots mentioned in the bluefish recipe is possible, but not necessary. Salt, pepper, and dot with flecks of butter (remember always to salt fish just before it goes into the broiler so that the salt will not draw juice out of the fish as it waits to be cooked). Ar-

range the shad on a platter with the roe placed around the fish and parsley sprigs and lemon wedges distributed around the platter.

BROILED SHAD ROE CANAPÉ
SERVES 8 TO 12

The advantage of this canapé is that you need serve no other with drinks.

3 pair shad roe
Salt and pepper
Bacon
2 medium-sized shallots, finely chopped
1 lemon
Toothpicks

The procedure is exactly the same as in the recipe for Broiled Shad Roe with Bacon (see page 56), except that when the roe is drained and patted dry, it is cut across into bite-size pieces. Then salt and pepper it. Place as many half-slices of bacon on the table as there are pieces of roe. Sprinkle the bacon with chopped shallots and place a piece of roe on each, cut side down. Wrap the bacon around the roe, and fasten with a toothpick. Place on the preheated slotted tray of the broiler pan, seam side down. Place the pan in preheated broiler at center position. When the bacon is brown, the roe will be ready to serve. Arrange them on a platter, squeeze lemon juice over all, pierce each with a toothpick, and serve.

This canapé can be prepared in advance and kept refrigerated until it is time to broil. I would much rather have the roe a little pink inside than too well done and dry.

BROILED FINNAN HADDIE
SERVES 6

2½ pounds finnan haddie
Water
Peanut or other light oil
6 pats of butter
Parsley sprigs

Preheat broiler. Cut the fish into portion-sized pieces and place in pot. Simmer gently in water for 15 minutes, or until a kitchen fork goes into the fish without resistance. Freshen under running cold water, drain, and pat dry with paper towels. Place on the oiled broiler pan. Pour oil on your fingertips and rub the top of the fish. Place the fish in the broiler as close as possible to the heating unit for about 10 minutes, or until the top of the fish begins to show dark brown or black places, but no longer than 12 minutes, as the fish is apt to dry out. Remove to a warm platter with a spatula. Place pats of butter on the pieces and use sprigs of parsley to decorate the platter.

Serve with Mashed or Riced Potatoes (see pages 170 and 171), a green salad, and follow with a pastry dessert. This is good for lunch.

SWORDFISH AMANDINE
SERVES 6

You don't need the almonds, but I do think they are better crispy brown on top of a juicy swordfish than white and soggy in somebody else's string beans.

4 pounds swordfish, 1 inch thick
Salt and pepper
Paprika
3 ounces sliced almonds
Beurre Maître d'Hôtel (see page 45)
Parsley, chopped
6 lemon wedges

Preheat broiler and broiler pan. Sprinkle salt, pepper, and paprika over both sides of the swordfish. Place it under broiler and cook for 6 minutes on each side. The broiler pan should be near enough to the heat to brown the surface of the swordfish. Before removing the fish from the broiler, sprinkle the almonds over the fish and then brown them under the heat. Pay attention, because the almonds will brown within seconds. Remove to a hot serving platter. Pour the Beurre Maître d'Hôtel over the swordfish and sprinkle with parsley. Serve the lemon wedges separately or around the fish as decoration.

CHARCOAL-BROILED THICK SWORDFISH STEAK
SERVES 6 TO 10

This delicious, large, thick swordfish steak makes an imposing main dish for a dinner party.

7–8-pound swordfish steak, 4 inches thick (without flank, if possible)
2 tablespoons oil
Salt and pepper
Juice of 1 lemon
1 teaspoon powdered ginger
Beurre Maître d'Hôtel (see page 45)

Prepare the coals. Coat both sides of the steak with oil. Sprinkle with salt and pepper. Put the steak into a wire-handled hinged grill. Slide the ring over the two handles to secure the fish within the grill. The coals should not be red-hot for such a thick piece of steak. Position the grill containing the steak about 6 inches from moderately hot coals. Both sides should be well browned in 20 minutes. Preheat oven to 350°. Remove to a platter or large oven-proof baking dish. Sprinkle with lemon juice and ginger. Place the fish in the oven for 20 minutes. Pour Beurre Maître d'Hôtel over the fish.

BROILED CHICKEN
SERVES 6

The average broiler pan will just hold 6 halves. This is a good recipe for the stove broiler.

3   2½-pound broilers, split in half
Salt and pepper
Beurre Maître d'Hôtel Butter (see page 45)

Preheat broiler. Sprinkle the chicken with salt and pepper. Arrange the cut sides to face the heat source. Most of the cooking time will be devoted to this side of the chicken. It can and should get a little burned. Be attentive when you turn the chicken, because the skin burns quickly and should be just brown. The cooking time is 30 to 35 minutes over medium-hot coals, or the same time in a preheated oven broiler. Serve the Beurre Maître d'Hôtel separately.

Half a chicken is a lot for one person, so depending on appetites, three chickens might easily serve eight. Serve with corn on the cob and a green salad, followed by Orange Mousse (see page 174).

BROILED RACK OF LAMB
SERVES 6

This is a real favorite of mine. The meat should be neither well-done nor blood-rare, but pink.

1 rack of lamb split, with the backbone removed, so that just the rib bone and meat remain
Aluminum foil
Salt and pepper
Watercress

Preheat broiler. Trim all the fat from the ribs so that just the eye of meat with some cover fat remains attached to the rib bone. Chop off the ends of the longer ribs so that they are all a uniform length (about 5 inches). Loosely cover the bare rib bone with strips of aluminum foil, since the bones are apt to burn and fall off. Salt and pepper the meat, and place it fat-side down on the hot broiler pan. Broil both sides until they are good and brown, even black in places (about 25 minutes). Remove to a platter, repose for 20 minutes, and put into a 400° oven for 5 minutes before serving. It is very easy to carve off the chops by cutting down between the bones. Use paper frills to decorate the ends of the ribs.

Serve the meat hot, garnished with a bouquet of watercress. If you like lamb gravy (recipe follows), it may be served separately. Serve with parsnips, Carrots Vichy (see page 165), and string beans (no salad)—preceded by creamed Mussels Marinière (see page 147)—and for dessert, Orange à l'Arabe (see page 172).

You may also serve the meat cold. Carve the cold rack evenly into chops and arrange them on a platter with the rib ends overlapping the edge of the platter and frills on the bones (white frills are the most attractive). Place a bouquet of watercress in the middle. Serve with tomato, endive, and avocado salad and sherbet for dessert.

Lamb Gravy

Follow the recipe for brown stock (see page 32). Barely cover the vegetables and browned bones with water. Simmer for 4 hours. Strain into a saucepan. Remove most of the fat from the top of the stock and reduce by boiling to ½-cup volume. Add salt and pepper if needed.

VEAL OR LAMB KIDNEYS
SERVES 6

These will be better if they are broiled over charcoal. You might even do a mixed grill of broiled single lamb chops, sweetbreads, miniature steaks, sausage, and kidneys. A mixed grill is a little tough on the cook, because all the meats have different cooking times, but it's fun for the guests.

3 pounds veal or lamb kidneys, split lengthways
Beurre Maître d'Hôtel (see page 45)
Salt and pepper

Get the coals hot. If you buy your kidneys from a butcher, the fat surrounding the kidneys should be pared down to ¼ inch and the membrane left on. If you buy them already peeled, paint the kidneys with a little of the Beurre Maître d'Hôtel. Salt and pepper the kidneys. Broil for about six minutes on each side. They should *not* be well done, but a little red in the middle and good and brown on both sides.

Serve with Endive Meunière (see page 119), Mashed Potatoes (see page 170), and Baked Pears (see page 97) for dessert.

SWEETBREADS
SERVES 6

It's important not to overcook sweetbreads. Before broiling, they must be blanched in boiling water so they're already cooked through. Then all they need is to be brown on the outside and hot through.

2½ pounds sweetbreads (soak in cold water for about 1 hour)
Water
1 lemon
Salt and pepper
Beurre Maître d'Hôtel (see page 45)
1 cup bread crumbs
12 large mushroom caps, sautéed (see page 119)
Watercress

Preheat broiler and broiler pan. Drain the sweetbreads. Put them into a pot and cover with fresh cold water. Cut the lemon in half, squeeze in the juice, and add the skins to the pot with one teaspoon of salt. Bring to a boil and simmer for ten minutes. Drain and let cool. Cut the sweetbreads in half lengthways and paint with some of the Beurre Maître d'Hôtel. Salt, pepper, and lightly bread them. Place on a pan and under the broiler, not too near the heat. When they are good and brown on both sides, arrange them on a platter with the sautéed mushroom caps on top. Spoon the Beurre Maître d'Hôtel over them just before serving. Place a bouquet of very fresh watercress at each end of the platter.

Serve with Mashed Potatoes (see page 170), Brussels sprouts, and ice cream with fresh strawberries in syrup for dessert.

PORK CHOPS
SERVES 6

Once you've tried broiled pork chops, you will never want to cook them any other way. Do not cook them too much. It is true that they must be well done, but they *do not* have to be cremated.

12 ¾-inch-thick pork chops
Salt and pepper
Beurre Maître d'Hôtel (see page 45)
Parsley, chopped

Preheat broiler. Salt and pepper the chops. Put them into the broiler as close as possible to the heat. They should get a few burned edges. Do not overcook. They should be juicy, not dry. Six min-

utes on each side is ample time. Arrange them on a platter. Pour the Beurre Maître d'Hôtel over them and sprinkle with parsley. A 5-minute repose before serving assures they will be well done.

Serve with string beans, Potatoes Gratin Dauphinoise (see page 92), and a fresh fruit dessert.

BROILED TOMATOES
SERVES 6 TO 8

Tomatoes are among the few red vegetables—color contrast is important when you're composing a menu. Do not overcook the tomatoes. They get mushy and collapse.

5 tomatoes, ripe but firm
1 teaspoon salt
½ teaspoon garlic, finely chopped
¼ cup bread crumbs
1 tablespoon olive oil
1 tablespoon parsley, chopped

Preheat broiler and broiler pan. Cut the tomatoes in half and put them into the pan, cut side up. Sprinkle them with salt. Mix the garlic, crumbs, and olive oil together and spread evenly over the tops of the tomatoes. Put them under the broiler until the tops get good and brown. Remove to the oven at 450° for about 4 minutes to heat through before serving.

Serve with broiled meats.

CHAPTER THREE

Roasting

THERE IS A SAYING in the French kitchen, *"On peut devenir saucier, mais on est né rotisseur."* ("You can become a sauce cook, but you must be born a roast cook.") It sounds good (anything does in French), but it just isn't true. Anyone can become an excellent roast cook. There is a method of roasting which is unique and foolproof, and I promise that if you understand and carefully follow this method, you will *never* have an underdone or overcooked roast. Instead, you will have a roast that is evenly cooked and moist throughout.

Now get this! It's not hard to understand and it's very important. All roasts go into a preheated 500° oven for 30 minutes. This extreme heat sears and browns the outside of the meat, forming a crust which holds in the juice. The heat is then reduced to 350° for the remainder of the cooking time. The oven rack should be placed as high as possible to allow the roast to come within 6 inches of the top. (Be sure the oven rack is inserted properly. It is designed to slide out as far as possible and stop before it falls.)

Roasting takes place in the oven. Because what's being roasted is surrounded by heat, the outside of the roast becomes brown all over. The heat penetrates the brown crust and gradually moves toward the center. (The heat carries with it the delicious taste of the crust.) While the center of the roast is still cold and raw, the outer portions, to a depth of an inch, are getting well done. But don't worry, because the interior meat will render juice as it gets hot. As this juice tries to get out of the roast (and let's face it; that's just what juice does in meat—it tries to escape), it reaches the well-done dry meat, where it is absorbed. Of course, the escape is also inhibited by the exterior crust of the roast. So that wonderful juice will be stopped and absorbed where it's needed most. For roasts that have to be pink, red juice will also color the well-done darker meat.

Now this is important; it is the key to perfect roasting. You must take the roast *out* of the oven before it's cooked through and *repose* it in a room-temperature, draft-free place for a certain length of time. The roast will continue to cook while the outside meat has a well-deserved rest. The interior heat will slowly continue to move toward the center of the roast. No additional time in the oven will hasten the slow progress of the heat toward the center of the roast. When you take something away from the heat (whether it's removing a roast from the oven or a steak from the broiler), it will continue to cook. Therefore the reposing time must be figured into the total cooking time. Some roasts must repose out of the oven for the same length of time they've spent in the oven. Of course, the outside of the roast will eventually grow cool, so it must be put back into a preheated 300° oven for 15 minutes before it is served.

As the roast reposes, the crisp brown outside meat on the other hand will act as an insulation for the interior heat, which is gradually making its way to the center. The roast should not be covered as it reposes, because the covering will create steam, which would soften the crisp exterior and permit the juice to leak out.

Some of my students have said they turn off the oven and leave the roast in it to repose. I must warn you against doing this. The oven is well insulated. It stays hot and will continue to cook and dry the outside of the roast, which is well done and dry enough.

There is one real danger when you repose meats. If the roast has had insufficient heat, it will not be just a little underdone; it will be raw. As the insufficient heat approaches the center, it diminishes and is used up by the cool meat. There must be sufficient heat to defeat (or cook) the cool center.

About 40 to 45 minutes before a roast is removed from the oven, roughly cut celery, carrots, and onion are distributed around the roast. They should get tinged with brown as they cook. This combination of vegetables is used extensively in the French kitchen and is called a *mirepoix*. It adds taste to the roast and to the sauce, which is prepared (after the meat has been removed) by simmering stock or water in the bottom of the pan with the vegetables. As this mixture cooks on top of the stove, a wooden spoon is used to loosen the bits clinging to the surface of the pan and blend them into the sauce. This unthickened juice (*jus*) of concentrated flavor is the best accompanying sauce for roasts. It should be strained before it is served.

Some roasts, such as pork, beef, and duck, render a lot of fat. The fat must be poured off before adding the vegetables. If this is not done, the vegetables give their flavor to the fat, which will be thrown away. (Duck and goose fat should be saved. Both are excellent for sautéeing potatoes.) The covering layer of fat on pork and beef roasts should be pared to a thickness of no more than ¼ inch. Meats that have little fat, such as veal, chicken, and turkey, should be smeared with soft butter or lightly oiled. They should also be basted frequently during roasting. This prevents the crust from getting too dry and breaking, which would permit the all-important juice to escape. If there are no drippings from the meat to use for basting, some melted butter can be poured over the roast.

Pay careful attention to the various time schedules for roasting in the following recipes. It is the thickness of the meat that dictates the cooking time, rather than the length or weight. There is a time chart given at the end of each of the following recipes (each chart is different) for both the length of cooking time in the oven and the length of cooking time out of the oven (reposing). Follow these charts carefully if you wish to cook perfect roasts.

ROAST CHICKEN

SERVES 2

I insist that you roast chicken with the breast down, although this direction is contrary to directions in all other cookbooks. It will keep the breast meat juicy. The back can stick up in the hot air and dry out because it has little meat on it.

1 2½-pound roasting chicken
½ stick butter
Salt and pepper
Watercress, with half the stems removed

Preheat oven to 500°. Truss the chicken (see pages 68–70). On top of the stove, heat the butter until it is brown, in an oval or round pot, pan, or casserole that will just contain the chicken. A small pot will hold the butter closer to the sides of the chicken. Salt and pepper the chicken. Place it in the sizzling brown butter, breast down. (The chicken will have to rest on one side of the breast.) Then put the chicken into the oven, as close to the top (where it is hottest) as possible, but without touching the top.

After 20 minutes, shift the chicken from one side of the breast to the other. If the bird is becoming good and brown, lower the oven heat to 450° and roast for another 20 minutes. (The total cooking time in the oven will be 40 minutes.) Remove from the oven and repose for 10 minutes. Then return the chicken to a 350° oven for 8 minutes and serve.

Serve the roast chicken breast side up on a platter. Pour half the butter from the pan over the chicken before serving. Garnish the platter with a bouquet of watercress. Serve with boiled new potatoes, Carrots Vichy (see page 165), and follow with a creamy dessert.

TIME CHART FOR ROASTING CHICKEN (FOR MEAT AT REFRIGERATOR TEMPERATURE)			
WEIGHT IN POUNDS	ROASTING TIME	REPOSE	SERVES
2½	40 MINUTES	10 MINUTES	2
3	50 MINUTES	15 MINUTES	3
4	70 MINUTES	20 MINUTES	5

ROAST TURKEY WITH CHESTNUT DRESSING

SERVES 6 TO 8

In this recipe you should play around with the stuffing. It should be your own concoction. All recipes for turkey demand too much cooking time in the oven. The reposing principle should be applied here, too.

First make turkey stock.

Liver, gizzard, and neck from turkey
Water
1 carrot, peeled and roughly cut
1 large onion, peeled and roughly cut
1 stalk celery, washed and roughly cut
2 bay leaves
Salt and pepper

Combine all the ingredients in a 2-quart saucepan. Cover with a quart of water and simmer uncovered for one hour. Reserve 2 cups of the resulting stock for the stuffing. Continue simmering the remaining stock over medium heat for at least 1¾ hours.

Chestnut Dressing

2 cups turkey stock
6 cups of stale French bread, broken in pieces no smaller than a golf ball and no larger than a tennis ball
1 pound chestnuts
1½ pounds sausage meat
4 onions, peeled and minced
1 teaspoon thyme leaves
½ teaspoon allspice
½ teaspoon sage
5 cloves garlic
Salt and pepper

Pour the 2 cups of turkey stock reserved for stuffing over the bread. After the bread has absorbed the stock, use your fingers to break it into pieces no larger than a nickel and reserve until needed.

Preheat oven to 500°. Make a ½-inch cut on the round side of each chestnut and place the nuts on a cooky sheet. Put into the hot oven for 10 minutes. Remove the nuts from the oven and allow them to cool off a bit. Peel the chestnuts. Both the outer shell and inner skin will come off quite easily. Reserve until needed. Sauté the sausage meat in a large frying pan over medium-high heat. As the meat begins to render fat, break it into small pieces with a spoon. Add the rest of the ingredients for the stuffing, except the chestnuts and the bread. Reduce the heat and simmer slowly for 15 minutes. Add to the soaked bread. Add the chestnuts and mix thoroughly. Add salt and pepper to taste.

Roasting the Turkey

10-pound turkey
2½ teaspoons salt
½ teaspoon pepper
½ stick butter
2 onions, peeled and roughly cut
1 carrot, peeled and roughly cut
1 stalk celery, washed and roughly cut
Aluminum foil

Clean the turkey under cold running water, taking care to rinse out the neck cavity as well as the inside cavity. Pluck any quills remaining on the skin. Put 2 handfuls of stuffing into the neck cavity and fasten the skin flap to the back of the turkey with a 4-inch skewer. Stuff the inside of the turkey and truss in the same manner shown on pages 68–70. No skewers or strings will be necessary to hold in the stuffing. You will find that little or none will fall out during roasting.

The oven has been preheated to 500° for the chestnuts. Place the turkey in the roasting pan, breast side up. Mix the salt and pepper with the butter, and rub it all over the bird. Put the turkey in the oven, as close to the top as possible, but without touching the oven. Since heat rises, the oven is hottest here. After 20 minutes, distribute the onions, carrot and celery around the turkey and reduce the heat to 450°. (For a larger turkey, put the *mirepoix* around the turkey 45 minutes before removing it from the oven.) The vegetables must be browned, but not burned. If burned, they give a bitter taste to the juice. Twenty minutes later, pour 1½ cups of water over the turkey breast. Loosely cover with foil and reduce heat to 350° for the remainder of the cooking time. (Tin foil pushed down over the breast of a turkey will keep the meat moist.) I would love to have you roast the turkey with the breast side down, but it's too hard to turn the larger ones. Another problem is that the skin on the breast is apt to soften too much and break.

Remove the turkey to a serving platter. Allow it to repose uncovered, in a warm, draft-free place.

After the turkey has had its repose, return it to 350° oven for ½ hour. Heat the sauce and serve it separately with kumquats, Mashed Potatoes (see page 170), Braised Butternut Squash (see page 141), and broccoli (see page 164). The meal could begin with Oyster Stew (see page 36). Serve Apple Pie Tatin (see page 96) for dessert.

Giblet Sauce

Stock
Liver, gizzard, and neck from stock
2 tablespoons cornstarch
½ cup water

Pour the remaining stock with the liver, gizzard, and neck into the roasting pan. Simmer for a minute on top of the stove, using a wooden spoon to scrape any brown bits from the bottom of the pan. These bits give color and taste to the juice. Strain the contents of the roasting pan into a saucepan. Bring to a simmer. Mix 2 tablespoons cornstarch with ½ cup of water and whisk into the simmering sauce. Adjust the seasoning of the sauce to taste. Pick the meat from the neck. Chop this, along with the liver and gizzard, quite finely. Add to the sauce and simmer for 10 minutes. The sauce may then be served separately.

TIME CHART FOR ROASTING TURKEY (FOR MEAT AT REFRIGERATOR TEMPERATURE)			
WEIGHT IN POUNDS	ROASTING TIME	REPOSE	SERVES
8 TO 12	12 MINUTES PER POUND	4 MINUTES PER POUND	5 TO 9
13 TO 15	11 MINUTES PER POUND	4 MINUTES PER POUND	10 TO 14
16 TO 22	9 MINUTES PER POUND	3 MINUTES PER POUND	15 TO 20

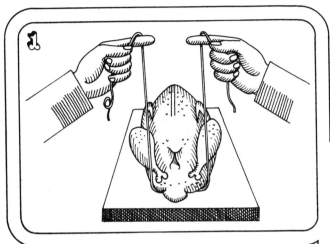

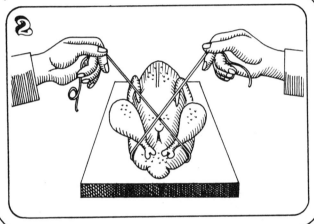

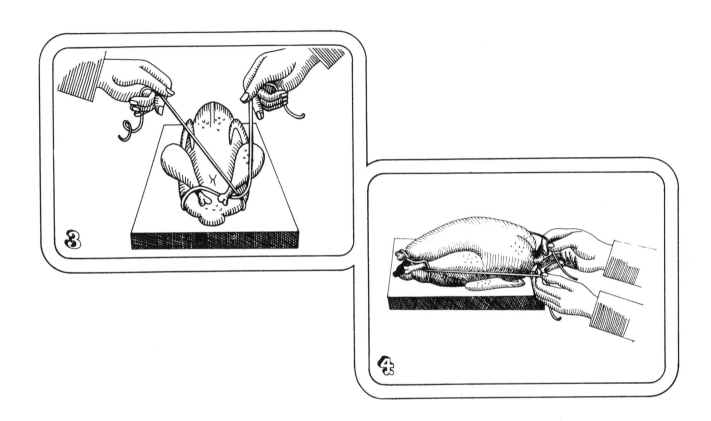

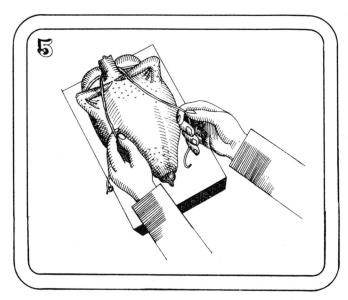

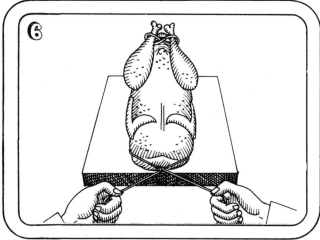

DUCK À L'ORANGE

SERVES 6 TO 8

The duck should be crisp and hot. The sauce should not be poured on until just before serving time. A plain roast duck is also delicious. You might try it sometime. This is a difficult dish to prepare. Lots of luck!

2   5-pound ducks
Salt and pepper
1 stalk celery, washed and roughly cut
1 carrot, peeled and roughly cut
2 onions, peeled and roughly cut

Preheat oven to 500°. Remove the wing tips from the ducks and reserve. Salt and pepper ducks, truss (pages 68–70) and set breast up on rack in roasting pan. Distribute the wing tips and 2 necks around the ducks. Place in the oven as near to the top as possible, but without touching the oven. After 45 minutes, pour off all the fat and add the celery, carrot, and onions. Reduce heat to 350°. Continue to roast for 40 minutes more. The vegetables must be brown, but not burned. They give a bitter taste to the sauce if they are burned. Remove the ducks to a serving platter to repose, uncovered, in a warm, draft-free place.

Orange Sauce

Necks, wings, and vegetables from roasted ducks
⅓ cup flour
1 cup water
2 bay leaves
2 cloves
½ teaspoon cinnamon
1 teaspoon allspice, ground
3 whole, unpeeled cloves of garlic
¼ cup tomato purée
8 oranges
1 lemon
7 ounces red currant jelly
⅓ cup wine vinegar
2 ounces Grand Marnier

Sprinkle the flour over the necks, wings, and vegetables in the roasting pan and stir until the white is no longer visible. Transfer the contents of the roasting pan to a 3-quart saucepan. Add the water to the roasting pan and deglaze by scraping the bottom and sides with a wooden spoon. Add the contents of the roasting pan to the saucepan. Stir in the bay leaves, cloves, cinnamon, allspice, garlic, and tomato purée. Cover with water. Simmer uncovered for one hour on top of the stove. Using a potato peeler, remove the skins of three oranges. Cut the skins into the finest strips possible (this is called *julienne*), place in a small saucepan, and cover with water. Simmer for 20 minutes. Run the skins under cold water, drain, and reserve. Section the three peeled oranges, and reserve.

Squeeze and combine the juice of four oranges and the lemon. Cook the jelly in a saucepan over medium-high heat, stirring constantly with a wooden spoon until the jelly becomes dark brown (carmelized). Add the vinegar, orange and lemon juice, plus the one remaining unpeeled orange, quartered. Let simmer until it liquefies. Add to the saucepan containing the necks, wingtips, and vegetables. Simmer the sauce for 15 minutes. Strain.

71

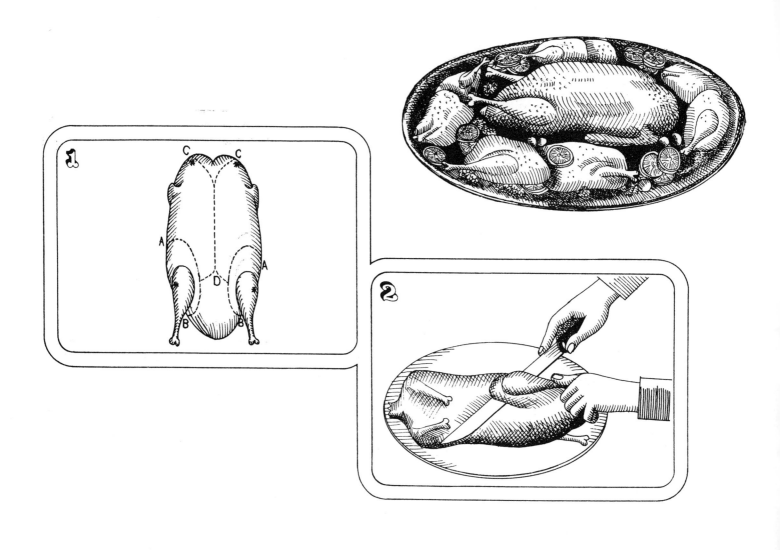

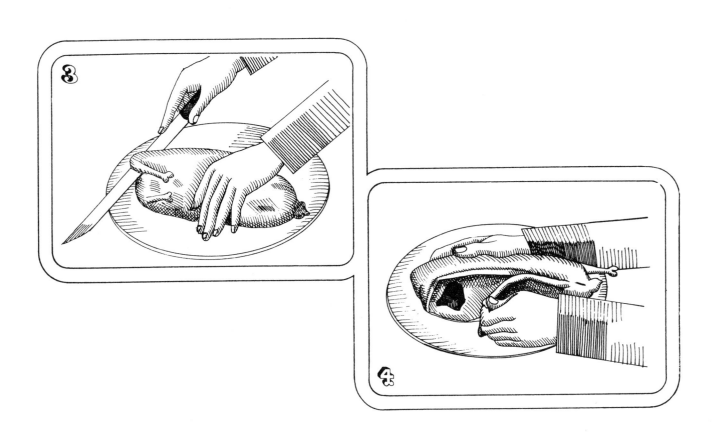

Add Grand Marnier to the sauce. If the sauce is not thick enough, mix a little cornstarch (one tablespoon) with ¼ cup water and stir into the simmering sauce. Pour a little sauce over the warmed ducks. Serve the rest separately or you will find the ducks are messy to carve. Add the remaining julienned peels and the orange sections to the sauce.

Begin the meal with Gazpacho (see page 37). Serve the duck with wild rice and sweet potatoes. Follow with Pears in Custard Tart (see page 96).

TIME CHART FOR ROASTING DUCK (FOR MEAT AT REFRIGERATOR TEMPERATURE)			
WEIGHT IN POUNDS	ROASTING TIME	REPOSE	SERVES
3½	1 HOUR	1 HOUR	2
4½	1¼ HOURS	1 HOUR	3
5½	1½ HOURS	1¼ HOURS	4

DUCK GRANDMÈRE

SERVES 6

This is a long, hard recipe, but I love it. It has a classic, simple taste—it tastes of what it is—duck. It is a pretty dish with mushrooms, onions, and carrots.

2   5-pound ducks
Salt and pepper
2 carrots, peeled and roughly cut
2 stalks celery, washed and roughly cut
3 onions, peeled and roughly cut

Preheat oven to 500°. Remove the second and third joints of the wings from the ducks and reserve. Truss the ducks as you would a chicken (page 68). Place in a roasting pan with the giblets, necks, and wing pieces. Salt and pepper the ducks. Place them in the oven as close to the top as possible, because that is where it is hottest. Roast for 30 minutes. Reduce heat to 350° and roast another 30 minutes. Pour the fat from the roasting pan and reserve. Add the carrots, celery, and onions, and continue roasting for ½ hour more. The vegetables must be browned, but not burned. Remove ducks to a warm, draft-free place.

Garnish

10 large carrots, peeled
Water
2 pounds white onions, peeled
Salt
½ tablespoon butter
Juice of one lemon
1 pound small mushrooms (quartered if large)

Cut the 10 carrots crossways into 3 equal parts. Cut the thick end pieces into quarters lengthways.

Cut the middle pieces in half, and leave their ends alone. Pare the edges of the pieces of carrot slightly so they resemble small carrots (see pages 167–168). Place them in a pot, cover with water, add salt, and bring to a boil. Lower the heat and simmer until just tender.

Brown the white onions in the reserved duck fat. Using a slotted spoon, remove the onions from the duck fat to a pot. Cover the onions with water, add salt, and simmer until they are just tender. Drain. Reserve the onion liquid. Heat the butter in a pan and add the mushrooms, salt, and lemon juice. Cover the pan and cook until the mushrooms render their juice. Uncover and continue cooking until the liquid has evaporated and the mushrooms are brown. Reserve.

Sauce

½ cup flour
1 cup water
2 bay leaves
1 tablespoon tomato paste
2 cloves garlic, peeled and minced
Salt and pepper
1 cup dry white wine

Remove the ducks from the roasting pan to a serving platter. Sprinkle ½ cup of flour over the giblets, necks, wing pieces, and vegetables in the roasting pan and stir until the white is no longer visible. Add one cup of water to the roasting pan, stirring with a wooden spoon to loosen the browned bits. This is called deglazing. The bits lend color and taste to the sauce. Pour the contents of the roasting pan into a large casserole. Add the bay leaves, tomato paste, garlic, salt, pepper, white wine, and cover with the reserved onion liquid. Simmer for 1½ hours. Strain into a saucepan. If the sauce is not thick enough, pour it into a large sauté pan and reduce to desired thickness. Skim off the fat.

Carve one duck as illustrated (see pages 72–73). Reheat the cooked carrots, browned onions, and mushrooms. Arrange them as garnish on and around the pieces of carved duck, with the whole duck in the center. Garnish around the whole duck with a few sprigs of parsley. Reheat the sauce and serve separately.

Serve with boiled rice and follow with Délice Lyonnaise (see page 95) for dessert.

ROAST PIGEONS
SERVES 6

It's almost impossible to use a knife and fork when you eat pigeons. As with lobster, it is great fun to use your fingers, so choose your guests accordingly.

6 1-pound squabs (or partridges), cleaned and trussed. Make sure all of the lungs have been removed. They have a very bitter taste if you happen on one while devouring your pigeon.
½ stick butter
Salt and pepper
⅓ cup dry white wine
1 cup seedless white grapes
Watercress, washed, drained, with half of the stems removed

Preheat oven to 500°. Salt and pepper squabs. Truss. Choose a roasting pan that will just contain them. Heat the butter in the roasting pan on top of the stove until it is brown. The smaller the pan, the deeper the butter will be. Place the squabs in the sizzling brown butter, breast down. Place them in the oven as close to the top as possible. Because heat rises, this is where it is hottest. After 20 minutes, tilt the birds so that the other parts of the breasts are against the bottom of the pan. Roast for 15 minutes more, then remove the roast pigeons to a serving platter. There is no need to repose pigeons, since they are so small. Place the roasting pan on top of the stove and add the wine. Cook for 3 minutes over high heat. Warm the grapes for a moment in this juice, and pour the juice and grapes over the birds. Garnish the platter with watercress.

This dish should be kept waiting in a warm 300° oven for no more than 15 minutes. The danger, as always, is that the pigeons will lose juice and be dry and stringy. In case of a delay in serving, it would be better to keep them breast down in the wine sauce and return them to a 300° oven before serving.

Begin the meal with a light cream soup, hot or cold. Serve pigeons with Spinach Timbale (see page 90), Rissole Potatoes (see page 124), and for dessert, Tarte Flambé aux Calvados (see page 94).

ROAST LEG OF VEAL

SERVES 15 TO 40 (DEPENDING ON SIZE)

This is perfect for a large party. If there is no trace of pink, the veal has been overcooked.

20–45-pound leg of veal, hip bone removed (shank end of leg bone cut to size of pan—take the pan to the butcher)
Salt and pepper
½ stick soft butter
3 onions, peeled and roughly cut
2 carrots, peeled and roughly cut
2 stalks celery, roughly cut
1 cup white wine
2 cups Demi-Glaze (page 32), or plan on a slight jus of white wine and a little water.
Watercress, washed and drained, with the stems removed

Preheat oven to 500°. Using your hand, smear the leg on both sides with butter, salt, and pepper. Since heat rises, place the leg of veal as close to the top of the oven as possible, where the oven is hottest. The roast must brown immediately to seal in the juice. After half an hour reduce the heat to 350°. See chart that follows for remainder of the cooking time. Add the vegetables 40 to 45 minutes before the roast is to come out of the oven. (The vegetables must be brown, but not burned. If burned, they give a bitter taste to the juice.)

Remove the roast to a serving platter and repose, uncovered, in a warm, draft-free place.

Add wine and demi-glaze to the roasting pan. Simmer on top of the stove. Scrape any brown bits from the bottom of the pan with a wooden spoon. They lend color and flavor to the juices. Strain into a saucepan and reserve.

Before serving, return the leg of veal to the roasting pan and put into a 300° oven for 15 minutes. Reheat the strained sauce and serve separately. Carve the roast as illustrated and garnish the platter with watercress.

Any veal roast can be cooked this way. Though veal should not be rare, I would prefer that the center be pink. Overcooked veal can be quite dry.

Serve Glazed Carrots (see page 166), Mama's Peas (see page 170), and Potatoes Parisienne (see page 124) with the veal. Follow immediately with a Bibb lettuce salad, and then a creamy dessert.

TIME CHART FOR ROASTING LEG OF VEAL (FOR MEAT AT REFRIGERATOR TEMPERATURE)			
WEIGHT IN POUNDS	ROASTING TIME	REPOSE	SERVES
20 TO 27*	7 MINUTES PER POUND	1½ HOURS	15 TO 24
28 TO 34	6 MINUTES PER POUND	1¾ HOURS	25 TO 34
35 TO 45	5 MINUTES PER POUND	2 HOURS	35 TO 40

* ROASTING TIMES TOWARD THE LIMITS OF THESE WEIGHT RANGES SHOULD BE ADJUSTED PROPORTIONATELY, E.G., A 26-POUND OR 27-POUND LEG SHOULD BE ROASTED 6½ MINUTES PER POUND.

STUFFED BREAST OF VEAL

SERVES 10 TO 12

This is an inexpensive dish and is good for a party. It is delicious served cold for a summer buffet. It's well worth a try. Most supermarkets have breasts of veal for stuffing.

1 breast of veal
2 pounds fresh spinach
4 medium onions, chopped
¼ stick butter
⅓ cup chopped parsley
1½ pounds ground veal
1 pound ground pork
1½ pounds ground raw chicken
4 cloves garlic, chopped
2 ounces Cognac

2 teaspoons salt
2 teaspoons pepper, freshly ground
2 eggs
½ cup peeled pistachio nuts (optional)
1 cup water

Have the butcher cut a pocket in the breast of veal. Put your hand into the pocket to make sure it extends to the full depth and breadth of the meat. Use a small, sharp knife or single-edge razor blade to extend the pocket if necessary. Preheat oven to 400°.

Remove the stems from the spinach. Wash thoroughly to remove all the sand. Place the spinach with one cup of water in a pot and boil for 3 minutes. Stir once during boiling. Rinse the cooked spinach under cold running water. Drain in a sieve and squeeze out all the water. Chop the spinach finely. Sauté the onions in butter until they are light brown. Combine the onions and spinach in a large bowl with all the remaining ingredients (except the cup of water) and mix thoroughly with your hands. Stuff into the pocket of the veal breast. Sew pocket, or close with skewers. Wrap veal tightly in a double thickness of cheesecloth. Twist and secure the ends of cloth with a string.

Cook the veal uncovered in the oven for ¾ hour. Then turn it and baste with one cup of water.

The entire cooking time should take 1½ hours. Repose for one hour, uncovered, in a warm place. Return to 300° oven for 15 minutes to reheat.

If served cold, the breast of veal should be glazed (see page 33).

Serve the hot breast of veal with broiled tomatoes, Cauliflower with Browned Bread Crumbs (see page 166), and Potatoes Boulangère (see page 91), followed by Crêpes Suzette (see page 126) for dessert.

TIME CHART FOR ROASTING BREAST OF VEAL (FOR MEAT AT REFRIGERATOR TEMPERATURE)			
WEIGHT	ROASTING TIME	REPOSE	SERVES
1 BREAST	1½ HOURS	1 HOUR	10 TO 12
½ BREAST	1 HOUR	¾ HOUR	6 TO 8

ROAST LEG OF LAMB

SERVES 6

When you carve the lamb, do not be alarmed if it seems a little too pink. Some or all of the pinkness disappears just seconds after it is carved. Don't forget that if you roast the lamb so long that there is no pinkness, the roast will not be as juicy. The hardest thing in the world is to turn out a *juicy* well-done piece of meat.

6-pound leg of lamb (Leg of lamb should not be peeled. The secondary skin covering the lamb is quite edible and holds in the juice.)
3 cloves garlic, peeled and slivered
Salt and pepper
1 stalk celery, roughly cut
2 medium onions, peeled and roughly cut
1 carrot, peeled and roughly cut
1 cup water
Few branches of fresh mint (optional)

Preheat oven to 500°. Make deep stabs into the meat in 10 places and insert a sliver of garlic into each. Push the garlic into the deep incisions with your little finger. Salt and pepper the roast quite liberally. Use about one tablespoon of salt, even more.

Since heat rises, place the roast right side up in the pan as close to the top of the oven as possible, without touching, because that is where it is hottest. The roast must brown immediately to seal in the juice. After half an hour, pour off all the grease. Reduce heat to 350°.

Add the vegetables to the pan approximately 45 minutes before the roast is removed from the oven. The vegetables must be browned, but not burned. If burned, they give a bitter taste to the sauce. After the roasting time is completed (see chart which follows), remove the roast to an oven-proof serving platter to repose, uncovered, in a warm, draft-free place for one hour, no matter how much it weighs.

Add one cup water to the pan with the vegetables and let simmer gently on top of the stove. With a wooden spoon, scrape any brown bits from the bottom of the pan. They lend color and taste to the juices. Then if you wish, simmer a few branches of fresh mint in the pan. Strain into a saucepan and reserve. Fifteen minutes before serving, reheat the roast in a 300° oven.

Since lamb has such a distinctive taste, interesting tasting vegetables go well with it. A tablespoon of fresh or dried rosemary leaves rissoléd with potatoes is good—if you haven't used mint in the sauce. Parsnips or kohlrabi with melted butter and parsley on top are good, too. Begin the meal with clams or oysters on the half shell. For dessert, serve vanilla ice cream with kumquats in a syrup served separately or spooned over the ice cream.

A half leg of lamb takes almost as long to cook as a whole one because it is, after all, the same thickness. Thickness is (as I've said before) the key factor in establishing cooking time. If a leg of lamb is boned, it needs much less time in the oven. Boned leg of lamb is easier to carve, but it is bad because the juice will leak out. It's like trying to hold water in a pot with holes in it. The more holes or cuts there are, the more juice runs out. For this same reason, it is bad to have the butcher cut chops partially through on the wide end of the leg.

TIME CHART FOR ROASTING LEG OF LAMB (FOR MEAT AT REFRIGERATOR TEMPERATURE)			
WEIGHT IN POUNDS	ROASTING TIME	REPOSE	SERVES
5	12 MINUTES PER POUND	1 HOUR	7
6	11 MINUTES PER POUND	1 HOUR	9
7 TO 10	10 MINUTES PER POUND	1 HOUR	11

SADDLE OF LAMB

SERVES 4 TO 6 (DEPENDING ON SIZE)

Saddles of lamb, dressed and ready for the oven, vary in size from 3½ pounds to 7 pounds. This is expensive, because the weight before dressing is double that of the meat oven-ready. A small saddle will serve four people, the largest will serve six. It shouldn't be served to people with huge appetites; there won't be enough. This lamb should be very pink or medium rare, but never well done.

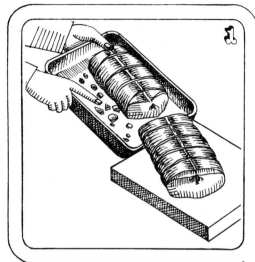

Cut straight down,
close to backbone,
as far as knife can go
(about 1 inch).

Remove roasted saddle
to cutting board.

3

Holding knife blade parallel
to cutting board,
cut in toward bone,
making ¼-inch slices.
Stack slices neatly
as you cut.

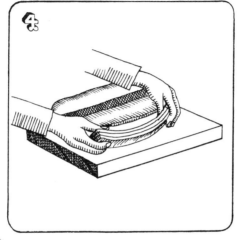

4

When one side is
completely carved,
replace the stack
of slices
next to the bone.

5

Repeat steps 2 through 4
with other side,
to produce finished carved saddle,
as shown.

1 saddle of lamb, without ribs
Salt and pepper
2 bay leaves or ½ teaspoon thyme
1 stalk celery, roughly cut
1 onion, peeled and roughly cut
½ carrot, peeled and roughly cut
½ cup water
Watercress, washed, drained, with half of the stems
  removed

Preheat oven to 500°. Cut away the kidneys and most of the fat and sinew against the inside of the backbone. Have the butcher peel off the outer skin and pare away all but ¼ inch of fat. The flanks are cut so they just meet under the inside of the backbone. Pepper the lamb inside and out. Cut the bay leaves lengthways, and arrange them against the inside of backbone, or sprinkle ½ teaspoon of thyme here. Bring the flanks together and secure with four pieces of string. Salt the roast just before it is put into the oven. Since heat rises, place the saddle of lamb down in the roasting pan, as close to the top of the oven as possible, where it is hottest.

The saddle must brown immediately to seal in the juice. After 25 minutes, pour off most of the accumulated grease and add the vegetables. Return to the oven. Reduce heat to 400° for the remainder of the cooking time. Follow the time chart for roasting and reposing. Remove the saddle of lamb to a serving platter to repose, uncovered, in a warm, draft-free place. Add half a cup of water to the vegetables in the roasting pan. Let it simmer on top of the stove for a few minutes. Scrape any brown bits from the bottom of the pan with a wooden spoon; they lend color and taste to the juices. Strain into a saucepan and reserve.

Fifteen minutes before serving, remove strings and return the roast to a preheated 300° oven for reheating. Carve and garnish platter with watercress. Reheat strained juice and serve separately.

To carve, keep the knife against one side of the backbone and cut along the length of the saddle. Then, with the flat of the knife held parallel to the table, cut in from the side, making slices about ¼ inch thick or less. To remove tenderloins, turn over the roast, open the flanks, and cut them out, keeping the knife edge in contact with the bone.

You might serve poached fish with either recipe for Beurre Blanc (pages 45–46) or Artichoke Surprise (see page 163) before the roast. Then, with the lamb, serve string beans and Potatoes Paillasson (see page 121), followed by Orange à l'Arabe (see page 172) for dessert.

TIME CHART FOR ROASTING SADDLE OF LAMB (FOR MEAT AT REFRIGERATOR TEMPERATURE)			
WEIGHT IN POUNDS	ROASTING TIME	REPOSE	SERVES
3½	40 MINUTES	30 MINUTES	4
5	55 MINUTES	45 MINUTES	6
7	1 HOUR	1 HOUR	7 TO 8

ROAST RIBS OF BEEF

SERVES 6

The principle of reposing really pays off when you roast beef.

6-pound rib roast
Salt and pepper
2 medium onions, peeled and roughly cut
1 celery stalk, roughly cut
1 carrot, roughly cut
1 cup water
1 bunch watercress, washed and dried

A 6-pound rib roast might be ample for eight, even ten, but for appearance's sake, I do feel that if you are serving a meal to guests, or even the family, a little nubbin of brown meat is a sad thing to behold. Even if it is enough, a few more dollars will buy a larger roast of more imposing and generous dimensions. If you're economizing, don't serve roast beef. The rib roast should have very little fat cover—no more than ¼ inch if possible, except where the meat joins the rib bone; there it has to be somewhat thicker. Of course, about 3 inches or more of the ribs are cut off. They are good braised.

Seven ribs make up the entire roast, which weighs about 20 pounds. From this, smaller roasts are cut; a 6-pound roast will have two ribs, a 10-pound roast will have three ribs, and so forth. Allow one pound of trimmed meat per person: a 5-pound roast for five, a 10-pound roast for ten. The small end, sometimes called "first cut," is the best. A roast cut from the middle to the large end has a wide strip of meat running over the top. This piece should be removed (your butcher will probably grind it up for you), and the fat cover brought down and tied to just cover the eye, or larger piece of meat. This gives a roast no more than 7 inches from the top of the fat side to the bottom. As I said in the introduction to roasting, the actual cooking time is dictated not so much by the weight as by the thickness.

Allow 2½ hours before mealtime for the 6-pound roast. Take the roast from the refrigerator. It must *not* be room temperature, or the time schedule that follows will not apply. Meat at room temperature will take less time to cook.

Preheat oven to 500°. Salt and pepper the roast quite liberally. Use about one teaspoon of salt, even more. The rib roast is placed *rib side up, fat side down,* and remains so throughout roasting. Since heat rises, place the roast as close to the top of the oven as possible, without touching, because that is where it is hottest. The roast must brown immediately to seal in the juice. After half an hour, pour off all the grease. Return pan to the oven. Reduce heat to 350° for remainder of cooking time.

Add the vegetables 30 to 45 minutes before removing the roast from the oven. The vegetables must be brown, but not burned. If burned, they give a bitter taste to the juice. Remove the roast to an oven-proof serving platter to repose, uncovered, in a warm, draft-free place.

Add one cup of water to the pan with the vegetables and let it simmer gently on top of the stove. Scrape any brown bits from the bottom of the pan with a wooden spoon, as they lend color and taste to the juices. Strain into a saucepan and reserve.

Fifteen minutes before serving, reheat the roast in a preheated 300° oven. Cut half the stems from the bunch of watercress and place a bouquet at one end of the platter. Slice the roast and reheat the strained juice, which should be served separately. Be sure to serve a few sprigs of watercress with each slice of beef.

Serve Oyster Stew (see page 36) to begin. Glazed onions, Potatoes Dauphine (see page 104) or Potatoes Sables (see page 124) are delicious with roast beef. Finish with Pears Poached in White Wine (see page 174) with some good, simple cookies.

If you have some roast beef left over, it is delicious cold. Serve it with Horseradish Sauce (see page 48) and a simple green salad.

TIME CHART FOR ROASTING RIBS OF BEEF (FOR MEAT AT REFRIGERATOR TEMPERATURE)			
WEIGHT IN POUNDS	ROASTING TIME	REPOSE	SERVES
5 TO 11	12 MINUTES PER POUND	1 HOUR	ALLOW
12 TO 16	10 MINUTES PER POUND	2 HOURS	1 POUND
17 TO 20	9 MINUTES PER POUND	2 HOURS	PER PERSON

All roasts go into a 500° oven for the first 30 minutes. The heat is then reduced to 350°. The total cooking time is calculated to include the first 30 minutes at 500°.

Use of this chart will result in a rare roast. For medium-rare, add 2 minutes per pound for roasts up to 10 pounds, and one minute per pound for roasts over 10 pounds.

ROAST PORK LOIN

SERVES 6

Please don't overcook pork. It's such good meat and does not have to be dry.

4-pound loin of pork (with bone cut to facilitate carving)
Salt and pepper
1 medium onion, peeled and roughly chopped
1 stalk celery, washed and roughly chopped
1 carrot, peeled and roughly chopped
⅓ cup dry white wine (or brown stock)

Preheat oven to 500°. Salt and pepper the loin of pork. Use a deep roasting pan and place it in the oven as close to the top as possible, without touching, because that is where it is hottest.

After ½ hour, pour off the rendered fat and return the roast to the oven. Reduce heat to 350° for the remainder of the cooking time. Add the vegetables 45 minutes before removing the roast from the oven. The vegetables must be brown, but not burned. If burned, they give a bitter taste to the juice.

Remove the roast to a serving platter to repose in a warm, draft-free place. Like roast beef and veal, the loin should rest out of the oven for at least one hour before serving. It then should be returned to a 300° oven for 15 minutes to reheat before serving.

Add wine to the pan and simmer for 3 or 4 minutes. Scrape any brown bits from the bottom of the pan with a wooden spoon. They will lend color and taste to the juices. Strain into a saucepan and reserve. Reheat the roast and strained juice and serve separately.

Serve with Mashed Potatoes (see page 170), Carrots Vichy (see page 165), and if peaches are in season, fresh Peaches in Custard Tart for dessert (see page 96).

TIME CHART FOR ROASTING PORK LOIN (FOR MEAT AT REFRIGERATOR TEMPERATURE)			
WEIGHT IN POUNDS	TIME IN OVEN	REPOSE	SERVES
4	1¼ HOURS	1 HOUR	6
6	1½ HOURS	1 HOUR	8
8	1¾ HOURS	1 HOUR	10

CHAPTER FOUR

Baking

Baking, like roasting and braising, takes place in the oven. Heat surrounds what's being baked, with the top, bottom, and sides all receiving an equal amount. Of course, something boiled or deep-fried is also surrounded by heat, but the vehicle for the heat is liquid, which is far less delicate than the hot air in the oven. A cake, for example, demands perfect tranquillity. As it bakes in the oven at a moderate temperature, it slowly dries out and browns evenly on all sides. A leavening agent such as yeast or baking powder makes it puff up. What was a basic liquid mixture of eggs, shortening, flour, and a leavening agent comes out of the oven a rigid, interconnected spongelike mass. It's really like magic.

Cakes are often too dry. People forget that the cake will continue to cook out of the oven, just like a roast of beef. A cookie, when first removed from the oven, is soggy. Moments later, outside of the oven, it will become just crisp enough. Therefore, whatever is being baked must be removed from the oven before it has achieved the desired consistency.

If the stove is not level, you will have lopsided cakes. It is important to preheat the oven so that the temperature will be even throughout. The oven rack should be in a central position so that cakes, cookies, or bread will brown evenly on top and bottom. Dark-colored foods bake faster than light-colored ones because they absorb heat more (in the same way as a dark-colored car parked in the sun gets hotter inside than a light-colored one).

I am not a pastry chef. That is why there are only a few recipes in this section. For instance, I've never made an angel food cake, and I think soufflés are a pain in the neck. Why go through all that aggravation when the same amount of energy can produce an entire meal of elegant proportions?

What is baked? Anything that goes into the oven uncovered at a moderate temperature. Cakes, custards, casserole dishes, fruit, Idaho potatoes, even a wet shoe. Whatever it is, it dries out as it bakes, and will continue to dry out and cook after it has been removed from the oven. So take out the shoe when it gets good and warm, because it will dry out as it cools.

CRAB MEAT NORFOLK

SERVES 4

This recipe has the fewest possible number of ingredients, and is easy to make. Serve it with fluffy white rice.

1 pound lump fresh crab meat
1½ sticks butter
¼ cup parsley, chopped

Preheat oven to 400°. Cover the bottom of a buttered baking dish with the lumps of crab meat; they can be close to each other but not piled up. Exactly 10 minutes before serving, put the dish of crab meat into the oven. Five minutes before serving, put the butter into a frying pan and put the pan over a medium-high heat. Wait until the butter is brown. After it melts it will foam up and you will be unable to tell if it is yellow or brown. Push the foam aside with a spoon and take a look; the foam usually disappears just when the butter turns brown. When the butter is brown, it will emit a most pleasant, nutty odor. Sprinkle the parsley over the hot crab meat. Serve immediately with the brown butter sauce apart in a preheated bowl.

Do not stir or bother the lumps of crab meat in any way; they are delicate and will break.

ESCARGOTS

SERVES 6

Once the snail shells and serving plates have been purchased, it is simply a question of buying the snails. The pincers used to hold the snail shells are unnecessary. The thumb and index finger do the job better. You could also buy the little forks to take the snails out of the shells, but a toothpick does just as well.

½ pound butter
2 tablespoons garlic, chopped (about 5 cloves)
2 tablespoons shallots, chopped (about 3 or 4 shallots)
½ teaspoon salt
½ teaspoon pepper, freshly ground
Juice of ½ lemon
⅓ cup parsley, chopped
36 snails
36 shells

Preheat oven to 400°. Using a fork or your fingers, mix together the butter, garlic, shallots, salt, pepper, lemon juice, and parsley. This mixture is called Escargot Butter. Push a piece of this butter as large as a marble into each shell. Push an escargot, tail end first, into each shell, the larger ones into the larger shells, the smaller ones into the smaller shells. Push them well into the shell and fill the remaining shell cavity with the rest of the Escargot Butter. Put the stuffed shells into the indented places on the plates, the open side up and level. If there is any remaining butter, it can be divided among the six plates. Just throw it on top. Cook in the oven for 6 or 7 minutes and serve immediately with lots of French bread to sop up the delicious Escargot Butter.

The escargots should be hot, but the butter must not burn or even get brown.

LITTLENECK CLAMS
WITH ESCARGOT BUTTER

SERVES 6

The only complaint I've ever had about this dish is that the clams seem tough. They will not be if they are just heated up and served immediately.

⅓ cup parsley, chopped
2 tablespoons garlic, chopped (about 5 cloves)
2 tablespoons shallots, chopped (3 or 4 shallots)
Juice of ½ lemon
½ teaspoon salt
½ teaspoon pepper, freshly ground
2 sticks butter
36 littleneck clams, on the half-shell

Preheat oven to 400°. To make the Escargot Butter (using a fork or your hand), mix together the parsley, garlic, shallots, lemon juice, salt, pepper, and butter. Tip the clams on the half-shell to drain the excess juice from them. Place on a pan. Dot each with Escargot Butter. This can be done ahead of time. When ready to serve, bake for 5 to 7 minutes. Serve immediately, with French bread to sop up the excess butter.

MUSSELS
WITH ESCARGOT BUTTER

SERVES 4 TO 6

French bread is a must with Escargot Butter.

36 mussels
Escargot Butter (see above)
⅓ cup bread crumbs

Preheat oven to 450°. Wash the mussels in lots of cold water. Then scrape each mussel by paring the seaweed beard with a small sharp knife. Put the mussels into a pot, cover tightly, and steam them until they open. They need no water to cook in. When they are open they are cooked. This should take about 12 minutes over a high heat. When they are cool enough to handle, throw away 36 half shells and arrange the others with the mussels inside on a pan. Dab the Escargot Butter on each mussel. Then sprinkle on bread crumbs. Bake in oven for 15 minutes.

PORGY (Scup) AU GRATIN

SERVES 6

These fish have fine texture and taste. It is almost as much fun to eat them as it is to catch them.

½ stick butter
1 large zucchini
3 medium tomatoes
12 porgy fillets
5 medium shallots, finely chopped
Juice of 1 lemon
3 tablespoons olive oil
Salt and pepper
½ cup grated Parmesan cheese
⅔ cup bread crumbs

Preheat oven to 400°. Rub butter on the inside of a shallow baking dish that is large enough to contain the above ingredients in a single layer. Slice the zucchini and tomatoes into rounds. Arrange these in the baking dish, alternating the fish, zucchini, and tomatoes in an overlapping pattern. Sprinkle the top with the shallots and lemon juice. Pour the olive oil over all. Add salt and pepper. Mix the grated cheese and bread crumbs together and sprinkle over the top. Dot the surface with butter. Bake for 45 minutes or until the top is golden brown.

STUFFED MUSHROOM CAPS

SERVES 8 TO 12

These mushroom caps could be served with broiled meats, with a roast or even with cocktails.

36 large mushrooms (1½-inch diameter)
⅓ stick butter
Salt
Juice of ½ lemon
Escargot Butter (see page 88)
⅓ cup bread crumbs

Preheat oven to 450°. Break out the stems of the mushrooms, wash and sauté them in hot butter with a pinch of salt and the lemon juice until they begin to shrink, about 3 minutes. Let them cool. Stuff them with the Escargot Butter. Put the mushrooms close together on the table and sprinkle them liberally with fresh bread crumbs. Put them on a pan and bake them in an oven for 10 minutes. It would save trouble if they could be served on the same pan or baking dish in which they were cooked.

SPINACH TIMBALE

This is a really fancy vegetable to perk up an otherwise plain meal, and is easy to prepare.

1 pound fresh spinach
1 cup water
2 cups light cream
2 cloves garlic, peeled
3 large, or 4 or 5 small eggs
1 egg yolk
1 teaspoon salt

Preheat oven to 375°. Wash the spinach thoroughly to get rid of sand. Place spinach in a pot with one cup of water and bring to a boil. Reduce heat. Stir and let simmer for 2 minutes. Cool the spinach under cold running water. Drain in a sieve and squeeze out the excess water with your hands. Roughly chop the spinach.

Heat the cream slowly with the cloves of garlic, allowing time for the garlic to impart a noticeable scent to the cream (about 20 minutes). Remove the garlic. Beat the eggs and yolk. Beat the cream, spinach, and salt into this. Pour into a buttered one-quart ring mold or individual timbales or ramekins.

Place the mold or timbales into a pan containing one inch of cold water. Bake for a minimum of 30 minutes for individual timbales, 45 minutes for a ring mold.

Once the timbale is ready to serve, it can rest for 30 minutes or more and then be reheated in the oven at 375° for 10 minutes before serving.

BAKED EGGPLANT

SERVES 6

This is stolen from my chef friend Pierre Abadie. Thank you, Pierre.

1 large eggplant
Salt
⅔ cup bread crumbs
4 large cloves garlic, finely chopped
⅓ cup olive oil
Pepper

Preheat oven to 425°. Cut the eggplant in half lengthways. Make several crisscross cuts, ½ inch deep, on the open face of each half. Do not cut skin. Sprinkle liberally with salt and set aside for 45 minutes. Rinse under cold water and gently squeeze. Pat dry. Combine the bread crumbs, garlic, oil, and pepper, and spread on each half. Bake the eggplant until it is brown and tender (about 45 minutes).

This is good with lamb and game.

BAKED POTATO

There is nothing better in the world. In the list of ingredients it says "butter"—it should be "lots of butter." Never bake potatoes wrapped in tin foil. The potato steams, causing the skin to lose its crispness. The baked skin is delicious and imparts taste to the interior of the potato.

Idaho potatoes (of equal size—½ pound)
Butter

Salt
Pepper, freshly ground

Preheat oven to 450°. Scrub the potatoes. Lightly prick each one with a kitchen fork or skewer. Put the potatoes directly on the rack in the oven for 45 minutes. Pinch one to see if it's soft inside. Serve as soon as possible, because baked potatoes start to dry out once they are cooked through.

Serve them piping hot and let each person cut his own. Mash in lots of butter, salt, and a good twist of pepper.

POTATOES BOULANGÈRE

SERVES 6

This dish does not have to be served immediately. It can be cooked in advance of the meal. Reheat in the oven at 400° for 20 minutes.

2½ pounds potatoes
5 medium onions, sliced
⅓ stick butter
10-ounce can of beef consommé
½ cup water (approximately)
Salt and pepper

Preheat oven to 425°. Peel and thinly slice the potatoes. Gently sauté the onions in butter until they are limp and translucent. Remove them from heat. Add potatoes, consommé, and enough water to barely cover. Salt and pepper to taste. Pour into a baking dish or casserole. Bake for 40 minutes, or until the potatoes are browned on top and tender.

POTATOES GRATIN DAUPHINOISE

SERVES 6

A specialty of the Restaurant de la Pyramide in Vienne, France. You can cook it 6 hours in advance of a meal. It almost tastes better warmed up.

1 clove garlic, peeled
½ stick butter, melted
2 pounds boiling potatoes
¼ teaspoon pepper
2 eggs
1 pint light cream
1 teaspoon salt

Preheat oven to 375°. Use a large enough flat-bottomed casserole or baking dish so that when the ingredients are evenly distributed they are no more than ½ inch thick. (A casserole 9 by 12 inches would be ideal.) Lightly rub the bottom of the casserole with garlic. No little pieces of garlic should remain in the dish; the taste of garlic must be very slight. Pour the melted butter into the dish and spread it around evenly with your fingers. Peel, wash, and finely slice the potatoes. Sprinkle them lightly with pepper and spread them evenly over the bottom of the dish.

Beat the eggs. Add the cream and salt to the eggs and beat in. Pour the mixture over the potatoes. Bake for 50 minutes, or until it is lightly brown on top. To warm up, place in 350° oven for 15 minutes.

FRENCH PIE CRUST

This will cover a pizza pan one foot in diameter.

2 cups flour
1 tablespoon sugar
1 teaspoon salt
¼ pound butter
3 egg yolks
3 tablespoons water

Mix the flour, sugar, and salt in a bowl. Pinch in a stick of cold butter. Rub the mixture together between your hands until it has a yellow-colored, sandy texture. Beat the egg yolks with 3 tablespoons of cold water and pour over the flour and butter mixture. Work the mixture together with the ends of your fingers to distribute the moisture. Put your fingers in some flour and rub them together over the bowl to get rid of the pastry sticking to them. Flour the palms of your hands and press the pastry into a ball. If it does not stick together, but crumbles apart, add 1 or 2 more tablespoons of water. Press into a ball and let rest for at least 15 minutes in the refrigerator.

Dust the table with flour and then flatten the pastry a little with your fist or bang it a few times with the roller. Dust the dough top and bottom with flour and roll it out to slightly more than the width of the pan. Roll the crust onto the roller and transfer it to the pan. Arrange the pastry to conform with the shape of the pan. Press the pastry against the rim of the pan using the end of a fork (or pinch it against the edge using your thumb and index finger). Put your fingers into flour so that they will not stick to the dough. Trim any excess pastry from the rim of the pan with a knife. Poke a few holes in the crust with a fork. Arrange a piece of tin foil over the crust and up the edges and distribute ⅔ pound of rice or dry beans over it. This will prevent the crust from rising in the center. Cook until golden brown in an oven preheated to 400° for 20 minutes. Remove the foil and beans and store them in an open mason jar for your next tart. At this point the crust will feel soft, but as it cools it will dry and become crisp. If you have the courage, the crust can be removed from the pan and placed on a more attractive flat platter, plank, or tray. It should fall out of the tin.

If the crust has broken (and you have had an impossible time with it) you can be assured that it will be flaky, cakelike, and delicious. If the filling to go into the crust is a very wet one, a long wait before garnishing the crust will make it less soggy.

Pie crusts cooked separately from the fillings are dry, crumbly, and delicious. Any number of fillings are possible for a precooked crust: baked pears or apples, fresh or poached peaches, baked mixed fruit, fresh strawberries, raspberries, plums, or sliced bananas.

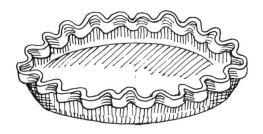

QUICHE LORRAINE

SERVES 6 TO 8

This is a good vehicle for experimentation—chopped ham, scrunched crispy bacon, olives, chicken, or with sugar and fruit you have a custard tart (page 96).

1 lightly browned crust (French Pie Crust, page 92)
4 slices Swiss cheese
1 pound fresh spinach
3 eggs
2 yolks
1½ cups light cream
1 tablespoon shallots, chopped
½ teaspoon salt
½ teaspoon pepper

Make the pie crust in a pan (square or round) with sides ¾–1 inch high. The crust should be baked no darker than light brown, since it has to bake again in the oven with the Quiche mixture in it. The prebaked crust should be dry and crisp within 2 hours after it has been removed from the oven, and ready for the Quiche mixture.

Preheat oven to 375°. Cut the cheese in strips and distribute them on the bottom of the crust. Wash and boil the spinach. Freshen under cold running water. Drain in a sieve, squeeze out additional water between your hands, and chop. Beat the eggs and yolks. Add the cream, shallots, salt and pepper to the eggs. Stir in the spinach. Taste the mixture and add more salt **and** pepper, if needed. Pour the mixture over the **cheese** and bake for 40 minutes or until the center of the Quiche is no longer liquid.

Warm up in 350° oven for 20 minutes and serve for lunch with a plain green salad and fruit for dessert. The Quiche makes an ideal cocktail snack when cut into one-inch cubes and served warm.

APPLE TART FLAMBÉ AU CALVADOS

SERVES 8 TO 12

I hate to say this so often, but *please* don't over-cook the apples.

The Pastry

¼ pound butter
1½ cups flour
1 tablespoon sugar
1 teaspoon salt
3 egg yolks
2 tablespoons water

Blend the butter into the flour, sugar, and salt. Blend the egg and water and pour around the dry ingredients. Blend. Form into a ball. Line a pizza pan with the pastry. Cover with aluminum foil. Press the pastry down to take the shape of the shell. Fill it with dry (or uncooked) rice. Bake in a 425° oven for 10 minutes. (The rice serves to hold the pastry in shape and should be removed later.)

Filling and Baking Tart

11 Golden Delicious apples
⅛ pound butter
1 cup sugar
Juice of 1 lemon
Water
⅓ cup Calvados

The apples should all be the same size. Peel and halve them and remove the cores with a melon-ball scoop. With the cut side down, carefully slice each half into six pieces, keeping the original shape. Butter the bottom of a shallow oven casserole. Place the apples in the shallow baking dish, keeping them in the shape of a half. The apples should completely cover the bottom of the casserole. It may be necessary to spread the slices apart, always keeping the round shape of an apple half. Sprinkle the sugar and lemon juice over the apples. Add a small amount of water (about ⅛ inch) and bake at 450° about 15 minutes (or until tender). This can be done ahead of time. Place in broiler to brown the tops.

Transfer the cooled, baked pastry shell to a round oven-proof platter. Fill the shell with the baked apples, arranging them in circles. The slices may have to be spread somewhat to fill the shell completely. Reduce the liquid used in baking the apples and pour over the apples.

Before serving, flame with the Calvados.

CHEESE RAMEKINS À LA CRÈME

SERVES 12 (USING CUSTARD CUPS OR RAMEKINS OF ½-CUP CAPACITY)

This is an excellent luncheon dish.

8 eggs
1 quart heavy cream
½ teaspoon salt
½ pound Swiss cheese, coarsely grated

Preheat oven to 420°. Beat the eggs until they are frothy. Add the cream and salt to the eggs and mix well. Distribute the cheese evenly in the bottoms of 4-ounce custard cups. Pour the egg mixture into a pitcher and then fill each cup almost to the top. Place the cups in a pan of cold water and bake for about 30 minutes.

Follow with a simple green salad and then a pastry dessert.

GENOISE

MAKES ONE 9-INCH CAKE
1 INCH HIGH

This is an awfully good cake. Be sure to beat the eggs until they are no longer warm before adding flour and butter.

4 eggs
¼ cup sugar
⅔ cup flour, sifted
⅓ stick butter, melted and cooled
½ teaspoon vanilla

Preheat oven to 400°. Beat the eggs and sugar together in a double-boiler over hot water until they are quite warm and double in volume. Continue beating, off the heat, until cool. Fold in the sifted flour, then the cooled butter. Pour into a greased, floured 9-inch pan. Bake for about 20 minutes, or until lightly browned. Cool on rack before removing from pan.

DÉLICE LYONNAISE

SERVES 10

Don't do this on a rainy day.

⅔ cup mixed candied fruit
⅓ cup Kirsch
Butter
Juice of ½ lemon
Salt
8 egg whites
⅓ cup sugar

Preheat oven to 400°. Chop the fruit into pieces no larger than a small pea. Cover the fruit with Kirsch and marinate (soak) overnight.

Butter a 2-quart mold; wipe it out with a paper towel. In a bowl, combine the lemon juice, salt, and egg whites. Beat until soft peaks are formed. Gradually add the sugar. Beat to stiff-peak stage. Drain the Kirsch from the fruit and reserve for sauce. Fold the candied fruit into the meringue, and transfer to mold. Smooth the top.

Use a skillet or pan that just contains the mold. Fill the skillet with water and bring to a boil. Place the mold in the skillet. Place the skillet with mold in the oven, and bake for 22 minutes, or until browned. Cool. Refrigerate before serving.

Gently pull the meringue (with your fingers) away from the sides of the mold. To unmold, place the serving platter face down on top of the mold. Grip the platter and the mold with both hands and invert. Gently remove the mold.

This recipe can be prepared 8 hours in advance of serving.

Sauce

⅔ cup light cream
8 egg yolks
⅓ cup sugar
1 teaspoon vanilla
1 tablespoon flour
Kirsch reserved from candied fruit
1 ounce Grand Marnier

Scald light cream by bringing it to a boil. Beat the egg yolks until frothy. Add the sugar and vanilla and beat until thick and light in color. Beat in the flour. While beating, slowly add some of the scalded cream to the egg mixture and then add the egg mixture to the remaining cream. Place on medium heat and continue beating until mixture is thick. Immediately pour into a bowl. Cool, mix in reserved Kirsch and Grand Marnier, and chill.

Spoon sauce over meringue.

PEARS IN CUSTARD TART

SERVES 6 TO 8

I say "ripe pears"—it should be "almost ripe," so that when they cook, they don't get mushy. The same is true if you make the custard tart with peaches or cherries.

1 prepared baked crust (French Pie Crust, page 92)
3–4 ripe pears
4 whole eggs
4 yolks
½ cup sugar
2 cups light cream

Preheat oven to 375°. Peel the pears, halve them lengthways, and core. Cut each half in thirds lengthwise. Arrange these pieces symmetrically on the prepared crust. Beat the eggs and yolks. Beat in the sugar. Heat the cream and beat in the egg-sugar mixture. Pour the mixture over the pears and bake in oven until the custard is slightly brown and firm —about 40 minutes. Cool and serve at room temperature. Do not refrigerate. If the tart is very cold it loses its delicate taste.

APPLE PIE TATIN

SERVES 8 TO 12

This was stolen from André Soltaer, chef at La Lutèce in New York. Thank you, André.

½ stick butter
1 cup vanilla sugar (vanilla beans will impart flavor to sugar if left together in a jar for several days)
10 apples (golden delicious or winesap)
1 unbaked crust (French Pie Crust, page 92)

Melt the butter over medium heat. Add the vanilla sugar, stirring almost continuously until the mixture is golden brown. Remove from heat. Pour into a 14-inch frying pan. Peel, quarter, and core the apples. Cut the quarters in half lengthways and arrange them, overlapping, on top of the caramelized sugar. Cover loosely with French Pie Crust. Do not press the crust to the edges of the pan. Cover with a damp cloth and refrigerate until one hour before serving time.

Preheat oven to 400° and bake for 45 minutes. Cool in the pan for 10 minutes. Then place a round platter face down on top of the frying pan. Get a firm grip on both pan and platter with both hands and turn upside down. Serve warm.

BAKED MIXED FRUIT

SERVES 8 TO 10

My grandmother made this often. She may have put in some grated orange and lemon peel.

½ pound large grapes
½ large pineapple or 1 small one
2 apples
1 large grapefruit
2 oranges
¼ pound purple plums
¼ pound fresh apricots
¼ pound seedless grapes
½ stick butter
Juice of 1 lemon
½ cup sugar
2 ounces Kirsch (optional)

Preheat oven to 425°. Wash and drain the fruit. Cut the large grapes in half lengthways and remove the seeds. Peel, core, and slice the pineapple and apples. Peel and section the grapefruit and oranges. Halve and pit the plums and apricots. Pick the stems from the seedless grapes. Do this work over a bowl or platter to catch as much juice as possible.

Smear half of the butter on the bottom of a shallow baking dish and add the fruit, arranging it attractively. Pour any accumulated juice over it. Add the lemon juice. Sprinkle on the sugar. Dot the fruit with the remaining butter. Bake for 30 minutes or until some of the fruit is tinged with brown. Remove from oven.

Using a suction baster or a small ladle, take as much juice as possible from the dish. Put it into a pot, add Kirsch and cook over medium heat until it reduces and becomes quite syrupy. Coat the top of the fruit with the syrup.

The taste of pineapple is indispensable. Citrus fruit is necessary for the juice it lends. Otherwise, substitutions and omissions are possible.

BAKED PEARS

SERVES 6

The juice in the pan should be poured over the fruit. If it is not syrupy, let it simmer until it is.

6 pears, with stems if possible
⅓ stick butter
½ cup sugar
Juice and grated rind of 1 lemon
⅓ cup water

Preheat oven to 400°. Use pears that are green, or just beginning to soften. The pears should be of the same hardness or they will require different cooking times. Peel the pears, cut in half lengthways, and core. With the tip of a paring knife, cut out the fibers that extend to the stem end. Leave the stems intact. Butter a baking dish, and arrange the halves flat side down. Sprinkle with sugar. Grate the skin of the lemon. Sprinkle the gratings, lemon juice, and water over all. Dot with the remaining butter.

Bake the pears for 45 minutes, or until tender. During the baking, baste at least once. The pears must stay in the oven until the sugar caramelizes or turns brown. Be careful toward the end of the cooking time—sugar turns black quickly.

Serve the pears hot or cold with heavy cream or ice cream. Apples, pineapple, or plums can be baked this way or, of course, Baked Mixed Fruit (see page 97).

BAKED ALASKA

SERVES 10 TO 12

This whole structure is in the shape of a volcano. This is a very difficult recipe. The first time I did it I omitted the cake, so the meringue had little to adhere to. As I was presenting it in the dining room, the meringue slid down the sides, out over the edges of the round platter, and onto the floor. I was so furious that I threw the whole thing out of the window.

9-inch cake—pound cake or Genoise (see page 95)
3 quarts ice cream (vanilla, strawberry, and orange sherbet)
3 ounces Grand Marnier
7 egg whites
4–5 egg yolks
1 cup sugar

The first step is to cut the cake into 3 layers. Place one layer on a heat-proof plate. Spread the bottom first with softened vanilla ice cream, then with the strawberry, and then the peak of the volcano with orange sherbet. Cut the other cake layers in half and place 3 halves along the sides of the ice cream. Cut the remaining half-layer into thirds and fill in the empty spaces. As if you were removing the small end of a soft-boiled egg with a sharp knife, remove the top of the small end of one of the eggs. Empty it and sink the shell halfway into the very top of the volcano, with the open end of the shell up. This will later be used to hold the Grand Marnier. Sprinkle the volcano with Grand Marnier. At this point, the cake can be frozen, wrapped and kept in the freezer for several weeks. Before baking, cover the cake with meringue.

For meringue, put yolks and ½ cup of the sugar into a bowl and beat until the yolks are very thick and light. Put the egg whites into a separate bowl and beat until they are foamy (low speed on and electric mixer). Then gradually add the remainder of the sugar at high speed. Beat to a very stiff stage. Blend the beaten egg yolks with the beaten whites. Remove the cake from the freezer and cover it completely with half of the meringue. The rest can be piped along the base and up the sides of the cake for a decorative touch. At this stage, the cake can again be placed in the freezer for a maximum of 8 hours. To bake, preheat oven to 450° and bake until browned—3 or 4 minutes. Remove at once.

This must be served immediately, so be ready to pour the barely warmed Grand Marnier into the empty eggshell. Ignite it. Just before serving, pick up the eggshell with tongs and pour the flaming liqueur over the browned meringue. Flames plummet down the sides like a volcano exploding.

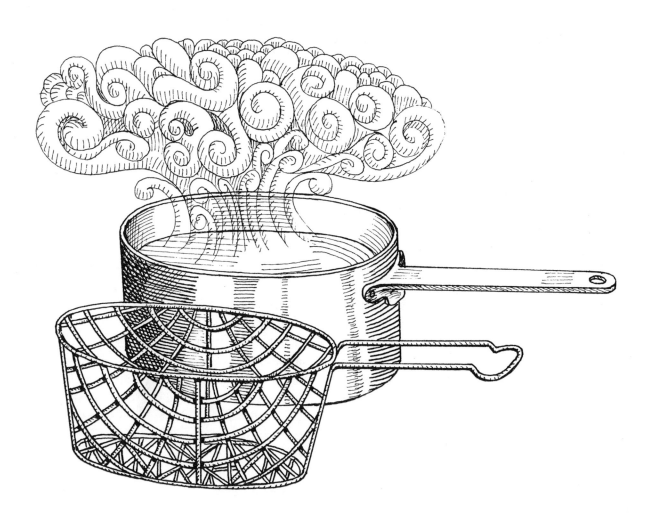

CHAPTER FIVE

Deep-fat Frying

Deep-fat frying is the fastest way to cook (except, of course, for the electronic oven). The heat of the smoking hot fat sears and browns the exterior of whatever it surrounds almost immediately. As in other methods of cooking, this seared exterior is of vital importance because it holds in the juice. However, the possibilities for deep-fat frying are limited to meats or vegetables no thicker than a chicken leg. Anything larger would become too crisp and brown on the outside before being cooked through. Here, too, as in roasting, the principle of reposing applies with things as thick as a chicken leg—when first given a certain time in the hot fat, of course. (Let's say 10 minutes.) The leg will be brown enough on the outside and the heat will have penetrated to a depth sufficient to cook the meat through to the bone during a repose of 10 minutes.

Inexpensive restaurants feature fried foods such as scallops, sole, clams, shrimps, and so on, because deep-fat frying is a fast and easy way to cook. My complaint is that usually the food has been left in the hot fat for too long, so that it is hard and dry.

You *must* know how to French or deep-fry *before* you try it. Why? Because it's very, very dangerous. In the actual frying there are a few things to keep well in mind that will mean the difference between complete success and total failure, with little room for error. Fill the pot with oil or shortening no more than two-thirds full. The shortening must be melted before the basket is inserted. About 4½ pounds of shortening or 3 quarts of oil are required. Heat the fat until smoke can barely be seen rising from the surface (about 385°). The odor from this smoke is not pleasant, so keep the exhaust fan going and shut the doors to the rest of the house. This is a perfect kind of cooking for a beach cottage where there is a good sea breeze and all the windows may be kept open.

When it is time to put in the food, your left hand must be kept on the basket handle while the food is placed carefully in the very hot fat. Don't splash. It is very important to *be ready* to lift the basket because the fat is likely to foam up and overflow. But as the basket is lifted out, the foam will go down. Repeat a third or even fourth time if necessary until the foam stays at a constant level without threatening to go over the top. If a lot of fat boils over onto the stove, it may catch on fire.

I can't stress too much how dangerous it could be to try to deep-fry any wet foods. Potatoes are dangerous. A student of mine once tried to make cherry tomato beignets. Fortunately, they didn't all explode at once. And, of course, water itself must be kept away from the frying pot. Cooking vegetables or a coffee pot on a unit too nearby might boil over into the hot fat. Also keep the fryer on a back burner with the handle out of the way of kitchen traffic; while you are frying, the kitchen should be off-limits to children.

First of all, the fat should be barely smoking. If it's smoking too much, it will be too hot and make what you're cooking *too* brown before it has a chance to cook through, unless you are frying tiny minnows or whitebait. They are so small that they're cooked through as soon as they are brown.

The quicker the better, so for them the smoke can be more than just barely visible.

Do not cool off the fat too much by putting in too much of what is to be fried at once. If you put too many potatoes into the hot fat at one time, the fat will cool; the potatoes will absorb the fat, get soggy, and simply fall apart. The fat or oil must be hot and stay as hot as possible. That's why you use such a quantity of fat; because once it gets very hot it will cool very little when the foods to be fried are put into it. Because there is such a high degree of heat in the fat, it takes no more than three seconds to fry something as delicate as parsley. It is brittle, lacy, and delicious when fried in deep fat, and makes a perfect garnish for fried fish.

WHITING EN COLÈRE

SERVES 4

The fish appears angry because it is biting its tail.

6 whole whiting (⅓–½ pound), cleaned and
  scaled, head and tail on, gills removed
1 cup beer
3 cups flour
4½ pounds shortening or 3 quarts oil
Parsley, chopped
1 lemon

Clamp the mouth of each fish across its tail. (Simply open the mouth with your fingers, put the tail into the mouth and press the jaws down so the teeth close on the tail.) Arrange them in a pan or bowl and pour the beer over them. Remove one at a time. Dredge each fish in flour, and drop into the smoking deep fat. Two fish should be fried at one time. When the fish is golden brown on one side, turn it to brown the other side. Remove the fish to a platter and sprinkle with chopped parsley. Serve with a wedge of lemon, Potato Chips (see opposite), a green salad, and a ripe cold melon for dessert.

WHITEBAIT

SERVES 6

These are easy to prepare and delicious. Perfect with drinks, these minnows, also known as shiners, do not have to be cleaned in any way and are cooked in a matter of seconds.

1 cup bread crumbs
1 cup flour
1 teaspoon salt
½ pound whitebait or shiners
1 bottle of beer
4½ pounds shortening or 3 quarts oil
1 cup parsley sprigs

Combine the bread crumbs, flour, and salt. Put the shiners into a bowl and pour half of the bottle of beer over them. Drain in a sieve. Dredge them in the flour mixture. Shake off the excess flour. Cook them no more than a handful at a time (about 20) in smoking-hot deep fat (450°) until they are slightly brown. Lift the basket and drain. Place the fish in a paper-lined straw basket. Put part of the parsley in the hot fat (this will make an awful noise) for just 3 seconds. Arrange it on top of the fish. Sprinkle with salt and serve.

POTATO CHIPS

SERVES 6

Like French-fried potatoes, your own home-made chips will be far better than any you have ever had before. Be sure to store them in a dry place. The oven with pilot light on is a perfect place. Of course, you have to remember they are there before you turn on the oven. Tie a dish towel around the oven door handle as a reminder.

1½ pounds baking potatoes
4½ pounds shortening
Salt

Preheat fat to 310°. Slice the potatoes ⅟₁₆ inch thick. Wash and drain them. Dry them by putting them in a towel. Grab the loose ends of the towel and shake. Fry no more than a handful of potatoes at a time. Make sure they don't stick during the first moments of frying. Use a slotted spoon to separate them. They are done when they are golden brown. It takes 4 minutes. Arrange them on several layers of paper towels. Sprinkle with salt. Store in a dry place until ready to serve.

POTATOES DAUPHINE

SERVES 6 TO 8

The nutmeg taste is delicious in these puffy potatoes. I prefer freshly grated nutmeg to the canned, preground variety. I love Potatoes Dauphine, but they are not easy to make, so try to keep the rest of the menu simple to prepare.

1½ pounds boiling potatoes
½ cup water
⅓ stick butter
⅓ cup flour
3–5 eggs
⅔ teaspoon nutmeg, freshly grated (1 teaspoon preground)
Salt and pepper
1 quart oil

Peel and wash the potatoes. Put them into a pot. Cover them and boil until they are tender. Meanwhile, in a saucepan, bring the water and the butter to a boil. Using a wooden spoon, stir in the flour over a low heat. Keep stirring until the mixture leaves the sides and the bottom of the pan and forms into a ball. Let the mixture cool for ½ hour or so. Using the wooden spoon, incorporate one egg into the ball of dough, then another egg, and another, until the mixture barely flows. Mix in the nutmeg, ½ teaspoon of salt, and a little pepper. This, minus the nutmeg, is called *pâte à choux.*

When the potatoes are tender, drain them and put them through a ricer. Mix the *pâte à choux* and riced potatoes together. The potatoes have to take on some form before being deep-fat fried. To do this, take an oval soup spoon in each hand. Remove half a spoonful of the mixture, using the length of the bowl of the other spoon to shape and mold. Lift from one spoon to the other until it looks like a small egg.

Use a deep skillet or French-fry pan and basket. Be careful. The shortening should be slightly smoking (375°). Gently drop the shaped potatoes into the fat. Do about 6 in each batch. When the potatoes are golden brown, remove them with a slotted spoon to a pan covered with several thicknesses of paper towels. They can be cooked one hour before serving.

Reheat them for 7 minutes in a 400° oven.

SOUFFLÉED POTATOES

SERVES 4

This is not difficult, but it is time-consuming. You must have two separate fats going at different temperatures. If you have trouble slicing the potatoes to ⅛-inch thickness, you can buy a slicer called a *Mandoline,* which will make the slicing job easier.

3 baking potatoes approximately 4 inches long, 2½ inches wide
6 pounds shortening or 4 quarts oil

Peel and wash the potatoes. Pare them so that the sides and top and bottom ends are flat. Pare the corners to flatten them. Cut the potatoes in slices ⅛ inch thick, cutting through the narrow side of the potato. The slice will look like this. Slices *must be* of uniform thickness, exactly ⅛ inch thick. You should get almost 36 slices. Wash them off. Pat them dry.

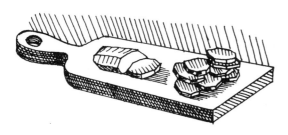

Heat 4½ pounds of fat in the fryer to 400° and 1½ pounds in a frying pan to 280°. (Adjust the flame in an attempt to keep the temperatures constant.) Put 9 slices of potato into the frying pan. Using a slotted spoon, gently turn the slices and keep them separate from one another. In 90 seconds small bubbles will form within the slices. As soon as you notice them, wait 6 more seconds, then transfer one slice into the hot fat. If it does not puff up completely, discard it or eat it, wait 4 seconds, and try again with another slice. If this trial slice puffs up completely, quickly transfer the remaining 7 slices. Occasionally they split or fail to inflate, but there is an 80 percent success, or 30 out of 36 slices. When the potatoes are transferred from the 285° fat to the hotter fat, they should be barely tinged with brown. NO MORE, or they will not inflate. As the potato fries slowly in the cooler fat, a skin or crust forms on the outside of each slice. The moisture inside the crust begins to steam.

The steam tries to get out of the potato, but it cannot because of the crust, so it makes a little bubble under the skin. The hot fat simply accelerates this bubbling and the *whole* slice of potato inflates. The skin must be strong enough to hold the steam, but elastic enough to stretch. The browner the skin gets, the more rigid and brittle it becomes.

Let them fry for about 5 seconds in the hot fat, then transfer them to a pan lined with paper towels. Do not let them touch, because they might stick together when cool. Repeat this process with the remaining slices. This can all be done a maximum of 5 hours before serving. The fry pan with fat will no longer be needed. The souffléed potatoes will deflate when they cool. Before serving, reheat the fat in the fryer to 380°. Put in 15 souffléed potatoes at one time. They will inflate again. Let them get golden brown. Remove to a basket lined with a paper or linen napkin. Serve immediately.

FRENCH-FRIED POTATOES

When they're good, they're very good. The French are ten times better at French-fried potatoes than we are. Too bad.

1 medium-large boiling potato per person
4½ pounds shortening or 3 quarts oil
Salt

Peel and wash the potatoes. Using a French knife (3-inch handle, 9-inch blade), pare a thin slice off one side of the potato. With this flat side down against the board, the potato will not rock as you cut it. Cut the potato into slices of uniform thickness, less than ½ inch thick. Cut these slices into strips of the same thickness. Rinse them well with hot water from the tap. Drain in a colander. Push a cloth or towel around in the potatoes to dry them as much as possible. Put a couple of handfuls in the fry basket and lower into the barely smoking fat (385°). When they are slightly brown and almost soft (lift out the basket and pinch one), collect the French fries in a pan lined with paper towels. Give the fat a chance to heat up again until it barely smokes, and repeat.

This blanching (precooking) of the potatoes can be done as much as 6 hours in advance of mealtime. Just before serving, the potatoes go back into the fat. The fat should be a little hotter, and a few more potatoes can be put in at one time. When they are golden brown, drain them and sprinkle with salt.

To repeat, the potatoes must come out of the fat as soon as they are soft, even if they are not brown enough. The fat must have a chance to recover heat before the potatoes get the brief final fry (either 10 minutes after the first, or hours later). It is also faster and easier to have the potatoes in a blanched state at mealtime, since you may need five batches to feed six people.

Serve the potatoes in a basket lined with a paper or linen napkin.

EGGPLANT BEIGNET

SERVES 6

This is not easy, so try it when the rest of the menu is quite easy.

1 eggplant (about 1 pound)
Beignet Batter
4½ pounds shortening
Salt

Heat the shortening to 425°. Peel the eggplant. Cut it into slices about ⅛ inch thick. The slices will be too large to work with, so cut them into rectangles about 2 inches wide and 3 inches long. Holding each slice by one end, dip it into the Beignet Batter to coat one side, then turn it and coat the other side. Gently drop the coated slice into the hot fat. Repeat. Fry about 6 at a time. Keep the slices warm in the oven at 350° in a pan lined with paper towels. Allow 3 slices of eggplant per person; 18 slices for six people should be ample. Serve as soon as all of the eggplant has been fried. Sprinkle the slices with salt before serving.

Beignet Batter

This is the best batter for deep-fat frying. It puffs up and browns beautifully.

2 eggs
⅓ cup milk
½ cup flour
¼ teaspoon salt

Separate the eggs. Whisk the egg yolks slightly.

Whisk in half of the milk, then the flour and salt. Whisk until the mixture is smooth. Stir in the remaining milk. Beat the whites until they are stiff. Fold them into the egg yolk mixture.

APPLE BEIGNET

SERVES 6

This will go very well with roast pork.

2 large McIntosh apples
Beignet Batter (see page 106)
4½ pounds shortening
½ cup sugar

Heat shortening to 425°. Core the apples. Do not peel them. Cut the apples across the core hole into rings about ½ inch thick. Dip the rings into the Beignet Batter, then gently drop them into the hot fat. Do about 4 rings at a time. Two apples should make about 12 rings (2 per person). Keep them warm in the oven in a pan lined with paper towels. Serve as soon as the last rings have been fried. Sprinkle the rings with granulated sugar before serving.

CHAPTER SIX

Sautéing

Sautéing is cooking in a small amount of fat in a shallow pan. What is sautéed? Meats, fish, and vegetables of uniform thickness, so that they will be evenly cooked throughout (no more than 2 inches thick). A chicken leg or 2-inch steak can be sautéed in a pan on top of the stove, but anything thicker would get too brown on the outside before it was cooked through. There are other methods of cooking thicker cuts. (Roasting is the most popular.) Sautéing, then, is for thin pieces of meat, fish, or vegetable.

How do you sauté? First the pan must be heated. Then a little butter or oil is put in—just enough to cover the bottom of the pan. When the butter or oil is hot, whatever is to be sautéed is put in. The film of hot butter sizzles, acting as a buffer between the pan and what is cooking. Little bubbles of sizzling hot fat repel what's being sautéed and thus prevent it from sticking to the pan. At the same time the underside of the meat or vegetable is allowed to brown gradually. This brown exterior seals in the juice.

It is very important that both the pan and the butter be hot. Meat will not brown if it is immediately added to an unheated pan on top of cold butter. Juice will ooze out, and the meat will boil in its own juice. Eventually it may brown, but that will occur too late; the juice will have boiled away. If both the pan and butter are hot, the cold meat will begin browning as soon as it hits the pan.

Most meats contain large amounts of water. Since you cannot pour a glass of water into a pan and expect it to brown, you cannot expect anything as wet as liver or fish to lend itself to browning. For this reason, a thin film of flour will keep the outside of the meat sufficiently dry for enough time to permit it to brown.

The heat of the pan and the butter tends to draw out, or render, the juice in the meat. This juice has nowhere to go but out. However, the protective coating of flour is there to seal it in. The slice of meat or fish is dropped into the plate of flour, and then is turned to get flour on the other side. Then it is picked up by one end, given a shake to rid it of any excess flour, and put into the hot pan. This flouring is done at the last minute. If it is done too far in advance, the flour adhering to the meat will soak up moisture like a blotter. What gets moist will stick to the meat (since that's where the moisture is coming from), and will be impossible to shake off. This is why so many fried things have such a thick, ugly crust. The flour coating or buffer should not be noticeable once the meat or vegetable is cooked.

Never put too much of anything into a pan to brown at one time. That is just as bad as failing to heat the pan before sautéing, and has the same disastrous result. Too much will cool down the pan. Whatever is supposed to be getting nice and brown will just stew or boil. When the fish or meat has been put into the pan, it should be left alone for awhile. Give it a chance to brown where it is. Don't stir it (for instance, cubes of stew meat), turn it over, or otherwise bother it. Let it be. The preheated pan and butter are trying hard to compensate for the coldness of the piece of meat touching them. If you expose another cold side of meat to the pan, it will cool down the pan, which not only

must be hot to begin with, but must also stay hot. Do not crowd the pieces, either. Any steam created needs to escape. Rather use two sauté pans. The heat in the pan must be as high as possible until you are sure the meat is browning. Then you may reduce the heat under the pan so that the meat does not burn. How do you know if the meat is browning? Listen. It will make a sizzling sound. Or, take a look under the meat by lifting it with a fork or spatula.

Often a sauce can be composed right on top of what is being sautéed. For example, you could add to slices of veal (that have been floured and sautéed until golden brown) chopped shallots, mushrooms, white wine, and finally, cream and lemon juice. There you have a fine main dish for a meal.

BAY SCALLOPS SAUTÉ MEUNIÈRE

SERVES 4 TO 6

You must know this recipe thoroughly before you start cooking the scallops, because it has to be done quickly and there will be no time to check the recipe. The floured scallops must spend no more than one minute in the hot pan. During that time they don't have to get completely brown on all sides, just tinged with brown. Do not overcook them, or they will be tough.

1 pound bay scallops
1 cup flour
1 teaspoon salt
1½ sticks butter
Juice of 1 lemon
2 tablespoons parsley, chopped

The scallops should be floured just before they are cooked. If too many are put into the pan at one time, the scallops will cool the pan and take too long to brown. Juice will escape, causing them to lose their tenderness. Scallops do have more than two sides, but they will be cooked through if the sides that are browned are opposite each other.

Drain—do not wash—the scallops and dry them on a few layers of paper towels. Put the flour on a large pie plate or platter and mix in the salt. Fluff the scallops around in the flour mixture. Heat a large 10–12-inch skillet (cast iron is best) over a high heat and put in ⅓ stick of butter. When the butter is hot and brown, add ⅓ of the scallops. (Just jiggle them around in a wire mesh sieve to rid them of excess flour.) They must cover the bottom of the frying pan. Do not budge them for at least 25 seconds, so that the surface of the scallops touching the pan will have a chance to brown. Then one by one, turn over the scallops that are brown, giving them all a chance to brown on another side. They will be brown enough and cooked within a minute. Put them on a warm platter, wipe out the pan, and repeat the process twice more. Brown the remaining ½ stick of butter over a medium-high heat. Squeeze the lemon juice over the scallops, pour the brown butter over all, sprinkle with the chopped parsley, and serve immediately with Mashed Potatoes (see page 170) or Boiled Rice (see page 171).

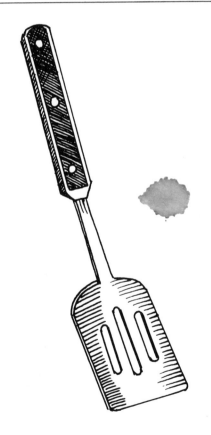

FILLET OF SOLE MEUNIÈRE

SERVES 2

Never diminish the amount of brown butter poured over the sole before it is served. I realize that it seems like a lot, but it isn't. The nutty taste of brown butter is delicious.

4 fillets of sole (gray sole, flounder, or fluke)
Salt
½ cup flour
1 stick butter
½ lemon
2 tablespoons parsley, chopped

Lightly salt and flour the fillets. Shake them to remove any excess flour. Heat up a frying pan and put in ⅓ of the stick of butter. Lay in the fillets as soon as the butter is brown. A ½-inch-thick fillet of sole should be attractively brown on both sides and done within 5 minutes. (The first down side, which must be golden brown, takes about 3 minutes to cook; the second side takes 2 minutes.) Then place the fillets side by side on a heated platter. If they cook too long, they will become either fragile and fall apart or will be leathery on the outside and dried out inside. Squeeze lemon juice over the top of the cooked fillets. Wipe out the pan and brown the rest of the butter. Pour the butter over the fillets. Sprinkle them with parsley and serve.

This dish can wait for 10 minutes in a moderate 250° oven, but I would prefer that it be served very soon after it is cooked. No green vegetable is needed. I suggest boiled new potatoes. Salad and cheese could be served as separate courses.

Large oval frying pans exist to sauté meunière whole large fish. Flour and then brown the fish in the pan on top of the stove, the same way you would the Fillet of Sole Meunière. Then finish cooking the fish in the oven, which has been preheated to 450°. Measure the fish at its thickest point to determine the cooking time. Allow 10 minutes for every inch of thickness. Quantities of brown butter make the perfect sauce for whole fish meunière.

FROGS' LEGS PROVENÇAL

The procedure for cooking frogs' legs is exactly the same as for the Fillet of Sole Meunière (see above) except that one tablespoon of chopped garlic is added to the brown butter and allowed to sizzle in it for just a second before it is poured over the frogs' legs. This procedure can also be used for blowfish, or chicken of the sea.

Figure one tablespoon of chopped garlic for each pound of frogs' legs. The legs should be as small as possible, about 12 pieces to a pound. Allow a half pound per person. As with Fillet of Sole Meunière, they must not be overcooked, or they will be dry.

COQ AU VIN

SERVES 8

I really apologize for including a recipe demanding nineteen ingredients and three phases of preparation, but Coq au Vin, though quite common, is delicious. In spite of the many ingredients, the sauce still tastes of chicken. While working in France, I made Coq au Vin for some restaurant friends, using rye whisky instead of wine. My French friends enjoyed this switch immensely.

The sauce for this dish must be prepared first.

Carcasses, necks, nubbins, and wings of chickens
1 stalk celery
2 carrots
3 medium onions
¼ cup flour
Water
¼ cup tomato purée
1 cup dry red wine
1 bay leaf
⅓ teaspoon thyme
3 cloves garlic, unpeeled
1 teaspoon salt

Preheat oven to 450°. Put the carcasses, nubbins, necks, and wings into a pan and under the broiler to brown. Add the celery, carrots, and onions. Place in the oven until the vegetables take on some brown color. Remove from the oven. Stir in the flour until the white no longer shows. Flour will absorb the fat present in the pan, and on the surfaces of the chicken bones and vegetables. (For brown stocks in general, the proportion of rendered warm fat, butter, or oil, to flour must be equal. For instance, in this recipe there should be no more than ¼ cup of rendered chicken fat present. If there is too much fat, the gravy will have a film of fat on it.) Remove to a 3-quart pot.

Add a little water to the broiling pan. Use a spoon or spatula to scrape the residue loose from the pan and add it to the pot. Add the tomato purée, wine, bay leaf, thyme, garlic, and salt to pot. Add enough water to cover contents. Simmer, uncovered, at least one hour.

Now continue with the chicken recipe.

¾ pound white onions, peeled
½ stick butter
Water
1 pound mushrooms
2½-pound chickens, breasts and legs removed
(The skin is left on pieces. Nubbins should be
removed from the drumsticks. Legs are cut into
two pieces at the joint between the drumstick
and second joint. Reserve the carcass, neck,
nubbins, and wings for sauce.)
Salt and pepper
⅓ cup flour
¼ cup Cognac
1 cup dry red wine

Brown the white onions in 2 tablespoons of butter. Remove them to a small saucepan. Barely cover them with water, and simmer the onions until they're just tender, but not falling apart. Reserve. Sauté the mushrooms in ½ the remaining butter until they are lightly browned and reserve. Salt and pepper the chicken pieces. Heat a large sauté pan over high heat. Add the remaining butter. When the butter turns brown, add the pieces of chicken, skin side down, and brown on both sides. If the pan is *not* cast iron (good for sautéeing, bad for making sauce), the rest of the procedure can take place in the same pan, *or* put the browned chicken pieces into a large 3–4-quart casserole and stir in the flour until all the white disappears. Add the Cognac. Ignite, and spoon it over until the flame dies. Then add the red wine, the reserved onions, and the mushrooms. Strain in the liquid

from the pot. Stir. Cook for 15 minutes. Add salt and pepper if needed. Let stand for at least one hour, then bring to a simmer, and serve.

Coq au Vin will keep very well in the refrigerator for as long as a week. In fact, the taste improves with standing. But if you plan on preparing it that far in advance, cook it for only 5 minutes after you combine all the ingredients. To reheat from refrigerator temperature, cover and place in a 400° oven for at least 50 minutes. Stir after 35 minutes.

Begin the meal with Mussels Marinière with cream (see page 147), and serve the Coq au Vin with Boiled Rice (see page 171), fresh peas (Mama's Peas, see page 170), and an apple tart for dessert.

CHICKEN LIVER PÂTÉ WITH TRUFFLES

SERVES 25

The subtle tastes of the Cognac and livers complement each other. The Cognac must be the very best. Serve this with an ample supply of Melba toast. No other canapés are necessary.

1 pound butter (4 sticks)
2 cups chicken livers (1 pound)
6 medium shallots, chopped
1 teaspoon salt
1 teaspoon pepper, freshly ground
½ cup Cognac
4 medium truffles, finely chopped

Remove butter from the refrigerator to soften. Drain the livers of any excess blood in a sieve. Brown a half stick of butter over high heat in a cast-iron frying pan. Add the livers and spread them out on the bottom of the pan, but do not stir them around until they have had time to brown. Then turn them over and brown them on the opposite side. The livers should be cooked no more than 4 minutes altogether. Remove the pan from the heat and mix in the shallots, salt, and freshly ground pepper. Pour in half the Cognac. Ignite it and stir gently with a spoon. When the flame dwindles, pass the contents of the pan through the finest sieve or food mill. Place in a bowl and cool to room temperature. Combine with the rest of the softened butter. Then add the remaining Cognac and the truffles. Mold and refrigerate. If the mold is lined with a plastic wrap, the pâté will come out more easily. This pâté can be made several days in advance, but should be tightly wrapped.

VEAL SCALLOPS À LA CRÈME

SERVES 6

I became acquainted with this dish on my first trip to Paris. I liked it so much that I had it for dinner eight days in a row.

1¼ pounds veal in 18 slices, pounded as thin as
   possible
Salt and pepper
½ stick butter, divided into 6 pieces
Flour
1 tablespoon shallots, chopped
½ cup white wine
⅔ cup heavy cream
Juice of 1 lemon

The veal must be pink—almost white—to be of excellent quality. The pieces of veal have to be so thin you can almost see through them, and 3 or 4 inches in diameter. If, when they come from the butcher, they are still more than ⅛ inch thick, they can be made thinner. Tear off 2 pieces of waxed paper 2 feet in length. Place one sheet of the paper on a heavy table top and place the thick pieces of veal on top of it. Place the other sheet on top of the veal. Pound the pieces with something heavy, such as a cleaver or a pot with a smooth, heavy bottom.

Salt and pepper the escalopes. Preheat a large, heavy-bottomed frying pan. Put in a piece of the butter. While the butter is browning, dredge the escalopes in flour. Shake off any excess flour. You will be able to cook only three or four pieces at a time. Lay the pieces in the hot butter, which should be brown, not black. As the slices brown, they will shrink. When they are brown on both sides, remove them to a hot platter. Repeat until all the escalopes are brown. Add the shallots to the pan, and return the escalopes. Add the white wine and simmer for 3 minutes. Add the cream and simmer for another 5 minutes, or until the sauce is of a pleasantly thick consistency (so that it evenly coats a spoon or finger). Taste and correct the seasoning, add the lemon juice, and serve.

When the dish is ready to be served, it can wait around for a maximum of one hour. If there seems to be a lessening in the amount of sauce, you could add more cream, but it is most important that the pieces be turned periodically to keep them moist. Begin the meal with Mussels Marinière (see page 147). Serve the veal with Broccoli (see page 164) and buttered noodles. Follow with a fruit dessert.

VEAL KIDNEYS BORDELAISE

SERVES 2 TO 3

These will be tough if you overcook them.

2 veal kidneys
Salt and pepper
1 cup flour
3 tablespoons butter
½ cup mushrooms, sliced
1½ tablespoons shallots, chopped
⅔ cup red Bordeaux wine
½ cup Demi-Glaze (see page 32)
1 teaspoon parsley, chopped

Remove membrane from kidneys if it has not been removed. Finely slice the kidneys (⅛ inch thick). Salt and pepper the slices and dredge them in flour. Heat a frying pan and put in two tablespoons of butter. When the butter is brown, shake the excess flour from the kidneys and put them into the pan to brown over high heat for about 2 minutes (a minute on each side). Add the mushrooms and shallots, sauté for another minute, and mix in 1½ tablespoons of flour. Add the wine and then the Demi-Glaze. Simmer uncovered until the liquid is reduced to one-half its original volume. Stir in the remaining butter, sprinkle with parsley, and serve.

Boiled potatoes and braised celery would go well with the kidneys. A red Bordeaux wine, of course. Follow with baked pears and cookies for dessert.

CALVES' LIVER WITH BLACK BUTTER

SERVES 3

Do not overcook liver. Once it has browned on one side, it is turned over to brown on the other. A small puddle of red juice often appears on the surface. This indicates that the slice of liver is cooked through. Heat has reached the center of the slice and forced the juice to the surface, like a pot of liquid boiling over. The liver must be eaten before all the juice comes out.

1 pound calves' liver (3 slices)
⅔ stick butter
Salt and pepper
Flour
2 tablespoons red wine vinegar

The calves' liver must be no more than ½ inch thick. Heat the frying pan; put a third of the butter into the hot pan. Salt, pepper, and flour the slices of liver. Shake any excess flour off and lay the liver in the brown butter. The slices should be well browned on the down side within a minute's time. Brown the other side and arrange on a warm platter or on individual warmed plates. Wipe out the pan and return it to a high heat. Put in the rest of the butter. When the butter turns black and begins to smoke, pour it over the pieces of liver. Put the vinegar in the hot pan. It will reduce by half of its original volume in several seconds. Pour it over the liver and serve immediately.

Do not cook liver for more than three or four persons unless you have two frying pans and are sure you can get it to the table with the accompanying vegetables, bread, and so forth very soon after the liver comes out of the pan.

Serve with Potatoes Gratin Dauphinoise (see page 92), a green salad (serve at the same time, but on separate plates), and Apple Pie Tatin (see page 96) for dessert.

CALVES' BRAINS IN BLACK BUTTER

SERVES 6 TO 8

Calves' brains have the most delicate consistency but little taste. The black butter sauce provides a sharp and delicious flavor.

3 pairs of calves' brains
1 lemon
Salt and pepper
1½ sticks butter
1 cup flour
1 tablespoon capers
⅓ cup red wine vinegar
3 tablespoons parsley, chopped

Disconnect the pairs. Peel off the outer membrane under a thin stream of cold water. Frozen brains are all right, but are impossible to peel. Just forget the peeling process—it's not essential. Put the brains into a pot and cover with cold water. Soak for 15 minutes, drain and cover with cold water again. Add the juice and skin of the lemon, one teaspoon of salt, bring to a boil, and cook for

5 minutes. Cool the brains under cold water in the same pot. They will be more rigid and manageable. Pat them dry and cut them in half lengthways. Salt and pepper them. Put a lump of butter (¼ stick) into a hot frying pan and let it begin to brown. Flour the brains. Gently pat the brains between your hands to rid them of any excess flour and put the halves flat side down in the pan. Cook over a medium-high heat. Rather than crowd them, do the sautéing in two shifts. When they are good and brown on both sides, remove them from the pan and arrange them on a platter. Wipe out the frying pan, put in the remaining butter, and wait until it smokes and is black. Turn off the heat as soon as the butter smokes. It is quite flammable at this stage, so be careful. Pour the black butter carefully over the brains. Then sizzle the capers and vinegar in the hot pan until the vinegar is reduced to half its original volume (about 10 seconds). Pour over the brains and sprinkle them with parsley.

Serve with boiled potatoes, French bread, and lots of Burgundy. Follow with a green salad and then Pears in Custard Tart (see page 96) for dessert.

SAUTÉED STEAK

Steaks can be sautéed in a black frying pan. This is sometimes called pan broiling. You won't get the same smoky taste you get from charcoal broiling, but sautéeing is easier. The degree of doneness of the steak is more predictable.

Steak
Butter
Salt and pepper

117

Heat a cast-iron frying pan. When it is hot, heat a tablespoon of butter in the hot pan. (Fat trimmed from the steak can also be used. Allow it to cook until it has rendered a tablespoon of fat—then discard.) Salt and pepper the steak and put it into the pan over a constant high heat. When the steak is good and brown on one side, turn it over to brown on the other side. Very thick steaks (2 inches or more) require some time in a 350° oven, and then a certain reposing time. See the time chart that follows.

Allow ⅔ pound of steak for each person. Cooking times vary according to the thickness. There are so many different cuts of steak of varying dimensions. A wide, long steak, one inch thick and weighing 6 pounds, would take half as long to cook as a steak weighing 3 pounds and 2 inches thick. If I suggested minutes per pound, the heavy steak would be overcooked, while the lighter but thicker steak would be almost raw.

A thick steak will brown on the outside as fast as a thin one. So, if a thick steak stays in the pan longer than is necessary to brown it (so that it's cooked, and not raw), it will get too black. Here's the answer to this problem. Thin steaks, less than 1½ inches thick, require a very hot pan or broiler throughout their short cooking time, a 5-minute repose, and no time in the oven. Very thick steaks require a very hot pan at first to sear both sides, and then the heat can be reduced. The steak will still sizzle, but not so violently. It will also continue to brown, but not as quickly.

TIME CHART FOR SAUTÉING STEAK			
THIS CHART CAN ALSO BE USED TO CALCULATE THE BROILING TIMES OF PIECES OF MEAT OVER MEDIUM-HOT COALS, AND ALSO UNDER GOOD HOME BROILERS (HOT ONES).			
TIME IN PAN 12 MINUTES PER INCH OF THICKNESS (OR 6 MINUTES PER INCH OF THICKNESS ON EACH SIDE)		TIME IN 350° OVEN 5 MINUTES PER INCH OF THICKNESS	REPOSE 5 MINUTES PER INCH OF THICKNESS
USING THIS TIME CHART WILL PRODUCE A MEDIUM-RARE STEAK. IF YOU WANT IT RARER OR MORE WELL DONE, REDUCE OR INCREASE THE TIME IN THE OVEN.			
THICKNESS 1½ INCHES	TIME IN PAN OR OVEN BROILER 16 MINUTES (8 MINUTES ON EACH SIDE)	TIME IN OVEN NO OVEN TIME REQUIRED	REPOSE 7 MINUTES
2 INCHES	24 MINUTES (12 MINUTES ON EACH SIDE)	10 MINUTES	10 MINUTES
3 INCHES	36 MINUTES (18 MINUTES ON EACH SIDE)	15 MINUTES	15 MINUTES

FRIED EGGS WITH BLACK BUTTER

SERVES 3

If you're good at frying eggs sunny side up, try this one.

⅔ stick butter
6 eggs
Salt and pepper
3 tablespoons red wine vinegar
2 tablespoons capers
1 tablespoon parsley, chopped

Preheat oven to 250°. Put about a third of the butter into a cold 10-inch frying pan and put the pan over medium heat. As the butter melts, tip the pan so that the butter covers the bottom evenly. When the butter begins to sizzle, break in three eggs very carefully so the yolks remain whole. Sprinkle with salt and pepper. The white of the "sunny side up" fried eggs should be slightly underdone. Remove them to a hot platter. Add a little more butter to the pan and fry the other three eggs. Arrange them on the platter and put the platter in the oven. Return the pan to high heat, and put in the remaining butter. When it is smoking and black, spoon it over the eggs, and turn off the heat. Add the vinegar and capers to the hot pan. Let the vinegar reduce to almost half its original volume. (This will happen within seconds in the hot pan. There is no need to have heat under the pan.) Pour this mixture evenly over the tops of the eggs. Sprinkle them with parsley and serve immediately.

Serve for lunch with hot French bread and red wine followed by a salad (vinegar and oil dressing), a good cheese, more hot bread, and more wine.

SAUTÉED MUSHROOMS

Wipe the mushrooms with a damp cloth. Sauté in butter, caps down. Sprinkle with one tablespoon of lemon juice. Cover the pan. Cook the mushrooms gently over medium heat until a lot of water has accumulated on the bottom of the pan. Once this water has come out of the mushrooms they can be browned by turning up the heat to medium-high and removing the cover from the pan.

ENDIVE MEUNIÈRE

SERVES 6

Do not eliminate the first boiling process. It removes the bitter taste of the endive.

1 pound endives (Belgian)
Water
½ stick butter
Salt
Juice of ½ lemon

Preheat oven to 275°. Put the endives into a pot and cover them with water. Bring to a boil and continue to boil for 15 minutes. Remove from heat and cool under cold running water. Remove each endive from the water, holding it by the root end. Reshape it and squeeze some of the water out. Place the endives in a baking dish, buttered with half of the butter. Sprinkle with salt and the lemon juice. Cover the dish tightly with tin foil and bake in the oven for 1½ hours.

The endives are now tender and can be sautéed in the remaining butter immediately or they can be cooled and stored in the refrigerator until you are ready to sauté them. The frying pan should be hot and the butter brown before you put in the endives. Let the endives get good and brown on both sides; turn them with a fork at the root end.

Arrange neatly on a platter and serve.

EGGPLANT
SERVES 6

There are a few good eggplant recipes. This is the first one to know. It is simple and basic.

2 small eggplants, 3 inches or less in diameter
   (*about 1 pound*)
Salt and pepper
Flour
½ stick butter
Juice of ½ lemon
Parsley, chopped

Cut the eggplant into round pieces about ⅔ inch thick. Salt and pepper them. Flour them on both sides. Shake off the excess flour. Brown the butter in a frying pan and sauté the pieces of eggplant over medium heat until they are brown on both sides and tender. Sprinkle the lemon juice and chopped parsley over the top and serve.

Do not overcook the eggplant or it will be mushy. This is one vegetable that must be cooked and served immediately, or it will look droopy.

ZUCCHINI
SERVES 6

This is a great vegetable—sautéed, boiled, even raw!

6 very small zucchini (3 to 4 inches long)
Salt and pepper
½ stick butter
Lemon juice

Cut the ends from the zucchini. Wash them thoroughly under cold water. Sand sometimes clings to the skin, so it's advisable to use a brush. Cut in half lengthways. Salt and pepper them. Heat the butter over medium heat. Sauté the zucchini, flat side down, until brown. Turn the zucchini and reduce the heat to medium-low. Cover the pan and cook the zucchini until it is tender (about 7 minutes). Sprinkle a little lemon juice over the top and serve.

This recipe would not be good with large zucchini, because the skin is too tough.

HASHED BROWN POTATOES
SERVES 6

You could boil and cool the potatoes left-over from the Potatoes Parisienne balls (see page 124).

2 pounds cold boiled potatoes
½ stick butter
Salt and pepper
Parsley, chopped

Put the cold cooked potatoes into a pan with a

high border. Using a beer can opener, put several holes in the closed end of a small empty soup can. Use the open end of the can to hash the potatoes. Heat a black seasoned fry pan, add the butter. When it is brown, add the potatoes, salt, and pepper. Let them get good and brown. Then turn them over with a spatula and push them to one side of the frying pan. You may want to put something under the handle or under the pan itself so that all the butter will flow to the side where the potatoes are. Since few stoves are level, this may be unnecessary. Tip the potatoes out onto an oval platter. Sprinkle with chopped parsley and serve.

POTATOES PAILLASSON

SERVES 4 TO 6

A favorite of M. Fernand Point, creator and owner of the famous Restaurant de la Pyramide in Vienne, France. These "straw mat" potatoes had to be thin, golden brown, and bubbling with butter when they arrived at his table. This recipe requires two 9–12-inch frying pans. They must be the same size.

2 pounds boiling potatoes
Salt and pepper
1½ sticks butter

Preheat oven to 400°. Peel the potatoes. Cut them in slices approximately ⅛ inch thick. Laying several slices one upon the other, cut them in strips about ⅛ inch wide. Put one of the frying pans over a high heat. Mix salt and a generous amount of freshly ground pepper into the potatoes. Put ½ stick of butter into the pan and, when it is almost brown, put in the potatoes. Distribute them evenly. Press them down with a spatula. Keep the heat on high until you hear the sound of frying. Then reduce the heat gradually to medium. Cook for 4 minutes. Using both hands and two pot holders, grasp the rim of the pan—not the handle but the rim—and give the pan a couple of vigorous quarter turns. If the potatoes move as a unit apart from the pan, you know they are not sticking. The heat is gradually lowered because the potatoes might burn. (It is not difficult to distinguish between the odor of browning and burning potatoes; one is pleasant and appetizing and the other is not.) No matter where the heat is—between medium or high—the sharp sizzling sound must persist.

In order to brown the other side of the potatoes, another pan is required. The problem is to turn the mat of potatoes over, so they can get brown on the other side. The use of a second pan makes this easier. Heat this other pan and put in about a tablespoon of butter. Spread the butter around the bottom of the pan. Lift up both pans at least a foot from the top of the stove. Tilt the pans toward each other, resting the edge of the pan containing the potatoes on the inside edge of the empty pan. But before the two pans meet, tip the full pan so that the potato mat flops into the empty pan. Return the potatoes to a high heat. Put the rest of the butter in pieces on top of the potatoes. Each side should take about 6 minutes to brown. Finish the cooking with 10 or 15 minutes in the oven. Take the pan from the oven and turn the potatoes out onto a round, flat platter and serve. These potatoes are perfect with roasts.

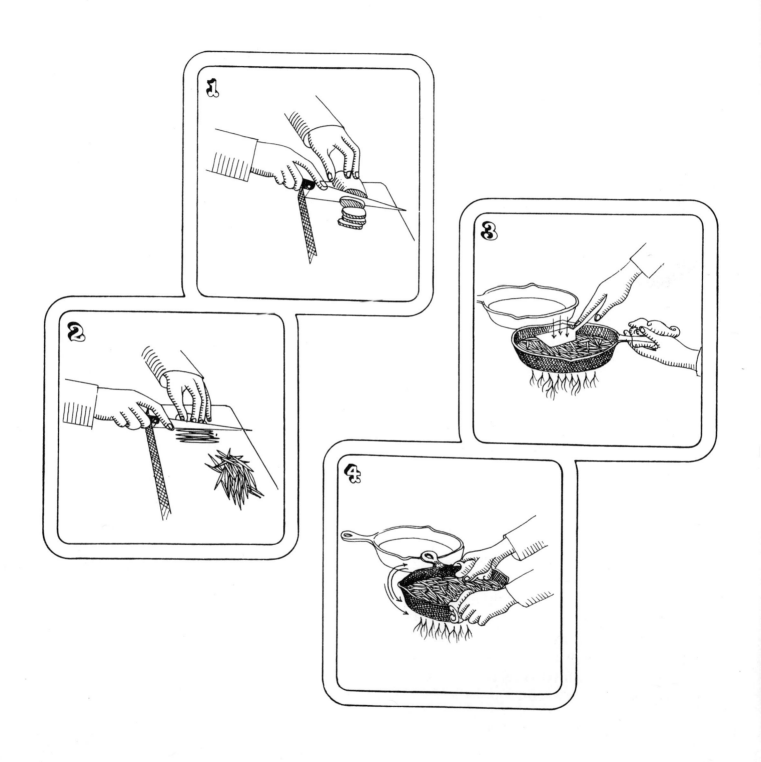

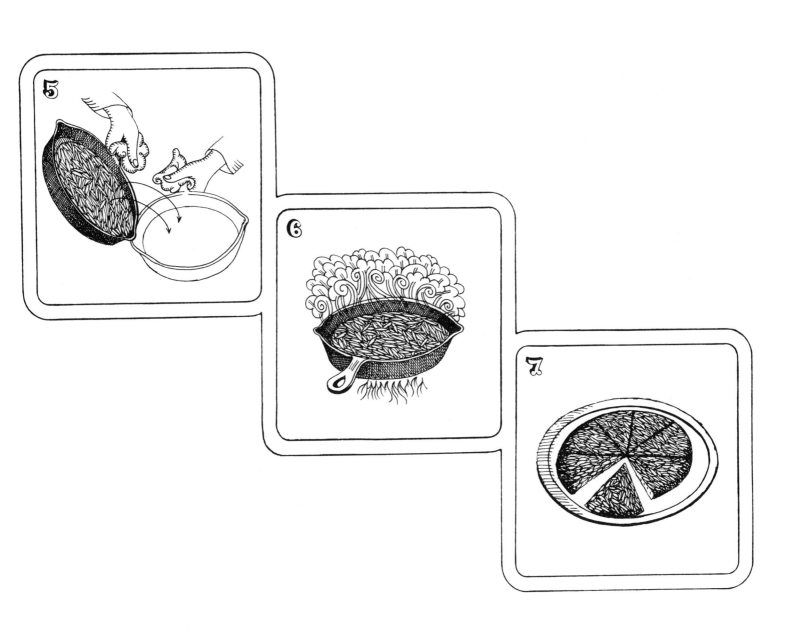

POTATOES PARISIENNE

SERVES 6 TO 8

Do not waste the remaining hole-filled potatoes. Use them for mashed or riced potatoes, or leek and potato soup. Store them covered with water in a container in the refrigerator until you are ready to use them.

3 pounds boiling potatoes
⅓ stick butter
Salt and pepper

Peel and wash the potatoes. Using a melon-baller, press the round cutting edge into the potato, turning it from side to side, and forward then backward. Finally, when it is well implanted, turn it completely. Collect the potato balls in a pot of cold water. Wash and drain them. Heat the butter in a frying pan until it is brown. Put in the potato balls. Sprinkle them with salt and pepper. Sauté until they are brown all over, then reduce the heat to low. Cover the pan. The potato balls will cook through within 8 minutes.

POTATOES SABLÉS

SERVES 6 TO 8

These can be prepared 1½ hours in advance of serving.

⅔ stick butter
1 pound mushrooms, washed, drained, and quartered
1½ pounds pearl onions, peeled

3 pounds boiling potatoes, peeled and diced in ¾-inch cubes
Salt and pepper

Preheat oven to 400°. Preheat frying pan. Add ½ the butter and heat. Put in the mushrooms and sauté until they are golden brown. Put them into a shallow roasting pan. Boil the onions in water until they are barely tender. Freshen under cold water and drain well. Add one tablespoon of butter to the frying pan and heat until it is smoking hot. Add the onions and sauté until they are lightly browned. Add the onions to the mushrooms. Heat the remaining butter in the frying pan until it is brown. Put in the potatoes, turning them from time to time until they are mostly browned. Add them to the mushrooms and onions. Sprinkle with salt and pepper.

Put the pan in the oven. Mix the ingredients around occasionally until the potatoes are tender. Remove from the oven. To heat, place in a 400° oven for 15 minutes.

RISSOLÉ POTATOES

SERVES 6

Raw potatoes, gently fried in butter until they are golden brown and tender, have a unique and pleasant taste.

2½ pounds boiling potatoes
½ stick butter
Salt and pepper
Parsley, chopped (or dill)

Peel the potatoes. Wash, dry, and cut them into ½ -inch cubes, potato balls, or fine slices. The tiny, tan-skinned new potatoes do not have to be peeled; they can be sautéed as is. A 10-inch cast-iron frying pan will just accommodate this quantity of potatoes. Preheat the pan over a medium-high heat; then, as you put in the butter, break it into several pieces. Salt and pepper the prepared potatoes. When the butter is partially brown, but not black, put in the potatoes. Add the parsley. When the potatoes are golden brown, turn them until they are evenly brown on all sides. Turn down the heat to very low, and cover the pan. Stir once or twice. Remove the cover as soon as they are tender. They can be cooked as much as ½ hour before serving. If you are serving these potatoes with lamb, sauté the potatoes with a teaspoon of fresh (or ¼ teaspoon dried) rosemary leaves.

SAUTÉED CHERRY TOMATOES

SERVES 6

This is an important recipe idea, because there are all too few red or orange vegetables. In composing a menu, you often need this color.

1 pint cherry tomatoes
2 tablespoons butter
Salt

Remove the stems; wash and dry the tomatoes. Sprinkle with salt, and then warm them in a saucepan in butter over a low heat for 4 minutes before serving. They must just be warmed up (not fried), or the skins will split.

CRÊPES AU CONFITURE

SERVES 6 OR 7

This makes a good snack.

1 cup flour
1 tablespoon sugar
½ teaspoon salt
3 eggs, beaten
1½ cups milk
¼ cup butter, melted
Raspberry, strawberry, apricot or cherry jam

Combine the flour, sugar, and salt in a large mixing bowl. Combine the beaten eggs and milk. Stir into the flour mixture and beat until smooth. Add the melted butter. The batter will be very thin, about the consistency of light cream. Preheat a 9-inch frying pan over medium heat. When the pan is hot, pour in 2 to 4 tablespoons of batter. Rotate the pan quickly to spread the batter. It must just coat the bottom of the pan. Pour off any excess. Cook about one minute on one side or until it is dry on top. Flip over and cook on the other side until it reaches the desired brownness.

If you are preparing the crêpes in advance, let them cool and stack them flat, one on top of the other. Cover with a damp towel and wrap in foil. Refrigerate or freeze until needed. Reheat briefly.

Spread jam on crêpes, roll or fold them, and put back in pan to heat. Or put into ovenproof dish and place in preheated 375° oven for about 10 minutes, until hot.

CRÊPES SUZETTE

SERVES 6 OR 7

Henry Charpentier claimed to be the inventor of this classic. I visited him in his tiny reservation —the only restaurant in Redondo Beach, California. A very charming man.

Crêpe Batter

1 cup flour
¾ cup milk
½ stick butter, melted
1 tablespoon sugar
2 eggs

To make the crêpe batter, mix all of the ingredients together in a bowl with ⅓ cup of milk. Whisk or beat the mixture until it is smooth. Add the rest of the milk or as much of it as it takes to achieve a mixture of the same consistency as heavy cream. Heat a frying pan (about 5 inches across the bottom). Holding the pan off the heat, pour 2 tablespoons of batter into the middle of it. Tip and slowly turn the pan to permit the batter to coat the bottom evenly. Crêpes have to be very thin, so there must be no excess batter floating around the surfaces of the crêpe; if the pan flares out, let this excess run up along the sides, or just pour it back into the bowl.

Return the pan to a medium heat. Within 20 seconds the underside of the crêpe will be brown. Take the pan from the heat and turn it upside down over a table. Tap the edge of the upside-down pan against the table and the crêpe should fall out. Use a spatula or your hand to put the crêpe back into the pan with the opposite side down. Better to let them get a little black than not brown at all.

The crêpes can be made far in advance and once cool can be kept, covered, in the refrigerator.

Suzette Mixture

½ cup confectioner's sugar
¼ pound butter
4 oranges
1 lemon
⅓ cup Grand Marnier
2 tablespoons Kirschwasser
2 tablespoons Cognac

The Suzette mixture is what the crêpe will eventually cook in and soak up. It also can be made in advance and kept in the refrigerator. Mix the sugar, butter, the grated peel of 2 oranges and one lemon together in a bowl. Squeeze the oranges and the lemon and strain the juice into a little pitcher. There should be about a cup of juice.

When ready to serve, fold the crêpes in half and then fold them again so that they have a quarter-moon shape. Arrange them on a platter. Now at the table at dessert time, there is a plateful of folded crêpes, a little bowl full of the butter mixture, a pitcher with the juice in it, and another pitcher into which you have measured the Grand Marnier, Kirsch, and Cognac. This dessert is flamed, served hot, and can be cooked at the table in an electric frying pan. Turn on the pan to 400° and put in ½ of the juice and ½ of the butter mixture. Put in the crêpes side by side, and before they have absorbed all the liquid, turn them over with two forks or a pair of food tongs.

Add the rest of the juice and the Suzette butter mixture. When all this has been absorbed by the crêpes, pull the plug and pour in the liquor. Keep your head to one side and approach the pan with a lighted match. When the flame dwindles and the simmering stops, there should be almost no liquid left. What is there will be thick and syrupy and should be spooned over the crêpes as they are served. This cooking process takes no more than 15 minutes. It can also be made in a chafing dish.

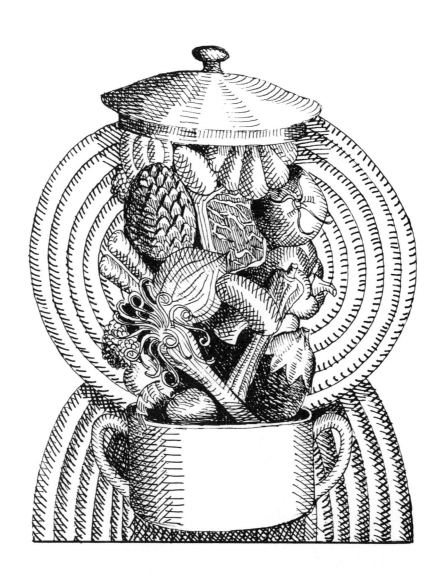

CHAPTER SEVEN

Braising

Braising (or stewing) is cooking meats, fish, or vegetables, or a combination of them, partially immersed in liquid. This is done in a moderate oven, in a covered baking pan or casserole with a border high enough to prevent the cover from interfering with the food. Braising is a combination of roasting or sautéing with simmering.

Meats that are braised are often those thick, relatively inexpensive cuts of beef, veal, or venison that would be tough and dry if roasted. With those varieties, the meat is first browned by searing in a 500° oven, or by sautéing over high heat on top of the stove. Then the meat gradually gets tender by slow boiling and then simmering for a long time, while it is partially covered with some liquid—wine, stock, or water—in a covered pan in the oven.

The advantage of braising is that the quantity of liquid can be kept at a minimum. It still has the same tenderizing effect as if the meat were completely surrounded by the simmering liquid (as in boiling), and the resulting sauce is concentrated and delicious.

The meat cooks in the oven where it is surrounded by heat, because, if it were cooked directly over heat, the meat would adhere to the bottom of the casserole or pan, causing it to burn. The cover is necessary to keep the small amount of juice from turning into steam and disappearing. The exposed parts of the meat keep moist, and as the meat is turned, it has a chance to be in the liquid.

The amount of juice or gravy that remains from the braising should be just enough to accompany the meat. If there is an excess, it can be reduced by boiling on top of the stove apart from the meat. As the juice reduces in volume, it will gain in flavor—a brown gravy will get browner, a thickened gravy will grow thicker. Celery, carrots, and onions should be cooked with braised meats to add flavor and thus achieve a good-tasting sauce.

Since it is such a fine way of cooking and getting a distinguished sauce at the same time, other meats than those requiring prolonged cooking time to be tender are often braised. Young chickens and sweetbreads, even expensive cuts of beef that are tender when roasted, are even more tender when braised. And then you have that great built-in sauce as well.

Turkey can be braised. The breast meat, which is usually so dry, will be juicy.

Fish, which gets cooked through and tender

very quickly, lends itself very well to braising. The delicate and subtle fish flavor imparted to the small amount of surrounding liquid (usually white wine and lemon juice) must be in the finished sauce. To dilute this limited taste by adding too much liquid would be a grave error. The character of the sauce would vanish.

Not all meats, fish, and poultry get seared or browned before braising, just those with no exterior covering of skin or fat. Searing helps to hold in the juice. Most cuts of beef require searing first.

Many vegetables are braised. Delicate vegetables—such as endive, celery, and butternut squash—braised in chicken stock or water retain their form. Some vegetables with delicate flavor lose a lot of their taste to the water if they are boiled. Braising the vegetables in a small amount of liquid keeps in the taste because it has nowhere else to go.

CHICKEN
À LA CRÈME TARRAGON

SERVES 6

In this dish it is better if the sauce is a little too thick than too thin. The juice from the string beans and additional juice coming out of the chicken will thin it.

⅓ cup dry tarragon or 2 handfuls of fresh tarragon
    sprigs with stems loosely bunched (about the
    size of a big apple)
Salt
2 2½-pound chickens, whole
1 cup dry white wine
⅓ cup cold water
2 medium onions, roughly cut
1 stalk celery, roughly cut
Beurre Manié (see page 44)
½ cup heavy cream
Juice of ½ lemon
2 egg yolks, beaten
1 package frozen string beans, cooked and drained

Preheat oven to 400°. If you use dried tarragon, divide it in half and tie it in two little cheesecloth bags. Place them in the cavities of the chickens. Fresh tarragon can be stuffed in as is. Salt the chickens and put them into a deep casserole that just contains them. Add the white wine, water, onions, and celery. Cover and cook for one hour.

Using a fork, lift one of the chickens from the casserole. If the juice that runs out is clear (not pink), the chickens are done. Remove the chickens from the casserole. There should be about 1½ cups of liquid in the bottom of the casserole. Strain the liquid into a saucepan. Discard the onion and celery. Squeeze the juice from the bags of tarragon and discard the bags. If you used fresh tarragon, leave it in. Simmer. Whisk in the Beurre Manié little by little until the sauce thickens. It should be a little thicker than heavy cream. Add the cream and the lemon juice. Let simmer for a few minutes. Whisk the sauce gradually into the beaten egg yolks. Stir in the string beans and spoon the sauce over the chickens.

Serve surrounded with a ring of Boiled Rice (see page 171), Endive Salad (see page 179), and followed by a fruit dessert.

131

BRAISED
ROLLED SHOULDER OF VEAL

SERVES 6

The trouble with this is that it tends to fall apart when it's carved. Well, as long as you know it's going to do that, why worry about it?

¼ stick butter
4 pounds boned and rolled shoulder of veal
Salt and pepper
1 stalk celery, roughly cut
3 medium onions, peeled and roughly cut
2 carrots, peeled and roughly cut
1 bay leaf
2 cloves garlic, peeled and roughly cut
3 tablespoons flour
1 cup dry white wine
1 cup water
2 tablespoons tomato purée

Preheat oven to 325°. Choose a pan or casserole of enameled ironware, thick aluminum, or cast iron, so the meat will brown uniformly where it touches the bottom of the pan. The casserole or pan should be at least 4 inches deep and just large enough to contain the meat. If your pan or casserole is inappropriate for browning meat, use a sauté pan, and then transfer the meat to the casserole you have chosen.

Heat the pan over a high flame. Add butter and cook until it is brown. Sprinkle all sides of the meat liberally with salt and pepper. Put the meat into the butter; cook until it is brown on all sides.

The meat will have several flat surfaces to be browned. When one side is brown, turn the meat to brown the other sides. If the meat is flat on both ends, stand the meat up to brown the ends. Lean it against the side of the pan or hold it upright with a fork. When the meat is browned, pour off all rendered fat, leaving approximately 2 tablespoons in the pan. Then add the celery, onions, and carrots. Lower heat to a medium flame. When these vegetables are tinged with brown, mix in the bay leaf and garlic. Sauté for another minute. Sprinkle the flour over all. Mix until the flour is no longer visible. Flour will absorb the fat present in the pan, and on the surfaces of the meat and vegetables. The amount of rendered warm fat, butter, or oil must be of equal proportion to the flour. If there is more fat, the gravy will have a film of it on top. For instance, in this recipe the proportions are 3 tablespoons flour to 3 tablespoons fat. There are approximately 2 tablespoons of fat left in the pan, and one tablespoon of fat clinging to the sides of the meat and vegetables.

Add the wine, tomato purée, and water, and stir. Bring to a simmer, cover, and put into the oven. Turn the meat every ½ hour. It should take about 2 hours to cook. Remove the meat to a serving platter. Repose the meat for at least one hour, turning it occasionally to keep the outer portions moistened by the juice which will inevitably gather on the platter.

Strain the gravy and serve it separately. Be sure to taste the gravy; add salt and pepper if necessary. Freshly ground pepper does wonders for heightening the taste of a brown sauce. If the gravy lacks character, reduce its quantity by boiling it rapidly over high heat. It will gain color, thickness, and depth of taste as its volume diminishes. Be careful not to let a gravy thickened with flour burn—it does easily. If the gravy is good after reducing, but lacks thickness, mix one tablespoon of cornstarch or arrowroot with ⅓ cup of white wine. Bring gravy to a simmer and stir or whisk this mixture into it.

For variation just before serving, add ½ pound sliced and lightly Sautéed Mushrooms (see page 119) to the sauce, and/or ½ cup of heavy cream.

VEAL AND KIDNEYS AU CINZANO

SERVES 8

The French countryside produces so many good wines of various tastes and colors. Since the French can't stand water, most of these wines find their way into regional specialties—red or white wine, sometimes champagne, and even Cinzano.

1 pound veal kidneys, peeled
1 pound veal in ¾-inch cubes (from shoulder, shin, or neck)
¼ stick butter
½ pound small white mushrooms
Juice of ½ lemon
¼ cup chopped shallots
3 tablespoons flour
½ cup dry Cinzano vermouth
1 tablespoon tomato purée or 1 teaspoon tomato paste
Salt and pepper
Water
½ cup sour cream
1 teaspoon chives, chopped or 1 tablespoon parsley, chopped

Preheat oven to 325°. Cut the kidneys into cubes the same size as the veal meat. Put a 10-inch frying pan over high heat. When the pan has become quite hot, add half the butter. Tip and turn to coat the pan evenly. When the butter is brown, distribute half of the cubes of meat and kidneys in the pan. Wait. Do not touch or disarrange the pieces until the undersides have time to brown. A cube of meat has six sides. Ideally, all six should be brown, but I find that impatience blended with experience produces three brown sides. Remove the meat and kidneys to a casserole and repeat with the remaining meat and kidneys.

Sauté the mushrooms over medium heat in the same pan in the remaining fat. They should be quartered if they are large. Squeeze lemon juice over them while they are cooking. Stir occasionally and add shallots when the mushrooms begin to brown. Permit this combination to sizzle or sauté for several minutes, stirring occasionally. Add to the meat in the casserole.

Stir in the flour until the white no longer shows. Add Cinzano, tomato purée, salt and pepper, and enough cold water to cover about ⅔ of the contents of the casserole. Bring to a boil, cover the casserole, and put into the oven for 1¼ hours. Put sour cream into a serving dish and gradually fold in the stew, which should be very hot, but not boiling. Sprinkle with chopped chives or parsley.

Serve with Riced Potatoes (see page 171), string beans, and hot French bread, followed by Pears poached in Red Wine (see page 174) for dessert.

PAUPIETTES OF VEAL

SERVES 8

I'm sure that once you are familiar with this recipe you will want to improvise your own stuffing, using ground ham or sausage, other vegetables, perhaps bell peppers. Be sure that at least one-third of the ground meat for the stuffing is uncooked. This is the whole principle of having meat loaf stay together and not crumble when you slice it—of course, some of the meat can be left-over cooked meat, but not all.

2 medium onions, finely chopped
⅓ stick butter
4 slices soft white bread
⅔ cup milk
½ cup parsley, chopped
1 3-pound chicken, skinned, boned, and ground
    (The butcher will do this if you also purchase a
    small amount of beef to chase the chicken out of
    his grinder.)
1 teaspoon salt
18 very thin scallops of veal (pounded out to approximately 2½ inches by 4 inches)

Salt and pepper
1 cup flour
2 tablespoons shallots, chopped
½ cup dry white wine
1 cup chicken broth
1 pound mushrooms, sliced

Preheated oven to 400°. Lightly brown the onions in two tablespoons of butter. Remove crusts from the bread and save them to use in making bread crumbs. In a medium-sized bowl, soak the remaining bread in milk. Add the browned onions, chopped parsley, ground raw chicken, and salt. Mix thoroughly with your hands and taste a bit of the mixture. Add more salt and pepper if needed.

Lay out the scallops of veal on the table. Put a heaping tablespoon of chicken mixture in the center of each scallop. Roll them as you would a rug, and secure both ends of each paupiette with white string.

Preheat a 12-inch sauté pan and put in the remaining butter. Salt and pepper the paupiettes and roll them in flour. Shake off the excess between your hands and put the paupiettes one by one into the hot butter. Brown all over. Add shallots and stir; add white wine, chicken broth, and sliced mushrooms. Bring to a simmer, cover the pan loosely with aluminum foil, and finish cooking the paupiettes in the oven for 25 minutes.

Before serving, if the sauce is thin, remove the paupiettes to a heated platter and cook the sauce slowly on top of the stove. It will thicken as it reduces in volume.

Serve with spinach and Mashed Potatoes (see page 170). Follow with seedless grapes in sour cream (topped with brown sugar) for dessert.

LAMB NAVARIN

SERVES 6

This stew blends two similar tastes—the taste of the lamb and that of the white turnips.

1½ sticks butter
2 pounds shoulder lamb in ¾-inch cubes
3 tablespoons flour
½ cup dry white wine
1 bay leaf
2 tablespoons tomato purée or 1 teaspoon tomato paste
Salt and pepper
Water
½ pound carrots, peeled, cut in 1-inch pieces
½ pound white turnips, peeled, cut in 1-inch pieces
½ pound small white onions, peeled
1 tablespoon sugar

When you are browning stew meat, the pan and fat have to be hot. When the meat hits the hot pan, the outside of the meat is seared, and the juice will stay in. Disaster strikes when you put the meat into a cold pan. As the pan heats gradually, the meat will start to boil, and all the juice will run out. Once the juice has escaped, there is no way of getting it back in, and the meat will be stringy and dry. Another hazard in stews or sautéed meat dishes is that if the meat cooks too long, it will disintegrate. I would rather have the stew meat a little underdone. If any kind of stew is to be cooled, refrigerated, and later reheated, you must deduct one-third of the cooking time, because as a very hot stew cools, though it's not boiling, it will still be cooking. The same is true when you reheat it.

Preheat oven to 350°. Place a 10-inch frying pan over high heat. After the pan has become quite hot, put in a half stick of butter, tipping and turning the pan to distribute it. When the butter is brown, evenly distribute half of the cubes of meat in the pan. Wait. Do not touch or disarrange the pieces until the sides that are down have become nice and brown. Then turn them one by one, again waiting until that down side gets brown. Remove the browned meat to a heavy casserole or a deep oven-proof pot. Repeat with the remaining meat and butter and add them to the pot. Sprinkle the meat with flour, mixing it around with a fork until you no longer see any white. Add white wine, bay leaf, tomato purée, salt, pepper, and enough cold water so that just the top pieces of meat are uncovered. Bring to a boil on top of the stove over medium heat. Push a wooden spoon against the bottom of the pot to make sure there is no burning or sticking.

Add the carrots. Cover the pot and place in the oven. Sauté the turnips in the remaining butter to a nice golden brown. Remove them with a slotted spoon and brown the onions in the same butter. A tablespoon of sugar sprinkled over the top will hasten the browning of the onions, but it is not essential. After the stew has been in the oven for about 15 minutes, stir in the browned vegetables and let the whole simmer in the oven for an hour, or until the meat is tender.

A sprinkling of green peas (Mama's Peas, see page 170) would be decorative on top. Serve with Boiled Rice (see page 171), green salad, and Pears Poached in White Wine (see page 174) for dessert.

BRAISED BEEF

SERVES 6

Oh that gravy! Don't forget to let it boil down some if it lacks taste.

1/4 stick butter
4-pound piece of beef (large end of brisket, second cut or crossrib, rump, or chuck—presence of exterior and/or interior fat makes for more tender meat)
Salt and pepper
1 stalk celery, roughly cut
2 carrots, peeled and roughly cut
3 medium onions, peeled and roughly cut
1 teaspoon paprika
1/4 teaspoon dried thyme leaves
1/2 bay leaf
4 cloves garlic, peeled and roughly cut
3 tablespoons flour
1 cup red wine
1/4 cup tomato purée
1 cup water

Preheat oven to 325°. Choose a pan or casserole of enameled ironware, thick aluminum, or cast iron with a cover. The casserole or pan should be at least 6 inches deep, and just large enough to contain the meat.

Heat the pan over high heat on top of the stove. Add butter and heat until it is brown. Sprinkle all sides of the meat liberally with salt and pepper. Put the meat into the butter; brown the meat well on all sides.

The meat will have at least three or four flat surfaces to be browned. When one side is brown, turn the meat to brown the other sides. If the meat is flat on both ends, stand the meat up to brown the ends. Lean it against the side of the pan or hold it upright with a fork. When the meat is browned, pour off all rendered fat, leaving approximately 2 tablespoons, then add the celery, carrots, and onions. Lower heat to medium. When these vegetables are tinged with brown, add the paprika, thyme, bay leaf, and garlic and mix. Sauté for another minute. Sprinkle the flour over all. Mix until the flour is no longer visible. Flour will absorb the fat present in the pan and on the surfaces of the meat and vegetables. The proportion of rendered warm fat, butter, or oil must be equal to the proportion of flour. If there is more fat, the gravy will have a film of it on top. For instance, in this recipe, the proportions are 3 tablespoons of flour to 3 tablespoons fat. There are approximately 2 tablespoons of fat left in pan, and one tablespoon of fat clinging to sides of meat and vegetables.

Add the wine, tomato purée, and water and stir. Bring to a simmer, cover, and put into the oven. Turn the meat every 1/2 hour. It might take as long as 3 hours for the meat to get tender. After 1 3/4 hours, push a kitchen fork into the meat. If it goes in quite easily, the meat is ready to be served. This can be prepared an hour or so in advance of mealtime. Remove the meat to serving platter.

Strain the gravy and serve separately. Be sure to taste the gravy; add salt and pepper if necessary. Freshly ground pepper does wonders for a brown sauce. If gravy lacks character, reduce by boiling it rapidly over high heat. It will gain color, thickness, and depth of taste as the volume diminishes. Be careful not to let a gravy thickened with flour

burn—it does easily. If the gravy is good after reducing, but lacks thickness, mix one tablespoon of
cornstarch or arrowroot with ⅓ cup of red wine.
Bring the gravy to a simmer and stir or whisk this
mixture into it.

Serve with Mashed Potatoes (see page 170)
and string beans, followed by vanilla ice cream
with strawberry sauce for dessert.

BRAISED PORK
WITH BAKED APPLE GLAZE
AND GARNISH

SERVES 8

This too is difficult, but it's fun and looks
pretty. Like Duck à l'Orange or Coq au Vin, this
recipe must be read through carefully before you
even begin.

*5-pound loin of pork (center cut—be sure the
butcher makes cuts through backbone at base of
ribs to fascilitate carving)*
Salt and pepper
1 stalk celery, roughly cut
2 carrots, peeled and roughly chopped
3 medium onions, peeled and roughly chopped
½ bay leaf
2 cloves garlic, peeled and roughly chopped
3 tablespoons flour
1 cup dry white wine
1 cup water
2 tablespoons tomato purée
½ cup finely diced dill pickle (optional, but good)
1 tablespoon fresh parsley, chopped
Watercress for garnish

Preheat oven to 500°. Brown the loin of pork
in the oven. It is easier than in a frying pan on top
of the stove, because of the pork's length and half-
moon shape. Put the fatty side up in an oval roasting pan (or diagonally in a rectangular pan) that
just contains it. You may have to bend and push
it to get it in. Sprinkle liberally with salt and pepper. Put it into the oven. After half an hour, pour
off rendered fat, leaving about 2 tablespoons fat in
the pan. Distribute celery, carrots, and onions
around the meat. Give it another 15 to 20 minutes
in the oven so that the vegetables can brown
lightly. Remove from oven and add the bay leaf
and garlic. Sprinkle flour over all. Mix and turn
meat until the flour is no longer visible. Flour will
absorb the fat present in the pan and on the surfaces of the meat and vegetables. The amount of
rendered warm fat, butter, or oil must be of equal
proportion to the flour. If there is more fat, there
will be a film of it on top of the gravy. For instance, the proportions here are 3 tablespoons of
flour to 3 tablespoons of fat. There are approximately 2 tablespoons of fat left in the pan, and one
tablespoon of fat clinging to the sides of the meat
and vegetables.

Add the wine, water, and tomato purée. Mix,
cover tightly, and return to the oven at 325° for
1½ hours. Turn the loin and stir the contents of
the pan every half an hour. Remove the loin to a
serving platter. The pork can repose in a warm,
draft-free place for an hour, or until the baked
apples and glaze are prepared.

Strain the sauce into a pot for heating up at
serving time. Serve the sauce separately. Be sure
to taste the gravy; add salt and pepper if necessary.
Freshly ground pepper does wonders for heighten-

137

ing the taste of a brown sauce. Taste the sauce, then give it a half-dozen twists of the pepper grinder, stir, and taste again. You'll see what I mean. The difference it makes is miraculous. If the gravy lacks character, reduce, by boiling it rapidly over high heat. It will gain color, thickness, and depth of taste as the volume diminishes. Be careful not to let a gravy thickened with flour burn—it does easily. If the gravy is good after reducing, but lacks thickness, mix one tablespoon of cornstarch or arrowroot with ⅓ cup of white wine. Bring the gravy to a simmer and stir or whisk this mixture into it. Add pickles and parsley to sauce just before serving.

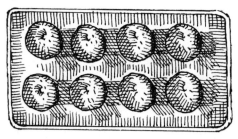

Baked Apple Garnish

8 red or golden Delicious apples (small ones)
⅓ cup water
Juice of 1 lemon (reserve skin)
½ cup sugar

Preheat oven to 450°. Core the apples. Peel about one inch of skin evenly from around the core hole at the small end of each apple. Reserve the peels and cores. Put the apples stem end down in pan. Pour the water and lemon juice over apples. Cut the lemon skins into quarters and add to the apples. Place the peels and cores around the apples. Sprinkle sugar over all, and put in the oven. Delicious apples will be brown on top and tender when poked with a fork, after about half an hour. Remove from oven when tender. The ideal apple for baking is the Roman Beauty, but it is too large to serve as a garnish. McIntosh are too juicy. When baked, they collapse like over-broiled tomatoes. Arrange the baked apples around the loin of pork. Reserve the juice in pan for glaze.

Baked Apple Glaze

4 ounces apple jelly
Juice of 2 oranges
Liquid from baked apple pan

Put the apple jelly into a small pot over medium-high heat. Stir constantly as it melts and begins to bubble. When it turns brown (caramelizes), add the orange juice to the pot. Strain in the juice from the baked apple pan. Let this boil. When it begins to thicken, pay close attention that it doesn't burn. Use a large kitchen spoon to put some of the glaze over the loin of pork. If most of it sticks to the pork and doesn't run off, pour the rest of the glaze evenly over the pork. The brilliant, shiny surface looks very appetizing, and it is well worth the trouble. The platter with apples and glazed pork should go into 300° oven for 15 minutes before serving. The glaze will not melt and run off. Garnish the platter with watercress.

Serve with Mashed Potatoes (see page 170) and Braised Celery (see page 139). Chocolate ice cream with almost-melted vanilla ice cream as sauce for dessert.

CHESTNUTS WITH RED CABBAGE

SERVES 8 TO 12

This dish is great for big holiday spreads or with game. But watch it! Peeling chestnuts is a pain in the neck.

30 chestnuts
4 pounds red cabbage
Boiling water
4 cloves
2 large onions
1 stalk celery, washed
1 carrot, peeled
3 tablespoons red wine vinegar
1 cup water
2 teaspoons salt
½ teaspoon pepper
1-pound slab bacon
1 tablespoon parsley, chopped

Preheat oven to 450°. Peel the chestnuts by making a slight gash on the round side of the nut. Place in the oven for 12 minutes. Cool slightly. Remove the shell with your fingers or a small, dull, pointed knife. To remove the second skin, put the chestnut into hot water for 5 minutes. Drain and peel while still hot. Since the peeling operation must be done while the chestnuts are hot or warm, it should be done in three shifts.

Remove the core and any tired outer leaves of the cabbage. Quarter the cabbage lengthways and then cut the quarters crossways into thirds. Cook, covered with boiling water, in a large pot, for 10 minutes. Drain and rinse under cold running water. Drain again in a colander and put into large oven-proof casserole or roasting pan. Stick 2 cloves into each onion. Place them in the cabbage. Add the peeled chestnuts, the stalk of celery, the carrot, vinegar, water, salt, and pepper. Remove the rind from the slab of bacon. Cut the bacon into ½-inch cubes and fry until golden brown. Add the fried bacon to the cabbage, and pour half of the rendered fat over the cabbage. Add the bacon rind. Cover the casserole or pan and cook in the oven for 1½ to 2 hours, stirring once or twice during this time.

The cabbage should be quite tender, but not mushy. Remove and discard the celery, carrot, onions, and bacon rind. Sprinkle with parsley and serve.

BRAISED CELERY

SERVES 6 TO 8

I always fix this when celery is on sale. Sometimes at supermarkets they put several bunches of celery with the outer branches and the tops trimmed in one package. This is a very easy and unusual vegetable dish.

3 large bunches celery
½ stick butter
Juice of 1 lemon
Salt
Cold water
3 tablespoons grated Parmesan or Swiss cheese

Preheat oven to 325°. Remove the outer circle

of celery branches and cut the celery bunches 5 inches from bottom, saving the tops and outer branches for soup stock. Pare off any brown from the bottom, but be sure to leave the celery root intact, or the branches will fall off in the cooking. Peel the outer branches of the bunch with a potato peeler. Split the bunches lengthways into quarters and wash.

Use 2 tablespoons of butter to coat the bottom of a baking dish that is large enough to contain the celery in one layer. Arrange celery neatly, cut side down. Dot the remaining butter over the celery. Sprinkle with lemon juice and salt. Add ½ inch of water and cover with aluminum foil. Cook until tender—about 1½ hours.

Sprinkle grated cheese over celery and place under broiler until lightly browned. Serve within half an hour.

This recipe may be prepared as much as a day in advance. Cook the celery until it is not quite tender. Cool and refrigerate with the aluminum foil still covering the baking dish. Reheat, covered, in a 325° oven. Sprinkle on the grated cheese and brown under broiler.

BRAISED LETTUCE

SERVES 10 TO 14

I don't like this very much unless the lettuce is right out of the garden.

8 heads of butter crunch lettuce (Bibb or Boston will do)
Water
¼ stick butter
2 onions, peeled and thinly sliced
3 slices bacon
Salt
2 cups beef stock
½ cup water
¼ cup Demi-Glaze (see page 32)

Preheat oven to 400°. Cut the brown from the base of each lettuce root and remove any tired or discolored leaves. Soak the lettuce heads down in a sink filled with cold water. Push the heads around occasionally, allowing plenty of time for the sand and dirt in them to soak out and settle to the bottom of the sink. Remove the lettuces from the sink and drain them stem side up. Place the heads in a pan large enough to contain them all. Pour enough boiling water over them to cover. Simmer for ½ hour. Drain and cool under a thin stream of cold running water.

Cut each root end in half and tear each head in two. Squeeze gently to get rid of excess water. Fold lengthways, with the torn part inside. Butter a baking dish large enough to contain the lettuce in one layer. Distribute the onion and bacon on the bottom. Place lettuce on top of this in a neat layer. Sprinkle with salt. Add beef stock and water. Cover loosely with aluminum foil and braise in oven for 45 minutes, or until almost all the liquid has evaporated.

Remove the lettuce from the baking dish and arrange it on a platter. Discard the onion and bacon. To serve, heat the Demi-Glaze and spoon over the top.

POTATOES FONDANTES

SERVES 10 TO 14

It is so nice to cook things and not have to worry about burning them. Here, potatoes cook slowly at a low temperature in the oven. They won't burn (famous last words). They should, however, be a little brown on top.

20–25 small new potatoes (about 6 pounds)
1 can consommé
⅓ cup water
Salt and pepper
⅓ stick of butter

Preheat oven to 400°. Peel and pare the potatoes so they're all the same size. Arrange in a 2-inch-deep pan that will just contain them without piling them one on top of another. Add consommé and water. Salt and pepper. Dot the top with butter. Cover loosely with aluminum foil. Bake in oven for 40 minutes, or until the liquid has evaporated. If the potatoes have not browned at the end of the cooking time, uncover them and continue baking until they are browned.

BRAISED BUTTERNUT SQUASH

SERVES 6

This has such delicate flavor, and the orange color is so valuable in menu planning.

3 butternut squash
1½ cups cold water
⅓ stick butter
Salt and pepper

Preheat oven to 425°. Peel the squash. Cut in half lengthways. Scoop out seeds. Pour water into a baking dish that is large enough to contain the squash in one layer. Add the squash, cut side up. Put equal amounts of butter in the cavities. Sprinkle with salt and pepper. Loosely cover with aluminum foil. Cook in the oven until tender (about one hour).

RATATOUILLE NIÇOISE

SERVES 8 TO 10

This should be done in the autumn when eggplant, zucchini, tomatoes, and peppers are readily available and cheap. Ratatouille can be prepared in advance. It tastes better the second day. It also freezes well.

1½ pounds onions, chopped
2 cups olive oil
6 fresh tomatoes, peeled and seeded (To peel a tomato, spear it with a fork and dunk it in boiling water for no more than 10 seconds. The skin will slip right off. To remove seeds, cut tomato in half crossways. Hold tomato half in on palm and gently squeeze out seeds. Cut halves into quarters.)
2 pounds eggplant, peeled and cut in ½-inch cubes
Salt and pepper
2 pounds zucchini (green squash), peeled and cut in ½-inch cubes
¼ pound red or green bell peppers, cut in ¾-inch squares
4 cloves garlic, finely chopped

Preheat oven to 325°. Lightly brown the

141

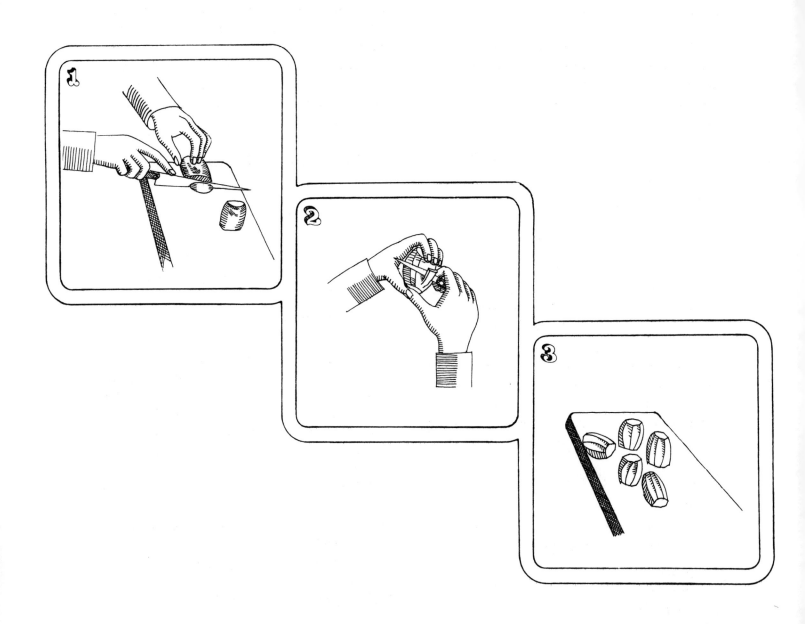

onions in two tablespoons of olive oil. Add the tomatoes and let them simmer slowly for half an hour, or until most of the juice has boiled away. Do not burn, so pay attention. Heat a frying pan, and put in a half cup of olive oil. When the oil is hot, put in a couple of handfuls of the eggplant. Salt and pepper and let the cubes get good and brown. Pour the contents of the pan into a colander, which should be placed in a cake tin, to recuperate the olive oil. Sauté the rest of the eggplant in the same way. Salt the zucchini, and brown in some olive oil (don't forget to use the oil recuperated from frying the eggplant) and drain in the same colander. Sauté the peppers and add to the other vegetables to drain. Gently dump the vegetables and tomatoes into a pot or casserole. Stir in the chopped garlic. Let simmer for 25 minutes in the oven. Add more salt and pepper if needed. Do not stir too much at this point. The vegetables are delicate, and the dish is far more attractive if they are recognizable.

Serve hot or cold. If served cold, decorate with slices of black olive, and/or wedges of tomato, hard-boiled egg, or a cold poached egg (soft) with catsup on top (Restaurant de la Pyramide in Vienne, France, does it this way).

CHAPTER EIGHT

Boiling

I CALL this chapter "Boiling," but it is really about all the ways of cooking in liquid.

Boiling, simmering, poaching, stewing—these are all alike in that in each case the liquid has been brought to a boil. Boiling liquid is very hot and is quite agitated with big bubbles; waves occur even in what is known as a rolling boil. Simmering liquid is not as hot and is less agitated, with very small bubbles. In poaching, the liquid is still cooler and is completely calm. Whole fish are poached rather than boiled because fish cooks quickly and because the bumping around the fish would get from boiling water might easily break it.

Boiling is an easy way to cook. Once the liquid (usually water) comes to a boil, and what is to be boiled is slowly simmering in the pot, no further attention is required. There are no encrusted pots to be scoured out. The whole main course can be cooked in one pot. Boiled beef, or what the French call *pot au feu,* begins with beef boiling in water to which leeks, celery, carrots, onions, potatoes, and other vegetables are added. It's all served on a large platter with a good vinaigrette or horseradish sauce. Bouillabaisse is another French speciality in which various fish, crustaceans, and bivalves are boiled together. In both cases the boiling liquid or broth is very good. In Marseilles the bouillabaisse broth is served first and followed by the fish.

Boiled meats or vegetables get heat from direct contact with a liquid which has been heated to its boiling point. Unlike foods cooked by sautéing, roasting, broiling, or frying, food that is boiled does not become brown from the heat. The taste of boiled food is therefore a milder version of the natural or raw taste of what is being boiled. Chicken tastes like chicken; onions taste like onions. But in both cases the flavor of the food after it has been boiled is more delicate.

What foods are boiled? Green beans, carrots, broccoli, asparagus, cauliflower, and many other vegetables. Spaghetti, its relatives, and other starches such as rice, potatoes, and dried beans need to soak up liquid to be palatable. Meats are often boiled, especially those that require long cooking to be tender, such as corned beef, short ribs, beef tongue, fowl, veal feet, ham hocks, pigs' feet, and tripe. All these meats take at least 2½ hours of simmering to be tender. They must also be kept moist to be tender, so surrounding them with a simmering liquid is an ideal way of cooking them. If these same meats were roasted, they would dry out and be inedible.

Steaming is like boiling, but it makes me nervous. Those who say that much taste is lost to the water during boiling might be right. In any case, I don't like those people. Since vegetables cook fast, very little of their flavor is lost to the water. Vegetables also retain more of their natural color in boiling, since they are contained in the liquid rather than being out in the air.

Any meat or vegetable that is boiled can also be braised. But braising is more complicated and is unnecessary, unless a concentrated accompanying sauce is desired. Braising produces such a sauce because the method requires less water than is used in boiling. For example, fresh brisket is delicious either boiled and then served with a vinaigrette sauce, or braised and served with the juice or sauce it cooked in. But butternut squash has such a delicious taste that it has to be braised.

Boiling, then, is not just a tenderizing process for tough meats. Fish, which is tender and cooks quickly, is often poached. In Lyons, France, a specialty is made of plump 2½-pound chickens from Bresse, which are simmered for under an hour.

What do you boil in? A pot with a lid that fits. For poaching fish you need a fish poacher—a long, deep pot with lid and a rack. The rack keeps the fish off the bottom of the pan and allows for removal of the fish without breaking it. The lid is necessary; otherwise the steam escapes into the air, decreasing the volume of the boiling liquid. If the volume of the liquid decreases, you will be forced to add more liquid in order to contain what you're boiling. If the liquid is red wine, it could cost you money, or if you are using sea water, it could mean another trip to the ocean. Since most meats and vegetables float to the top of the liquid, a portion of them often sticks out of the water like an iceberg. What protrudes from the water will not cook unless the pot's covered. Then the steam between the boiling liquid and the lid will cook them.

What kind of liquid do you use for boiling? Although the liquid is usually plain water, spices, herbs, celery, carrots, and onions are often added to lend flavor not just to the food being boiled, but also to the liquid or bouillon. A clove of garlic added to spaghetti water flavors the spaghetti. Lobsters can be boiled in tap water, but they taste better when boiled in sea water. They also taste delicious when boiled in dry white wine. Some lemon juice or vinegar should always be added to the water when seafood is boiled. It keeps the meat firm and white. Liquids used in boiling are always salted except when garden vegetables are being cooked. Green vegetables are likely to be less green if the water is salted. A little baking soda may be used to keep them green. Water for boiling corn on the cob is never salted; the salt makes the kernels tough.

Most vegetables can be cooked well in advance of a meal. If they are then cooked or even refrigerated, they may be reheated in a pan with some butter over moderate heat at mealtime.

PERIWINKLES

SERVES 6 TO 15

These are perfect for cocktails. They look like snails, only they are smaller, about ½ inch in diameter. They can be found at the shore on rocks that are partially covered at high tide.

2 pounds periwinkles
Water
1 large onion stuck with 3 cloves
Salt
1 stick butter
Juice of ½ lemon

Wash the periwinkles very well. Put them into a pot, cover with water, and bring to a boil. Discard the water, rinse and drain the periwinkles, and return them to the pot. Add the onion stuck with cloves, and cover again with salted water (do not add salt if sea water is used). Bring to a boil, and let simmer for about 30 minutes. Drain and serve them in their shells with a dip made of melted butter and lemon juice.

Periwinkles are also delicious cold. Chill and store them in their stock, then drain and serve with a vinaigrette dip made of chopped onions, salt and pepper, oil and vinegar. Or serve them with a hot dip made of ⅓ stick of butter melted with one tablespoon of chopped parsley, the juice of ½ lemon, and one teaspoon of chopped garlic.

Guests should be provided with straight pins to extract the periwinkles from their shells. The pins can be stuck into a large, handsome lemon. Pare a slice off the broad side of the lemon so that it won't roll. Gold straight pins might be used. The periwinkles will never have had it so good.

MUSSELS MARINIÈRE

SERVES 6

Roughly translated into English, this means mussels like the sailor's wife makes. If you visit the beaches in the summertime, you may want to gather your own mussels. Fresh mussels can be a real treat, and soothing to the budget. You can find them clinging to rocks below the high-tide mark.

5 pounds mussels
2 medium-sized onions, finely chopped
⅔ stick butter
½ cup dry white wine
½ lemon
½ cup parsley, freshly chopped
1 cup heavy cream (optional)

The only hard job is cleaning the mussels. First rinse them, then scrub them with a brush in lots of cold water. Pick off the beard from each mussel with a sharp paring knife. Any open mussels should be discarded. In every batch there are a few mussels full of sand or mud that have a peculiar desire to stay together like their healthy brothers. As you scrub the mussels, give each one a twist between index finger and thumb, as if you were snapping your fingers, but with the flat sides of the broad end of the mussel between them. The muddy ones will fall open. Discard them. Rinse the mussels several times and put them into a large pot. Add the onions, butter, wine, and the juice of half a lemon. Cover the pot. (You can delay cooking them for one hour maximum.) Fifteen minutes before serving, put them over high heat. When they have cooked for 10 minutes, stir them around once with a large spoon. Cover the pot again and continue cooking until the mussels are completely open. Mix in the chopped parsley (and cream) just before serving.

In some places it is very dangerous to eat mussels during the warmer months, May through August. You should find out from the health authorities in your area when it is safe to eat mussels. We eat them all year round in Cape Cod. The meat of the mussel is particularly big and fat when the water is cold, like in winter.

Serve the mussels as a first course. Use soup plates or larger chowder bowls. An empty shell is useful for drinking the broth from.

HOT POACHED WHOLE FISH

SERVES 8 TO 10

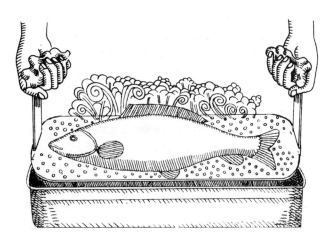

The best way to cook fish is to poach it whole. Like a big roast beef, leg of lamb, or turkey, its size and beautiful form make a whole fish an impressive main event for a dinner party. The other important advantage in poaching the fish whole is that the skin holds in the juice, to such a degree that once, when I was catering a dinner party in New York City, a hostess complained that the poached fish wasn't done because it was so juicy. People have simply gotten used to fish being dry, because it is so often served that way.

1   8-pound fish, scaled, with gills removed, but head and tail fins still on (striped bass, red snapper, large trout, pike—a salmon has more meat, so it can be smaller—allow ½ to ⅔ pound per person.)

To poach a large fish with its head and tail on requires a long, deep fish poacher. It must be at least 24 inches long. The fish poacher should have a lid and a rack that rests against the bottom, with two handles for lifting out the fish.

Court Bouillon for Poaching Fish

Four gallons water—how much depends on the size of the fish and the dimensions of the poacher—there must be enough liquid to cover the fish. This liquid, because of ingredients added to it, is called a bouillon—*court* because it's easy or short (or at least I find it so) to prepare.

The tasty bouillon gives the poached fish a good flavor.

2 carrots, peeled and finely sliced
3 onions, peeled and finely sliced
1 stalk celery, finely sliced
¼ cup salt
3 bay leaves
2 tablespoons whole peppercorns
½ cup red wine vinegar

Place the poacher over two heating units on the stove. Combine all the ingredients in the poacher except the vinegar. Bring to a boil and let simmer for one hour. Then, when you are ready to poach the fish, mix in the vinegar, and put the fish onto the poaching rack. Lower it into the bouillon. Be sure it is in the position described below when you put it in the poacher, because, once cooked, it will be almost impossible to turn over without breaking.

The position of the fish when it is presented on the platter in front of the carver will be the same as in the poacher (see illustration). The fish is poached on its side. The back of the fish should face the guests, because it is more handsome than the stomach. So when placing the fish in the hot bouillon, the stomach should be toward you, the back away, the head on your left, and the tail on your right. This will take time to figure out, but you have to like what you're doing, even the fish. Just don't try it while it's still wiggling.

The bouillon should just cover the fish. (If not, add water.) Turn both units on high, and when the liquid simmers, turn the heat down so that the water barely moves. When the fish is cooked, it is very fragile. Should the bouillon boil, the motion of the water might break up the fish.

Poaching time for fish is figured according to thickness, rather than weight. (Figure approximate thickness.) For poaching whole fish to be served hot, allow 15 minutes for every inch of thickness. Remove the poacher from the burners and allow the fish to repose (remain) in the hot bouillon for about half the time it took to cook it. When you are ready to serve, lift the rack above the top of the poacher, turn it slightly so it can be rested on the sides of the poacher for 30 seconds for the bouillon to drain off. Then bring the rack with the fish up parallel to, and slightly above, the platter. Tip the rack a little toward the platter. The fish should slide gently onto the platter. If it sticks to the rack, get a helping hand to give the fish a slight push, or you may have to slip a spatula or thin knife between the rack and the fish.

What kind of sauce for hot poached fish? Sauce Mousseline (see page 47), or Hollandaise (see page 46), or Beurre Blanc #1 or #2 (pages 45 or 46) with lemon juice. Serve with fresh peas or asparagus and boiled potatoes.

COLD POACHED FISH

For poaching whole fish to be served cold, the procedure is the same as for serving the fish hot, but the fish is cooled and refrigerated in the Court Bouillon. The cooking time should be reduced to 13 minutes for each inch of thickness, since the fish will spend more time in the hot bouillon. Cooling the fish in the bouillon is very important, because the bouillon holds the juice in. Once the juice in the fish is cold, it congeals, since it contains gelatin. The meat of the fish will therefore be moist, not dry. When cooling to room temperature, keep the lid off the poacher. The air passing over the bouillon helps to cool it. How to refrigerate the fish in its poacher is the only omission I'd like to make in this book. It's hard. A poacher that is 2 feet long will just fit diagonally in your refrigerator. With a longer poacher for a bigger fish, you're on your own—try the bathtub with a truckload of ice. Outdoors works best in the winter. Because of all this cooking and cooling time, you have to cook the fish the day before it is to be served.

The sauce for cold poached fish could be Mayonnaise (page 47) or Vinaigrette (page 49), Russian Dressing (see page 51), or the Green Sauce (see page 48). (Roquefort would not be good—ugh.) Serve with a cold vegetable salad and/or other salads and HOT bread.

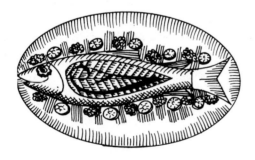

Decorating Cold Whole Poached Fish

1 cold whole fish
1 leek and/or 4 black olives, and/or 20 large tarragon leaves and/or a hard-boiled egg, and/or carrot
½ cup aspic (see Aspic Coating, opposite)

Remove the green leaves from the leek (keep white of leek for soup). Place in boiling water for 40 seconds. Cool the green strips under a stream of cold water and drain. If you wish to use fresh tarragon leaves, treat them the same as the leek, giving them 15 seconds in boiling water. The boiling water makes them very green and pliable. Melt the aspic and pour ½ cup of it onto a platter or plate. Any piece of decoration should be dipped into this warm aspic before being arranged on the fish, so it will stick and not move when the decorated fish is later coated with aspic. To provide a clean background for decoration, you can remove an oval section of skin from the side of the fish (see illustration). Make an oval cut ⅛ inch deep, using a sharp and pointed paring knife. Peel off the skin, then gently scrape away any brown meat until you get to the white (or pink in the case of salmon).

Cut the leek into strips; it makes beautiful branches and leaves. The slices of carrot rescued from the Court Bouillon can be cut out to make flowers. Use an olive slice for the eye, or a slice of hard-boiled egg. Below are some illustrations of ideas for decorating a fish; but of course you may have your own ideas, and I hope you do. I suggest, though, that you keep your decoration simple and symmetrical, with no minute detail.

Aspic Coating for Cold Poached Fish

½ cup water
5 envelopes of unflavored gelatin
3 cups bouillon
Ice cubes
A very cold fish in its Court Bouillon

150

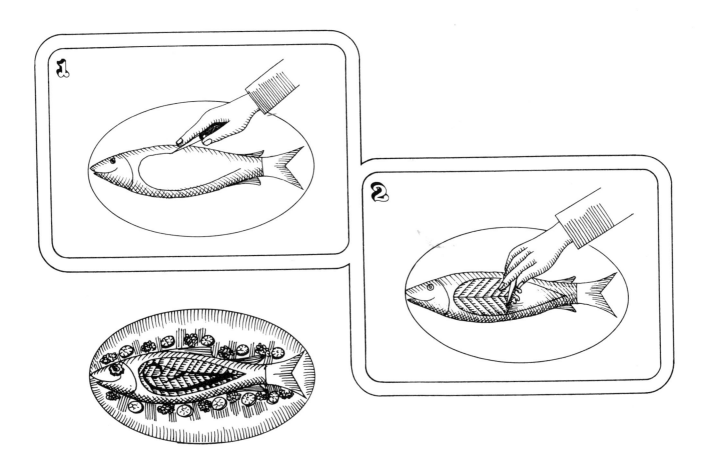

Put the water into a pot and stir in the gelatin. Let it stand for several minutes until the gelatin has melted. Carefully remove 3 cups of bouillon and strain it through a cheesecloth into the pot containing the gelatin and water mixture. Care is necessary, because, if the bouillon is stirred up, sediment from the bottom of the poacher will cloud it. Bring the contents of the pot to a simmer and set it aside until the fish is decorated and ready for the aspic coating. Then put the pot containing the aspic into a large bowl. (If the aspic has cooled and congealed, it will have to be liquefied first over medium heat.) Surround the pot with ice cubes and cover the ice with water. Stir the fluid aspic slowly with a ladle. As it cools, it will gradually get thicker. When the aspic is a good deal thicker than heavy cream (but not lumpy), hold the pot in one hand and the ladle in the other. Coat the fish. Don't splash it on. Think of the ladle as a paintbrush, and pour the aspic, using long, extended strokes almost the length of the fish.

If you don't let the aspic get thick enough, it will run off the fish. If it is too thick, there will be lumps. The idea is to coat the fish when the aspic is of exactly the right consistency. There is very little time, because the aspic does not stop thickening when it achieves this correct consistency. You have about 3 to 5 seconds to do the job, but don't abandon the project because it sounds too difficult. I have a couple of suggestions if you're doing this for the first time. First: remove 3 additional cups of the bouillon so that you can make another lot of aspic if you must. Second: because it's so hard to judge when the aspic has achieved the proper consistency for coating the fish, why not cool the

aspic once with no thought of coating the fish—just as a trial run. See what the proper consistency is, and get an idea of how thick it gets before it becomes lumpy. (You might even practice by coating a cold bowl turned upside down on a platter.) The aspic can always be liquefied again and re-cooled in the ice water. In general, you will find aspic a little too thick is better for coating the fish than aspic that is too thin, even if there are a few lumps. If a few lumps do appear, they can be leveled with the flat side of the blade of a knife heated under hot water or over a gas flame.

POACHED FISH FILLETS

SERVES 6

Fish is really best cooked whole. Sometimes, however, it is not feasible for you to cook the fish whole, or you may not want to cope with bones and skin. Or perhaps the fish store has little to offer but fillets of fish. The liquid surrounding the fillets will help to hold in the juice.

3 pounds fresh fish, filleted and skinned (flounder, sole, striped bass, red snapper, halibut, pike, cod, etc.—any fish but swordfish would be all right)
1 tablespoon butter
1 lemon
1 large onion
Water
Salt

Most fish markets sell portion-sized cuts of fish called "steaks." I don't like this way of cutting fish.

The portions are cut at right angles to the fish so that there is a section of the backbone in the middle of each piece. When these "steaks" are cut from the stomach end of the fish, there are two flaps extending from each piece. The stomach used to be between these flank pieces. Once cooked, these extremities invariably fall off. This popular method of cutting the fish is not as neat as cutting the portions from the skinned fillet, and there will be no bone or skin to contend with.

Preheat oven to 350°. Cut the fillets into portion-sized pieces of about ½ pound each. If you leave the fillets whole, they are large and it is difficult to transfer them from cooking pan to platter because they are very fragile and break easily once cooked. Unless, of course, you have an oversized spatula. If, however, the fillets are small (½ pound), they should be folded in half or thirds with the smoothest part (skin side) on the inside. Some fillets, especially members of the flat fish family of flounder, are thin enough to be rolled up. Again, skin side on the inside. Folded otherwise, the fillet will unfold as it cooks. Done correctly, it actually tightens up. Study both sides of the fish and you will see that one side is slightly smoother than the other. It's not easy to see the difference; sometimes there's a trace of skin that helps.

Butter the bottom of a broad pan that is large enough to contain the pieces of fish when placed side by side. Arrange the fish with the skin side down. Sprinkle with lemon juice; cut the lemon skin in quarters and distribute it between the fillets. Slice the onion and arrange it on top of the fish. Add enough water to barely cover, and about one teaspoon of salt. Cover the pan with aluminum foil and bring the liquid to a boil. If the pan is large, use two burners. Turn down the heat so the fillets are just simmering. Place in the oven to simmer for the remainder of the cooking time. For fish pieces one inch thick, simmer for 10 minutes. Add 10 minutes for each additional inch of thickness. Before serving, let the fillets repose in the liquid for a period approximately equal to the cooking time. For example, the one-inch-thick pieces should repose for 10 minutes.

If fillets or pieces of fillets are to be served cold, leave them in their liquid for cooling and refrigeration. This way they will stay moist. If the fillets are drained immediately after cooking, the juice will simply run out of the fish, and the fish will be very dry. The liquid surrounding the fish holds the juice in. Once cold, this juice, which is full of gelatin, will congeal. No fish at all is better than serving dry fish. If you wish to arrange the fish attractively on a platter well before mealtime, you can (without loss of juice), once the fish and surrounding liquid have been refrigerated for about 6 hours.

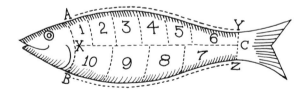

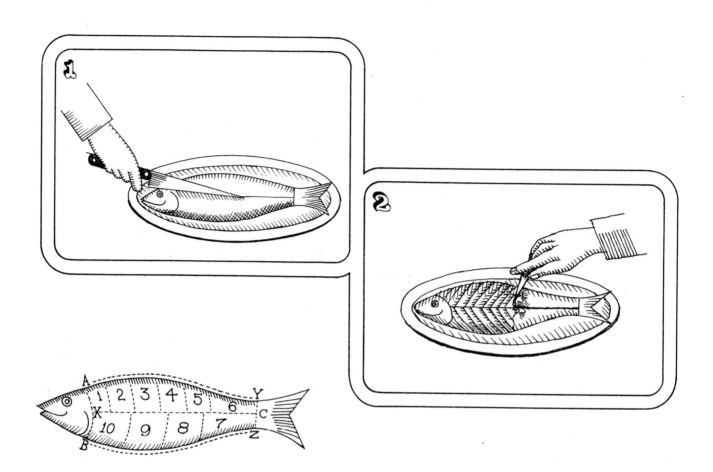

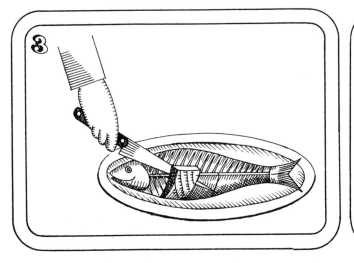 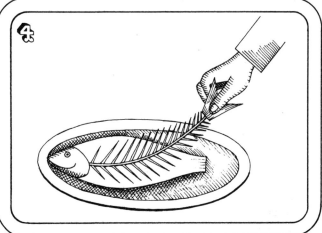

FILLET OF SOLE BONNE FEMME

SERVES 6

This is not easy to prepare, but when it's done right it's simply delicious.

3 pounds fillet of sole
3 tablespoons shallots, finely chopped
Salt
½ cup water (½ cup fish stock [see page 31] is
*   better)*
1 cup dry white wine
1 pound mushrooms (as white as possible), washed
Juice of 1 lemon
Hollandaise Sauce (see page 46)
Beurre Manié (see page 44)
½ pint heavy cream, whipped

Roll up the fillets with the skin side (smooth side) on the inside. This prevents the delicate fillets from unfolding as they poach. (You may slice the fillets diagonally lengthways for smaller servings.) Place the fillets in a buttered flat pan that just contains them. Sprinkle the shallots over the sole. Sprinkle with salt. Add the water (or stock) and the wine. Slice the mushrooms and add them to the pan. Sprinkle with the lemon juice. Cover and bring to a simmer on top of stove. Cover the pan and continue cooking at a simmer for 15 minutes (or, judging the thickness of the rolled fillets, 10 minutes for every inch of thickness). Remove the fillets to a heated platter.

Bring the stock and mushrooms to a boil. Whisk the Beurre Manié into the juice. Add the cream and bring to a boil. Salt to taste. Remove from the heat and cool for four minutes. Whisk in the Hollandaise Sauce. Spoon all the sauce over the fish. Broil for a very short time. The top of the sauce will become golden brown within seconds (don't take your eyes off it).

155

RAY WITH BLACK BUTTER

SERVES 6

It may be an ugly fish, but the meat of the ray is the most delicate of all. The soft, gelatinous bones almost melt as the fish poaches, keeping the meat very juicy. It's really worth trying. Ask your fish man to get you some.

3 pounds ray, cleaned and cut into ½-pound
  pieces (just the wings can be used)
1 teaspoon butter
1 cup dry white wine
1 lemon
Salt
3 tablespoons parsley, chopped
Water

Preheat oven to 350°. To remove the skin from the fish pieces, put into boiling water for 5 minutes, then under cold running water. Peel the skin from both sides of each piece. This can all be done as much as a day in advance. Arrange the pieces of fish in a buttered pan, wide enough to hold them in one layer. Pour the wine, the juice of one lemon, and one tablespoon of salt over the pieces. Cover with water. Bring to a boil, cover with a lid, or aluminum foil, and place in oven for 25 minutes. Lift the pieces from the pan with a spatula and let them drain a moment before arranging them on a platter. Sprinkle with chopped parsley.

While you make the Black Butter Sauce, keep the fish (loosely covered with aluminum foil), warm in the oven at 250°. Before pouring the hot sauce over the fish, slightly tip the platter into the sink to pour off any juice or water that might have accumulated.

Black Butter Sauce

I love this sauce.

⅔ stick butter
2 tablespoons capers
3 tablespoons red wine vinegar
Chopped parsley

Put a black frying pan on high heat. Put in the butter. When it is black and smoking, pour it over the fish. Turn off heat. Put the capers and vinegar into the hot pan. Simmer for 2 seconds, then pour over fish. Sprinkle with chopped parsley and serve with boiled potatoes.

BOILED CHICKEN

SERVES 6

A bite of this tender meat with the crunchy crystals of salt makes it understandable why it is the specialty of the city of Lyons, known to be the gastronomic capital of the world. This is a most delicate and refined dish.

2 2½-pound chickens whole
4 leeks
2 onions
1 stalk celery
Salt (for water)
Water
Kosher or coarse salt (to be served in glass bowl on
  the table)

In this country a 2½-pound chicken is called a broiler, a chicken weighing about 3½ pounds is called a fryer, and larger chickens are called roasters.

Put the chickens into a pot that just contains them side by side or head to tail. Split the leeks lengthways and wash well. Roughly cut the celery, and pack the vegetables into the empty spaces around the chickens. Salt and barely cover with water. Cover the pot. Simmer for one hour. Cut up and serve the chickens with their broth in soup plates. Sprinkle with coarse salt at the table.

The broth will be stronger if the space in and around the chicken is filled with vegetables, thus requiring less water.

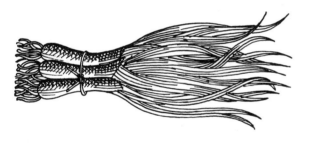

BLANQUETTE DE VEAU

SERVES 6

Blanquette means white and *veau* is veal— very popular in France. The creamed sauce of this stew has a subtle lemon taste. It has become a favorite of many of my students. It is perfect as a lunch or supper dish when you are expecting lots of guests. Make sure the sauce is thick before you beat it into the egg yolks!

2 pounds veal shoulder. breast or shank, cubed
Water
½ pound small white onions
½ pound mushrooms
1 large onion, peeled and stuck with 3 cloves
1 stalk celery, cut in half
1 teaspoon salt
1 cup dry white wine
¼ stick butter
¼ cup flour
½ cup heavy cream
2 tablespoons lemon juice (to taste)
Salt (to taste)
3 egg yolks

Cover the veal with water. Bring it to a boil, stir it around, wash it off under running cold water, and drain. Wash out the pot. Add peeled small white onions, mushrooms (if large, cut them in half), onion stuck with cloves, the celery, and salt. Add the wine and enough water to barely cover the ingredients. Cover the pot and simmer for an hour and a quarter. Stir at least once. Strain off the liquid into another pot. Simmer liquid over medium-high heat. Using your hand, mix the butter and flour into a paste. Whisk it into the simmering liquid. When the sauce is thick, add cream, and bring back to boiling point. Lower the heat, and add lemon juice and salt if needed.

The sauce at this point should be thicker than heavy cream. The flour and butter combination is called Beurre Manié. Whisk in more of it at this point if it is needed to thicken the sauce. Whisk the egg yolks slightly in a bowl and gradually whisk the simmering sauce into them. Discard the large onion with cloves and celery. Fold in the meat, onions, mushrooms, and serve. Or keep it warm on top of a pan of water over a very low heat until you are ready to serve.

Serve with rice, green salad afterward, hot French bread, and follow with a simple fruit dessert.

BOILED BEEF OR BEEF TONGUE

SERVES 6

Do this with brisket or beef tongue. Tongue takes a little more cooking time. Of course, it must be peeled before serving.

2 medium onions, peeled and each stuck with 2 cloves
4 pounds brisket (or tongue)
6 carrots, peeled
1 cabbage (small)
6–8 boiling potatoes of uniform size (small), peeled
Salt

Bring about one gallon of water and the onions to a boil in a 2-gallon pot. Put in the brisket. Simmer, covered, for 2½ hours. Add the carrots. Half an hour later, add the cabbage, cut into sixths from top to bottom, so that each section contains some of the bottom root system to hold the pieces together. Add the potatoes 15 minutes later. The total cooking time should be 3¾ hours. Add a tablespoon of salt 10 minutes before serving.

Arrange all the vegetables (except the onions) around the meat on a platter. Serve with Horseradish Sauce (see below) or the Sauce Vinaigrette that is used with whole artichokes (see page 50).

Horseradish Sauce for Boiled Beef

2 tablespoons butter
3 tablespoons flour
1–1½ cups boiled beef (or tongue) stock
2–4 tablespoons horseradish
Salt

Melt the butter in a saucepan over low heat. Whisk in the flour. Add stock from the pot little by little, whisking constantly. Keep the sauce quite thick. Add the horseradish and salt to taste, just before serving. The sauce should be thicker than heavy cream, but if it is too thick, more stock can always be added to thin it.

IRISH STEW

SERVES 6

I learned to make this from an aged retired chef who taught cooking two afternoons a week to all the thirteen-year-old apprentices in Lyons. I was working at Restaurant Chez Nandron, 26 Quai Jean Moulin. At the time, I was twenty-five, but since I was also an apprentice, my chef, M. Nandron, insisted that I attend the classes with all the thirteen-year-olds. We walked to class together. I told them about Indians, cowboys, and dollars. I clearly remember the old chef making Irish stew, because he made such a fuss over adding what he called *La Sauce Anglaise* (English Sauce or Worcestershire Sauce).

2 pounds lamb stew meat, shoulder, or neck, cut
   into 1½-inch cubes
Water
⅔ pound onions, roughly chopped
1½ pounds baking potatoes, each potato peeled
   and rough-cut into 8 pieces
1 bay leaf
Salt and pepper
1 teaspoon chopped garlic
1 tablespoon Worcestershire Sauce
3 tablespoons parsley, freshly chopped

Cover the meat with water and bring to a boil, rinse off, drain, and return the meat to the pot. Add chopped onions, potatoes, bay leaf, salt, and pepper to meat in pot. Cover half the contents of pot with water; cover and simmer slowly about 1¼ hours or until meat is tender. To thicken the broth, gently press the potatoes against the side of the pot with the round side of a kitchen spoon. Stew can keep as long as an hour before serving. Before serving, reheat and stir in the chopped garlic, Worcestershire Sauce, and parsley. Serve immediately.

SMOKED TONGUE WITH CREOLE SAUCE

SERVES 6 TO 8

Even if tongue is a distant relative of the macabre family, it's always been my favorite meat —even when I was very young and should have been appalled.

1 smoked beef tongue
Water
2 onions, peeled and roughly cut
1 carrot, peeled and roughly cut
1 branch celery, roughly cut
2 cloves
Creole Sauce (see page 49)

Put the tongue into a large pot. Put in more than enough water to cover the tongue and put the pot on the stove to boil. Peel the onions and carrot and throw them in with the celery. Put in the cloves. Cover the pot. It will take at least 3½ hours of simmering before the tongue is tender. Poke a kitchen fork into it. The fork should go in as easily as it would into a ripe peach. Remove the tongue from the pot and let it cool. Cut away the bones and fat from the base. Peel it and return it to the pot. Heat it up in the liquid when you are ready to serve. If you plan to serve it cold, cool and refrigerate in broth.

Be careful when you remove the tongue from the boiling water. It is slippery. Lift one end with a slotted spoon and grab the other with a pot holder, cloth, or a bunch of crumpled paper towels. Do not use two flat spatulas or spoons; it might slip.

Attractive presentation is particularly important. Pour enough of the Creole Sauce on the platter so that when you spread it out it will cover the base of the platter and be about ¼ inch thick. Drain the warmed tongue briefly and cut 8 or 9 even slices about ¼ inch thick, starting at the base of the tongue. Later (when you continue to carve the tongue), as you approach the tip, cut at an angle so that the tip pieces will not be too small.

Put the tongue on the platter and arrange the slices evenly, *en cheval* (stepped out from the base, overlapping). Return the platter to the oven briefly (2 minutes). Decorate with parsley sprigs and serve.

BEEF MARROW ON TOAST

SERVES 4

The taste and consistency are so distinguished that you must try this.

4 slices firm, good quality bread
1 cup consommé (see page 33)
Ask butcher to remove enough beef marrow bone
    to make ¼–½ pound sliced ¼ inch thick. Al-
    low the sawed pieces of marrow bone to reach
    room temperature. Then use your thumb or the
    butt of a paring knife to push out the marrow.
    Store it in cold water until you are ready to use it.

Preheat oven to 200°. Toast the bread. Put a piece of toast on each plate. Put plates in oven to warm. Heat the Consommé in a shallow sauté pan over high heat. Distribute the pieces of marrow in the Consommé and simmer for 25 seconds (do not turn them). Using a slotted spoon, arrange the pieces of marrow on the toast more or less to cover the surface. Sprinkle with parsley and serve immediately. Serve for lunch with salad and a fresh fruit dessert or, for canapés, on cut-out rounds of toast (one piece of warmed marrow to each round of toast). Warm the toast on a serving platter before putting on the marrow—try it.

TRIPE LYONNAISE

SERVES 6

This dish tastes good—it's good for you and cheap to buy. But like brains, ray, and pigs' feet, it puts a lot of people off. You just have to force yourself to try some of these creepy things. You'll be missing the best if you don't. Your bad feelings will be banished by the pleasure you get. Eating with the chefs at Chez Nandron in Lyons, it took two sessions with tripe before I stopped gagging. Then I grew to like it. Now I adore tripe—it's a real love story.

3 pounds beef tripe
Water
7 onions
2 stalks celery
2 carrots, roughly chopped
1 bay leaf
3 cloves garlic, peeled
1 teaspoon salt
⅓ stick butter
2 cups Brown Stock (see page 32)
Salt and pepper

Boil the tripe in water for 15 minutes. Rinse it off and cover with fresh water. Put in two onions, two stalks of celery, two carrots, the bay leaf, the garlic, and a teaspoon of salt. Cover the pot tightly and simmer very slowly for at least 5 hours or until the tripe is very, very soft and tender. It must not burn, so perhaps you should bring it to a boil, cover it, and cook in the oven at 300°. Let it cool, drain, preserve the stock, and cut the tripe into ½-inch-wide strips. Peel, slice, and fry the remaining onions in the butter until they are golden brown. Combine the tripe and onions and simmer in 2 cups of brown veal stock and one cup of the stock from the tripe. Grind in some pepper. Let it simmer until the liquid barely covers the tripe. Add salt if needed.

Serve with boiled potatoes, hot French bread, a simple green salad, and lemon sherbet for dessert. Be sure to invite your mother-in-law.

PARSLIED HAM

SERVES 10 TO 16

Since this mixture will fill four one-quart containers or molds, have them out and ready to fill. It would be nice if one of them were decorated to serve as a centerpiece.

6 pounds smoked ham, precooked and diced in
¼-inch cubes
3 cups consommé
11 packages gelatin (each package equals one
tablespoon)
2 cups cold water
2 cups fresh parsley, roughly chopped
1 tablespoon garlic, chopped
Salt and pepper to taste

Add the gelatin to the cold water in a pot and stir. Let it rest for 5 minutes or until the gelatin dissolves. Place over medium heat until the contents just begin to simmer. Remove from heat, add consommé, and cool by placing the pot in a bowl with some ice cubes and cold water.

Mix the diced ham, parsley, and garlic in a large bowl. When the gelatin and consommé mixture is cool, but before it begins to set, mix well with the ham. Add salt and pepper to taste. Add some finely chopped dill pickle if you wish.

Put the mixture into molds and refrigerate for at least one full day before serving. This much time is needed for the gelatin to set up. When cutting the parslied ham, use a long, thin, sharp knife and a sawing motion to cut (rather than pressing the knife straight down).

POLISH SAUSAGE

SERVES 8

In Lyonnaise restaurants they serve a delicious *Saucisson à Cuire* (sausage which must be cooked as opposed to the one that is cured and can be eaten as is—like salami). The Polish sausage to be found in this country in almost any market is as good and even better. The hot sausage in France is accompanied by a very hot boiled potato, sliced just before serving, and sprinkled with salt and a little peanut oil. What a quick and pleasant meal! If you like mustard, there's a very good one made in the United States. It's called Mr. Mustard. It is better than the real Dijon mustard. Recently I hit on some tired Polish sausage—it's hard to judge age when the sausage is packaged in cellophane. All I can suggest is that sausage should be reddish in color, not brownish gray.

2 pounds new potatoes
2 Polish sausages (Kielbasy)
Water
Salt
⅓ cup peanut oil
1 tablespoon parsley, chopped

Peel the potatoes, rinse them off, and put them into a 4-quart pot. Prick each sausage 10 times in various places with a kitchen fork. Put them into the pot. Cover all with water. Cover the pot tightly and simmer until the potatoes are done. Drain and thickly slice the potatoes onto a serving platter. Sprinkle them with salt and coat with oil. Cut each sausage into four parts and distribute around the potatoes. Sprinkle parsley over the potatoes before serving.

This is a delicious quick luncheon or supper dish. Follow it with fruit dessert or fresh fruit tart. Or serve a salad and no dessert—but don't make a production out of it, or you miss the point.

POACHED EGGS

Use enough water in a skillet almost to cover the eggs. Add one tablespoon of vinegar or lemon juice for each 2 quarts of water. Bring the water to the boiling point and slip each egg into the water individually. Allow the eggs to cook for 2 to 3 minutes, depending on the degree of doneness desired. Remove the eggs with a slotted spoon in the order in which they were placed into the skillet. A soft, warm terry towel is excellent for draining a large quantity of poached eggs.

If the eggs are to be used later, freshen them under cold running water and refrigerate in cold water. To heat, place the eggs in simmering water for 2 minutes.

MUSHROOMS À LA GRECQUE
SERVES 6 TO 10

Serve these with drinks, or as a part of a vegetable salad.

1½ pounds white mushrooms
⅓ cup olive oil
¼ teaspoon thyme
3 tablespoons lemon juice
1 teaspoon salt
¼ teaspoon pepper
4 cloves garlic, finely chopped
1 tablespoon parsley, chopped

Wash and drain the mushrooms. Cut the very large ones in half. Combine in a pot with the other ingredients. Cover. Bring to the simmering point and stir with a wooden spoon. Uncover the pot and simmer, stirring from time to time, until the mushrooms have diminished in size and are cooked through. Leave the mushrooms in the juice in which they cooked. Cool, and then refrigerate. Serve them with drinks in a pretty glass bowl. Stick some handsome toothpicks into the mushrooms on top.

During the summer, serve them with a cold buffet.

ARTICHOKE SURPRISE

SERVES 6

This recipe, stolen from my mother-in-law, may seem long, hard, and tedious. It's not. It will take you half as long as you think, and will be half as difficult.

6 large artichokes
Water
Salt
1 lemon
1 tablespoon butter
Hollandaise Sauce (see page 46)

The artichokes should float in lots of water in a large pot to which you add two teaspoons of salt and the juice and skins of one lemon. Boil gently. Artichokes are cooked when they no longer float in the boiling water, but sink to the bottom of the pot. Drain and cool. Cut off the stem where it joins and begins to spread out into the broad base, or heart, of the artichoke. Remove some of the lower leaves in order to see clearly where to cut. Make a straight cut so that the artichoke will stand upright and not teeter. Peel off all the leaves; then, holding the fragile base in the cup of your hand, scoop out the choke with a spoon. With a dull table knife, lightly scrape off the tender part of each individual leaf. The centers of the stems are also tender and should be collected. Using a fork, mash one tablespoon of butter and a sprinkling of salt into these scrapings. Stuff the bases with this mixture, rounding off the top with the same fork. You can do all this hours before serving. Just reheat them in the oven at 350° for 15 minutes in a covered pan containing ⅛ inch of water.

Arrange them on a warm platter or on individual plain white dishes. An even coating of Hollandaise on each conceals the identity of this most delicate surprise.

If the base breaks, the stuffing will hold it together. A perfect first course, but don't involve many other vegetables in the rest of the menu, since the first course is a vegetable.

ARTICHOKE VINAIGRETTE

This can be made days in advance. It is good with Boiled Beef (see page 158).

Cut off the stem, tip, and bark from the artichoke, using a sharp knife. Remove the spikes from the leaves. Place a thin slice of lemon on the stem end and tie in place with a string. Place the artichokes on their sides in a pan, cover with water, and add one teaspoon of salt. They should float half out of the water. Boil 30–45 minutes, until tender, and the leaves fall out easily.

Cool them under running water and drain them upside down. Separate the leaves and scoop out the choke. Fill the center of each with Vinaigrette #1 (see page 49), adding to the recipe one finely chopped hard-boiled egg, one tablespoon each of finely chopped parsley and finely chopped onion.

ASPARAGUS

SERVES 6

Fat, skinny, white or green—served hot or cold—asparagus is always welcome when it appears in the markets in early spring.

5 pounds asparagus
Water

With the asparagus flat on a board, hold the tips and cut about ½ inch off the butt ends. Peel a maximum of ⅛ of an inch from the asparagus beginning ⅔ of the way from tip to butt. Then most of, or even all of, the asparagus can be chewed and eaten. Tie them in bunches of six to eight with two strings, one below tips and one above butts (or use an asparagus cooker). Drop them into as much boiling water as possible (3 gallons). The more boiling water, the sooner the water will reboil after the cool asparagus has been put in. The faster they cook, the greener they'll be. They should take about 10 to 20 minutes to cook. Better that they should have a little bite to them than be falling apart from having overcooked. Lift them out by the strings. Arrange them on a platter and snip the strings with a pair of scissors. Serve with a moderately lemony Hollandaise (see page 46) or cold with Vinaigrette #1 or #2 (see page 49).

If you prefer to serve them cold, as soon as they are cooked, put them into a basin of cold water to stop the cooking. Run water over them until they are cold. Drain, arrange on a platter, cover, and refrigerate. This can be done six hours before mealtime.

BROCCOLI

SERVES 6

Soft and green, with a delicate cauliflower-cabbage taste, broccoli is very good served cold.

4 pounds broccoli
Baking soda
Salt
Water

One quarter of an inch should be cut from the butt end of the broccoli, and the tough outer skin of the stem should be pared down. Broccoli are often thick and should be split or quartered lengthways, starting at the stem. The flower will come apart, so cut the stem just to where the flower begins. Place the broccoli side by side in a rectangular pan that will just contain them. Sprinkle ¼ teaspoon of baking soda and one teaspoon of salt over the top for every 2 pounds of broccoli. Cover with boiling water and cook for 10 to 15 minutes on one or two burners, depending on the size of the pan. A clean kitchen towel tucked around the inside of the pan will make a good cover. Drain and serve hot with Hollandaise Sauce (see page 46), or cool under cold, running water and serve the broccoli cold with Vinaigrette #2 (see page 49).

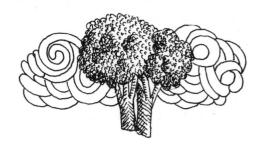

BROCCOLI RABE

SERVES 6

This is a leafy animal. It looks something like mustard greens or kale. It is good with game or fowl.

3 pounds broccoli rabe
½ cup olive oil
⅔ cup water
1 clove garlic, chopped
¼ cup lemon juice
Salt and pepper

Cut off and discard any stems over ¼ inch in diameter. Wash the broccoli in lots of cold water and drain it in a colander. Cut the greens roughly into thirds. Put the olive oil, garlic, water, and greens into a pot. Pour the lemon over the greens. Sprinkle with salt and pepper, cover the pot, and cook over medium-high heat. After 15 minutes, stir and reduce the heat so the greens just simmer. They should be tender and ready to serve within 35 minutes.

CARROTS VICHY

SERVES 6

Carrots Vichy are a good accompaniment to any meat, fish, or fowl dish of delicate taste. Their bright orange color also improves the appearance of a meal.

2 pounds carrots
Juice of 1 lemon
1 teaspoon salt
⅔ stick butter
¼ cup chopped parsley

Peel and slice the carrots into pieces about ⅛ inch thick and put into a saucepan. Barely cover them with water and add the lemon juice and salt. Boil them uncovered over a medium heat until they are tender. If the water goes below the level of the carrots, gently shake the pot so that the top slices will be in the water. Shake the pot as if you were trying to flip a pancake. The cooking time should be no more than 20 minutes. Pour off the water and add the butter. Keep them over very low heat (flipping them from time to time) until you are ready to serve. The carrots should stew around in the butter for at least 15 minutes. Mix in half of the chopped parsley just before serving. Sprinkle the rest of the parsley over the top.

Never serve carrots mixed with peas. This mixture is served so frequently in restaurants it could easily have an adverse effect on your guests.

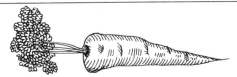

GLAZED CARROTS

SERVES 6

Do not leave the stove once the caramelizing process has started.

2 pounds carrots
Water
2 tablespoons sugar
Juice of 1 lemon
⅓ stick butter
1 teaspoon salt

Cut the carrots into batons about 1½ inches long and ¼ inch square on the ends. Cover with water, add sugar, and cook them until the water has almost all boiled away. Add lemon, the butter, and salt, and, keeping a close eye on the pot, let them cook over high heat until the butter and sugar begin to caramelize. Flip the pot gently so the carrots will be uniformly brown. The butter and sugar could get black, so take the pot off the heat as soon as the mixture achieves a pleasant shade of brown.

CAULIFLOWER

SERVES 6 TO 8

Cauliflower served whole on a platter surrounded by other vegetables, hot or cold, makes an attractive centerpiece.

1 large 3–4-pound cauliflower
Water
2 cups milk
¼ cup chopped parsley

Remove the green leaves from the cauliflower. Cut the stem flush with the bottom flowers so the cauliflower will rest firmly on its bottom and not teeter. The cauliflower should be boiled whole until tender in a pot that just contains it. For every quart of water necessary to cover the cauliflower, add one cup of milk. This keeps the cauliflower white.

It may be served hot with Hollandaise Sauce (see page 46).

To serve cold, cool under running water, drain, put in plastic bag, and store in refrigerator.

CAULIFLOWER WITH BROWNED BREAD CRUMBS

SERVES 4 TO 6

But why cook the cauliflower whole? Because it looks so much better. It looks like a cauliflower. It has more personality. Whenever possible, things you cook should look like what they are. This cauliflower recipe can be made hours in advance and heated up for a mealtime. The crunchy, browned bread crumbs and soft cauliflower make an interesting combination.

1 cauliflower
Water
Salt
2 cups milk
⅔ stick butter
1 cup bread crumbs
2 tablespoons chopped shallots

Remove the green leaves from the cauliflower. Cut the stem flush with the bottom flowers. Place

166

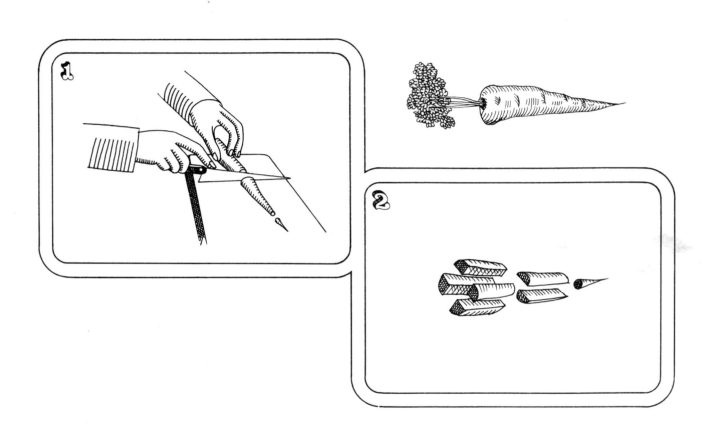

in a pot and cover with water. Add one teaspoon of salt and the milk and simmer for about 45 minutes, until it is tender but not falling apart. Freshen under running cold water. Drain and place on a pan or a round oven-proof serving platter. Heat the butter in a frying pan until it is almost brown. Put in bread crumbs. Reduce heat to medium and stir the crumbs constantly until they get brown. Stir in the shallots; cook for several more seconds or until the shallots are tinged with brown. Pour contents evenly over the cauliflower. This can be prepared in advance. To reheat, put into the oven at 350° for 40 minutes.

Two or more vegetables should be served with this: green peas and Sautéed Cherry Tomatoes (see page 125), Carrots Vichy (see page 165) and string beans, all with the cauliflower in the center.

KOHLRABI

SERVES 6

These remind me of some Martian device.

2 pounds kohlrabi
Salt
2 tablespoons butter

Peel and quarter the kohlrabi (if they're big, cut them into eighths). Boil them in lightly salted water until they are tender. Drain, cool, and warm in butter over medium heat before serving.

PARSNIPS

SERVES 6

These are great with lamb or game.

2 pounds parsnips
Salt
1 tablespoon butter
1 teaspoon parsley, chopped

Peel the parsnips. Cut them into quarters lengthways. Using a paring knife, cut away the center core, which is likely to be tough. It can be left in if the parsnips are very slender and young-looking. (Darling, there was this charming young parsnip who etc., etc.) Cut the quarters into pieces 1½ inches long or, if you have the inclination, pare them as you would the carrots in the illustration (pages 167–168). It might be pretty to combine the orange carrots with white parsnips.

Boil the parsnips in lightly salted water until they are just tender. Freshen under cold water. At mealtime, warm them in butter over medium heat. Sprinkle with parsley before serving.

Be careful—when parsnips are overcooked, they tend to get mushy. It would be better to undercook them.

MAMA'S PEAS

SERVES 6

On several occasions my guests have remarked, "Those peas were just delicious. Didn't it take forever to peel them?" My mother taught me the recipe when I was nine years old.

6 pounds fresh peas
1 teaspoon baking soda
Water
⅔ stick butter
1 teaspoon salt

Shell the peas into a pot. Sprinkle the soda on top. Barely cover with boiling water. Cover the pot. Bring the contents to a boil. Peas boil over, so keep an eye on them. Skim the foam from the top when they boil. Cook uncovered until the peas are tender (about 3 minutes). Pour off most of the water, leaving about 2 or 3 tablespoons in the pot with the peas. Add the butter and salt. At this point there can be a delay of a maximum of 20 minutes. The peas should then stew over a very low heat for at least 10 minutes before serving.

BOILED POTATOES

SERVES 6 TO 8

Boiled potatoes are a perfect accompaniment to any fish, fowl, or meat dish. Perfect because their delicate taste and consistency reflect and accentuate the savory qualities of the main dish. They must, however, have a pleasing appearance. Rather than just cutting them into chunks, scoop them out with a melon-baller or quarter them lengthways with the edges pared slightly to give them an oval sculptured look. Of course, if small new potatoes are used, you need only peel them.

3 pounds boiling potatoes
Water
1 teaspoon salt
¼ stick butter (optional)
Juice of ½ lemon (optional)
1 tablespoon chopped parsley

Thoroughly wash the prepared potatoes and keep them covered with cold water until cooking time. Then salt the water and simmer the potatoes until a fork can be pushed through one of the pieces with no effort. If they are not to be served for ½ hour or so, the heat should be turned off while the center of the potato still offers resistance to the fork. They will continue to cook in the hot water. Drain the potatoes; pour melted butter and the juice of half a lemon over them. Sprinkle with parsley and serve.

The Swiss-cheese-like remnant from the making of potato balls can be used for Mashed Potatoes (see below), Riced Potatoes (see page 171), Leek and Potato Soup (see page 37), or Clam Chowder (see page 35).

MASHED POTATOES

SERVES 4 TO 6

"Everybody knows how to make mashed potatoes," my editor said. "No, they don't," I say. Mashed potatoes are usually awful, and they can be so good. The whole secret is to mix lots of butter into them before adding the hot milk. Don't just stir in the butter with a few twists of the wooden spoon—I mean really mix it in thoroughly.

1½ pounds potatoes (boiling, not baking, potatoes)
Water
1 stick butter
½ cup milk
Salt and pepper

Peel the potatoes. Cut them in half or, if they are very large, into quarters. Cook them until tender in salted water. Drain them well and then pass them through a food mill. Heat the milk and reserve. Mix the butter into the potatoes thoroughly with a wooden spoon. Then beat the hot milk into the potatoes, first using the wooden spoon, and then a small whisk. Add salt and freshly ground black pepper to taste. Mashed potatoes can be kept warm in a double boiler. Flatten them on top with a spoon or spatula and pour a thin film of warm milk over them. This will act as a cover and prevent the surface of the mashed potatoes from becoming dry. They should be served within an hour from the time they are made.

There should be no lumps if the butter has been well mixed with the potatoes before beating in the milk. If you have a pepper mill with white pepper, use it. If not, use black pepper. The added taste of freshly ground pepper more than compensates for the small visual distraction of a few black specks.

RICED POTATOES
SERVES 6

This is such a simple dish and is easily made—

so don't make it in advance and try to keep it warm, as it would dry out and be ugly. It is perfect as an accompaniment to meat with a brown sauce, roast chicken with tarragon, French veal scallopini, or braised veal.

2 pounds boiling potatoes
Water
Salt
1 teaspoon parsley, chopped

Cut the potatoes to equal size. (Cut the larger ones into halves or quarters so they will be equal in size to smaller ones, and will cook in the same length of time.) Boil in salted water for about ½ hour, or until a table fork pushes into the potatoes with little resistance. Drain them well. Pass them through the ricer directly into a pretty vegetable dish (preheated). Sprinkle with parsley and serve immediately.

BOILED RICE
SERVES 6

If you let the rice come to a boil in a covered pot, you can then turn off the heat and the rice will cook by itself with no additional boiling. Otherwise you have to worry about it boiling over or burning. Rice does both very easily.

1 cup rice
2½ cups cold water
1 teaspoon salt

Let the rice and salted water come to a boil in covered pan. Remove from heat. Let stand 20 minutes (still covered) before serving.

171

GRANNY'S SPAGHETTI

SERVES 8 TO 10

A favorite of my grandmother's for large gatherings. It is best when served with hot or cold baked ham, or roast turkey and a green salad.

3 gallons water
4 cloves garlic
2½ tablespoons salt
2 pounds spaghetti
1 stick butter
1 cup freshly grated Parmesan cheese
Pepper (freshly ground)

Bring 2 gallons of water to a boil with 4 peeled cloves of garlic and enough salt so that you can taste it in the water. Put in the spaghetti and stir for 2 minutes to be sure it does not stick together. The heat should be high until water returns to a boil. Boil briskly, uncovered, until tender but still with a trace of bite to it (anything from 5 to 12 minutes). Take off the fire and drain into a colander waiting in the sink. Discard the pieces of garlic. Return spaghetti to the pot and, using a fork, stir in the butter, Parmesan cheese, and a very liberal amount of freshly ground pepper. Add salt if needed. Arrange in a casserole. Cover loosely with aluminum foil and keep warm in an oven at 300° for a maximum of one hour. (If tightly covered, the spaghetti will steam and stick together.) Stir occasionally.

A supplementary sauce would ruin the dish. Use only freshly grated Parmesan. Most Italian stores or cheese shops will grate it before your eyes.

Do not use Romano cheese, which resembles Parmesan, unless you happen to like it. I do not. It is more suited to southern Italian cooking, while this spaghetti dish is from the northern Italian kitchen.

ORANGE À L'ARABE

SERVES 12

This is a very refreshing dessert. It can be prepared 24 hours in advance.

16 seedless oranges
Water
1¼ cups sugar
1 vanilla bean
2–3 ounces Grand Marnier

Using a potato peeler, peel the skins from 8 of the oranges. Slice these thin peels as finely as you can. They should be no larger than toothpicks. Cover with water and bring to a boil in a saucepan. Drain and re-cover with cold water. Boil and drain. Cover a third time with cold water. Add the sugar and the vanilla bean and simmer the slivers until they become translucent and the liquid is syrupy. Set aside.

Using a long, thin, sharp knife, peel all of the skin from the oranges (and I mean all)—the orange skin, the white underneath, and the very membrane of the orange itself—do a neat job. Cut the oranges crossways into slices ¼ inch thick. Pour the skin slivers (called *julienne*), syrup (but remove vanilla bean), and Grand Marnier over the orange slices. Cover and refrigerate.

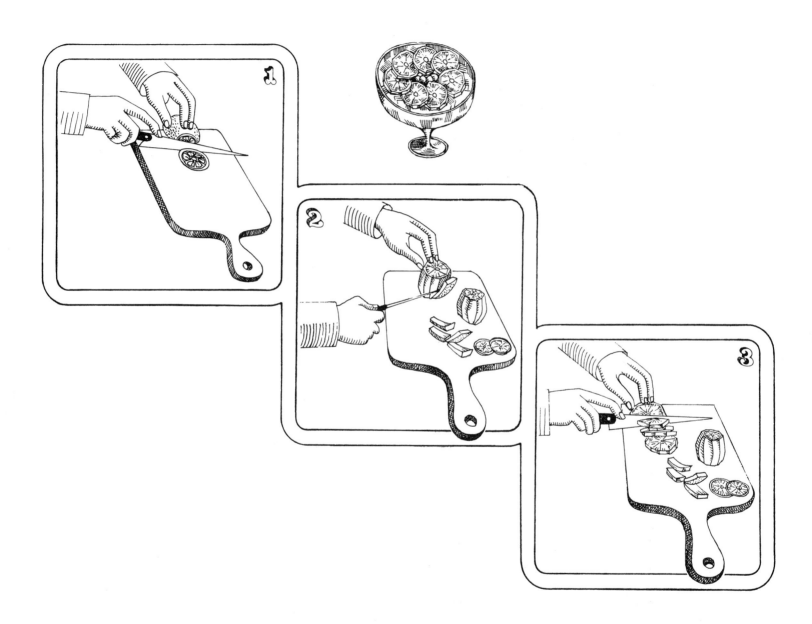

ORANGE MOUSSE

SERVES 8 TO 10

Juice of 9 oranges (3 cups), room temperature
Juice of 2 lemons (⅓ cup)
3 envelopes unflavored gelatin
1 cup sugar, divided into thirds
4 egg whites (¾ cup)
1 pint heavy cream
2 tablespoons Grand Marnier
1 tablespoon Kirschwasser
1 teaspoon vanilla

Combine orange and lemon juice. Pour ½ cup of the juice into a small saucepan. Sprinkle with gelatin and let stand until softened. Heat, stirring, until gelatin is dissolved. Stir hot gelatin mixture into rest of juice. Add ⅓ of the sugar, blend well and chill in refrigerator for about ½ hour—until very slightly thickened. Meanwhile, beat egg

whites until they form soft peaks. Beat in ⅓ cup of sugar. Whip the cream (not too much—it should still flow). Then beat the remaining sugar into the cream. Sprinkle the Grand Marnier, Kirsch, and vanilla over the whipped cream. Pour the slightly jelled juice over the egg whites and blend with whisk or wooden spoon. Fold in the whipped cream.

Let set for 10 to 15 minutes at room temperature. Then fold over a few times from top to bottom, pour into a 3-quart mold and chill (5 hours at least).

To remove from the mold, dip the mold in warm water, count to three slowly, and invert onto a serving platter.

PEARS POACHED
IN RED OR WHITE WINE
(or Just Plain Water)

SERVES 6

Vite et bien! (Quick and good!) The pears should be unripe.

6 pears, peeled whole, with the stem on if possible
4 cloves
1 quart red or white wine or water
2 cups sugar
Juice and thinly peeled rind of 1 lemon

Put the pears into a pot with the rest of the ingredients. Simmer until the pears are soft (45 minutes). Remove the pears to a serving dish. Reduce (boil down) the cooking juice until syrupy. Pour over the pears, cool, and serve.

FRESH PINEAPPLE SHERBET

SERVES 6

This is a light and pretty dessert.

1½ cups sugar
½ cup water
Juice of 2 pineapples
Juice of 1 lemon
⅓ teaspoon salt
3 ounces Kirschwasser (to taste)
4 egg whites

Combine the sugar and water in a saucepan. Dissolve them over low heat. Set aside to cool. Split the pineapples (including the crown) and cut out the meat of the fruit. Scrape out 2 halves and set them in the freezer to harden. Cut the fruit into chunks and place them in the blender. Blend at high speed to purée fruit. Then pass it through a strainer or food mill to remove all the pulp from the juice. Combine the juice with the lemon juice, salt, Kirsch, and sugar syrup.

Pour the mixture into an ice cream freezer. Pack ice and salt around the can (3 quarts crushed ice to one cup rock salt). Turn the freezer on. While the freezer is running, beat the egg whites until they form soft peaks. Stop the freezer when the mixture is partially frozen (slush stage—about 10 minutes). Add the egg whites. Continue turning in the freezer until the mixture has doubled in volume and is fairly firm. Heap the sherbet into the frozen pineapple shells and freeze until serving time.

CHAPTER NINE

Salads

Things must look like what they are. Whenever possible, lettuce leaves should be whole. Fastidious feeders can always fold pieces of lettuce with their forks before eating them. The pieces should be no smaller than a playing card, except for iceberg lettuce, which is best cut into hunks about 1–2 inches in size. Iceberg is such a dense, meaty lettuce that the pieces are fun to bite into; it's a mistake to break it into leaves. The leaves look sort of silly, anyway.

Lettuce must be washed in lots of cold water. If you pack too much of it into a small potful of cold water, the sand will have no room to fall to the bottom of the pot. Be gentle with lettuce; it bruises easily. Push the lettuce around in the water for 3 seconds, then let it rest for a few seconds to give the sand time to fall to the bottom. Push it around again, let it rest, and remove it to a colander; if you have a drain board that slants toward the sink, put the lettuce on it to drain. Rub your hands against the bottom of the pot. If you feel any sand, the lettuce should be washed a second time and even a third time, if there is still sand after the second washing. After the lettuce has drained for 5 minutes on one side in the colander or on the drain board, turn it over so water can drain from the other sides of the leaves. Put several layers of paper towels in your salad bowl. Put half of the drained lettuce on top. Then cover with several more layers of towels and the rest of the lettuce on top. Cover with a few more paper towels and refrigerate, or put the bowl in a cool place until you are ready to serve it. Pull the towels out of the salad and briefly mix the towels with the lettuce to absorb any remaining water. Some leaves will still be damp or wet, but they should be dried as much as possible, because water will dilute the dressing.

A salad must be a thing of beauty. Rather than always using a bowl, try cutting wedges of different kinds of lettuce and arranging them around a plate. Serve the sauce separately.

There are lots of vegetables that are good in a vegetable salad, cooked and uncooked. Here are a few: scallions, red onions, avocado, broccoli, Brussels sprouts, corn, lima beans, celery root, mushrooms, green spinach, fresh peas, and new potatoes. Don't use them all: it would be too confusing. Any combination of six is ample. The orange carrots and red tomatoes are important because they are two of the all too few vegetables from the red end of the color spectrum. Red onion slices are handsome if cut and placed just before serving the salad. Beets taste good, but I don't use them because the red juice gets all over the plate and discolors the other vegetables.

Children love raw vegetables. For adults, serve raw vegetables as hors d'oeuvres, arranged on a platter. Scallions, strips of bell pepper and cucumber, radishes, mushrooms (small and white), cherry tomatoes, branches of cauliflower and broccoli, celery and carrot sticks, fennel, or green squash are all attractive and tasty with cocktails. In the sauce section there is a dip (Russian Dressing, page 51) which is excellent with these raw vegetables and also with shrimp.

Vegetable salads are beautiful and delicious in the summer served with cold poached fish, lobster, and sliced roast meats. Cold roast duck is very good. Cold broiled rack of lamb or leg of lamb, smoked tongue, even a leg of veal for a large group, and, of course, cold roast beef. The cooking of all these meats is the same as if they were to be served hot, except that once they are cool they should be refrigerated for at least 12 hours before serving. Salt the meat before cooking so that its taste will be a part of the crust.

How about dressings for salads? There are many kinds. A dressing of salt, pepper from the grinder, red wine vinegar, and olive oil is the best. It's good on any salad, but I must admit I love Russian Dressing, too. There are recipes for salad dressings in the Sauce section (page 42).

There are so many possibilities for salads, using one main ingredient (other than the dressing) or a variety of ingredients, this is fertile ground for you to exercise your imagination. Do not forget the possibilities of fruits in salad, with sour cream or mayonnaise as a dressing.

ENDIVE SALAD

SERVES 6 TO 8

This salad, imported from Belgium, grows under at least a foot of earth. It's expensive, but well worth the money.

1½ pounds endive
Salt and pepper
¼ cup lemon juice
½ cup olive oil

Trim any brown leaves from the endives. Rinse and dry off with paper towels. Cut each endive in two lengthways. Arrange the halves, round side down, symmetrically on a platter. Sprinkle with salt and pepper. Pour over the lemon juice and then the oil. This salad must be made at least 2 hours or as much as 8 before serving. Keep in a cool place and baste it once or twice.

CHEVILLOT SALAD

If my friend M. Charles Chevillot doesn't mind, I will steal his salad. This is a good combination and it's simple.

2 parts endive cut into thirds crossways, with the stem third cut again in thirds, crossways

TO

1 part watercress (⅔ of stems removed)
A few fresh very white mushrooms, washed, drained, and finely sliced on top

Serve with a plain vinaigrette of salt, pepper, vinegar, and oil.

DANDELION SALAD

SERVES 6

You'll be happy you have dandelions on your lawn. This greatest of all salads should come first in a meal.

1 pound dandelion greens
Water
1½-ounce can anchovies, drained
Salt and pepper
¼ cup wine vinegar
¼ cup olive oil

Wash the dandelions in a large pot in lots of cold water at least three times. Push them around and let them soak for an hour in the first water. After you push them around in the second water, wait for five minutes to allow the dirt and sand that have been dislodged to fall to the bottom of the pot. Lift the dandelions out of the pot with your fingers. Put them into a colander. Wash out the pot, fill it with cold water, and start again. Drain the dandelions, then dry them with a dish towel. Place in a salad bowl. Roughly cut the anchovies and sprinkle them on top. Then add salt and pepper, the vinegar, and oil.

Most lawns will offer an ample supply of dandelions, which should be picked in the early spring as soon as the leaves are green—early April. Come in from the side of the dandelion with a paring knife and hit deep to get the whole root system, which should stay together. Peel down the outer leaves and cut just where the brown root begins.

DANDELION SALAD WITH BACON

SERVES 6

This is a *hot* salad. The rendered fat of the bacon replaces the oil used for cold salads.

1 pound dandelion greens
Salt and pepper
3 tablespoons red wine vinegar
⅓-pound slab bacon

Wash and dry the dandelions as directed in the preceding recipe. Lightly salt and pepper the dandelions. Pour over the vinegar. Remove the rind from the bacon and cut into ½-inch cubes. Fry. When the cubes are golden brown, pour them and ⅓ cup of the rendered fat evenly over the top of the dandelions. Toss and serve as a first course, or as the main course for lunch with cheese and a pastry for dessert.

POTATO SALAD

SERVES 6 TO 8

2 pounds new potatoes
2 scallions, thinly sliced crossways, or 1 teaspoon
 parsley, chopped, or 1 teaspoon chives, chopped
Salt and pepper
3 tablespoons white vinegar
¼ cup peanut oil

Wash, boil, cool, and peel the potatoes. Slice them ¼ inch thick into a bowl. Put in the scallions, finely sliced. Add salt, pepper, vinegar, and oil. Mix and serve.

Never use baking potatoes for potato salad, because they are starchier and drier inside than a boiling potato, and soak up water. When mixed, the slices break up and the salad turns to mush.

TOMATO SALAD

SERVES 6 TO 8

The only way to eat a tomato that is better than described in this recipe would be to eat one right in the garden, picked from the vine and warmed by the sun.

6 ripe, firm tomatoes
2 onions
Salt and pepper
½ cup red wine vinegar
⅔ cup peanut oil
⅓ cup parsley, chopped

Slice the tomatoes less than ¼ inch thick. Arrange them in neat rows on a flat platter with one slice overlapping half of the preceding slice. Throw away the butt ends or keep them for a soup or stock. Peel and slice the onions across the grain. Undo these slices into rings, using your fingers, and arrange them on top of the rows of tomato slices, starting with the large rings and finishing the row with the smallest. Sprinkle liberally with salt (tomatoes can take a lot of salt), and a good grind of pepper over all. Pour the vinegar and then the oil evenly over the top. Let the salad rest in a cool place (but not in the refrigerator), for at least one hour before serving. Tip the platter and baste the tomatoes with a kitchen spoon at least once during the hour's rest. Sprinkle them with parsley before serving.

SALADE NICOISE
SERVES 6 TO 8

This is complicated, but it looks beautiful and tastes very good.

1½ cups olive oil
¾ cup red wine vinegar
2 prepared artichoke hearts (see page 163)
½ pound Mushrooms à la Grecque (see page 162)
½ cup black olives, chopped
4 whole scallions, minced
1 red bell pepper, chopped, or 8 cherry tomatoes, halved
¼ cup capers, drained
1 red onion, minced
8 anchovies, chopped
2 cloves garlic, finely chopped
Salt and pepper
1 hard-boiled egg, quartered
4 radishes, sliced

Use a glass serving bowl—glass because you can see more of the salad, which is pretty. Put the olive oil and vinegar into it. Then add all the other ingredients, except the egg and radishes. Let them marinate for several hours at room temperature. Place the egg and radishes around the top before it is served. This salad goes with cold poached fish.

VEGETABLE SALAD

SERVES 12 TO 16

In this salad you could put a large, cooked cauliflower in the center with whole and very green string beans around it or on either side. A pile of carrots would go well on either side of the string beans.

12 scallions
2 cucumbers
6 endives
3 pounds string beans
2 stalks celery
1 pint cherry tomatoes
2 pounds new potatoes
1 pound Brussels sprouts
3 heads romaine lettuce
2 bell peppers
2 carrots
1 medium-sized red onion

Snip the roots and most of the upper leaves off the scallions and wash. Set aside.

Wash cucumbers and score the sides with the tines of a fork. Cut into slices ¼ inch thick. Set aside.

Pare any brown from the roots of the endives and remove any brown outer leaves. Cut in half lengthways and set aside.

To retain the green, boil the string beans in at least 2 gallons of water (unsalted), in at least two batches. The water must be boiling hard so that, when the beans are added, the water barely stops boiling (pot should be covered). Cool the beans immediately in cold water when they are removed from pot. Drain and set aside.

Remove the outer branches of the celery, keeping only the white heart of the stalk. Cut these small white branches in half lengthways. Set aside.

Pick the stems off the cherry tomatoes, wash, and set aside.

Peel and cut the potatoes to size, paring sharp corners to give the potatoes an oval shape. Boil, cool, and set aside.

Cut the brown from the stems of the Brussels sprouts, removing the outer wilted leaves. Put into one quart of boiling water. Simmer for no more than 15 minutes and freshen under cold running water. Set aside.

Cut some of the root system from the lettuce and remove all of the outer leaves, keeping just the hearts of the lettuce. Cut in quarters lengthways. Wash, drain, and set aside.

Cut bell peppers in half, top to bottom. Discard seed pod. Cut into vertical slices, ¼ inch wide. Wash and set aside.

Peel and cut the carrots crossways. Slice them as finely as possible. Wash and set aside.

Peel the onions and cut into thin slices to decorate the salad.

Beginning with the cauliflower described in the introduction to this recipe, continue placing the vegetables, alternating shapes and colors. The onion slices are handsome if they are cut and placed just before serving the salad.

Place the endive and romaine lettuce around the vegetables, again keeping in mind shapes and colors so that each vegetable will complement the other.

Index

Abadie, Pierre, 91
Almonds, Sauce Amandine, 45
Anchovy Butter, 56
Appearance, the Menu and, 13
Apple Beignet, 107
Apple Corers, 26
Apple Glaze, 138
Apple Pie Tatin, 96–97
Apple Tart Flambé aux Calvados, 94
Apples,
    Baked, 96–97, 138
    Selecting, 138
Arrowroot, 34
Artichoke Surprise, 163
Artichoke Vinaigrette, 163
    Sauce for, 50
Asparagus, 164
    Soup, Cream of, 33
Aspic Coating for Cold Poached Fish, 150–151

Baked Alaska, 99
Baked Apple Garnish, 138
Baked Apple Glaze, 138
Baking; Baked Foods, 87–99
    Apple Garnish, 138
    Apple Glaze, 138
    Apple Tart Flambé aux Calvados, 94
    Baked Alaska, 99
    Cheese Ramekins à la Crème, 94–95
    Clams with Escargot Butter, 89
    Crab Meat Norfolk, 88
    Délice Lyonnaise, 95–96
    Eggplant, 91
    Escargots, 88
    Fruit, Mixed, 97
    Genoise, 95
    Mousse of Fillets of Sole, 155
    Mushroom Caps, Stuffed, 90
    Mussels with Escargot Butter, 89
    Porgy au Gratin, 89–90
    Pears, 97–99
        in Custard Tart, 96
    Pie Crust, French, 92–93
    Potatoes, 91
        Boulangère, 91
        Gratin Dauphinoise, 92
    Quiche Lorraine, 93–94
    Snails (Escargots), 88

Sole Mousse, 155
Spinach Timbales, 90
Baking Dishes, 27
Bass,
    Poached Fillets, 152–153
    Poached Whole, 148–149
    Stock, 31
Batter,
    Beignet, 106–107
    Crêpe, 126
Béarnaise Sauce, 47
Beaters, 23
Béchamel Sauce, Described, 44
Beef,
    Boiled, 158
        Discussed, 145
    Bone Marrow on Toast, 160
    Braised, 136–137
        Discussed, 129, 130
    Broiling of Steak, 58–59
    Roast Ribs of, 83–84
    Roasting Discussed, 11–12, 64
    Sautéed Steak, 117–118
    Selecting, 17
    Shallot Sauce for, 44–45
    Stock, 30
        Consommé of, 33
    Tongue with Creole Sauce, Smoked, 159–160
    Tripe Lyonnaise, 160–161
Beignets,
    Apple, 107
    Batter for, 106–107
    Eggplant, 106
Beurre Blanc, 45–46
Beurre Maître d'Hôtel, 45
Beurre Manié, 44
Beurre Travaillé, 43
Bisque, Lobster, 34
Black Butter Sauce, 156
    for Calves' Brains, 117
    for Calves' Liver, 116–117
    for Fried Eggs, 119
Blanquette de Veau, 157–158
Blenders, 23
Bluefish, Broiled, with Anchovy Butter, 55–56
Boiling; Boiled Foods, 145–175
    Artichoke Surprise, 163
    Artichoke Vinaigrette, 163

Asparagus, 164
Beef, 158
Blanquette de Veau, 157–158
Bone Marrow on Toast, 160
Broccoli, 164
Broccoli Rabe, 165
Carrots,
    Glazed, 166
    Vichy, 165
Cauliflower, 166
    with Browned Bread Crumbs, 166–167
Chicken, 156–157
Eggs, Poached, 162
Fish, Poached, 11, 148–149
    Cold, 149–150
    Cold, Aspic Coating for, 150–151
    Cold, Decorating Whole, 150
    Court Bouillon for, 148–149
    Fillets, 152–153
    Whole, 148–149
    Whole, Decorating, 150
Ham, Parslied, 161
Irish Stew, 158–159
Kohlrabi, 169
Lamb Stew, Irish, 158–159
Marrow on Toast, 160
Mushrooms à la Grecque, 162
Mussels Marinière, 147–148
Orange à l'Arabe, 172
Orange Mousse, 174
Parsnips, 169
Pears, Poached in Red or White Wine, 174
Peas, Mama's, 170
Periwinkles, 147
Pineapple Sherbet, 175
Potatoes, 170
    Mashed, 170–171
    Riced, 171
Ray with Black Butter, 156
Rice, 171
Sausage, Polish, 161–162
Spaghetti, Granny's, 172
Tongue with Creole Sauce, Smoked, 159–160
Tripe Lyonnaise, 160–161
Veal, Blanquette de Veau, 157–158
Bone Marrow on Toast, 160
Bouillabaisse, Discussed, 145

Bouillon, 33
    Court, 148–149
Bowls, 13
    Mixing, 26
Brains with Black Butter, Calves', 117
Braising; Braised Foods, 129–143
    Beef, 136–137
    Cabbage, Chestnuts with Red, 139
    Celery, 139–140
    Chicken à la Crème Tarragon, 131
    Lamb Navarin, 135
    Lettuce, 140
    Pork with Baked Apples, 137–138
    Potatoes Fondantes, 141
    Ratatouille Niçoise, 141–143
    Squash, Butternut, 141
    Veal,
        and Kidneys Cinzano, 133–134
        Paupiettes, 134
        Rolled Shoulder of, 132–133
Bread Crumbs, Browned, 166–167
Bread Knives, 26
Broccoli, 164
Broccoli Rabe, 165
Broilers, 23
Broiling; Broiled Foods, 53–61
    Bluefish with Anchovy Butter, 55–56
    Chicken, 59
    Finnan Haddie, 58
    Kidneys, 60
    Lamb,
        Kidneys, 60
        Rack of, 59–60
    Lobster, 55
    Pork Chops, 61
    Shad, 57
    Shad Roe,
        with Bacon, 56–57
        Canapé, 57
    Sweetbreads, 60–61
    Swordfish,
        Amandine, 58
        Steak, 58–59
    Tomatoes, 61
    Veal Kidney, 60
Broth, Discussed, 33
Brown Stock, 32
    Discussed, 29, 30
Butternut Squash, Braised, 141
Butters; Butter Sauces, 43, 44–47
    Anchovy, 56
    Beurre Blanc, 45–46
    Beurre Mâitre d'Hôtel, 45
    Beurre Manié, 44

Black, 156
    for Calves' Brains, 117
    for Calves' Liver, 116–117
    for Fried Eggs, 119
Escargots, 88
    Clams with, 89
    Mussels with, 89
Lemon,
    Dip, 147
    for Sole Mousse, 155

Cabbage, Chestnuts with Red, 139
Cakes,
    for Baked Alaska, 99
    Baking, Discussed, 87
    Genoise, 95
California, University of, at Los Angeles,
    8–9
Calves' Liver; etc. See Veal
Camp Cook (California), 3–4
Camp Schimmelpfennig (Sendai, Japan), 4
Can Openers, 26
Canapé, Broiled Shad Roe, 57
Canisters, 23
Carrots, 14
    Garnish for Duck Grandmère, 75
    Glazed, 166
    Vichy, 165
Casseroles, 26
Cauliflower, 166
    with Browned Bread Crumbs, 166–167
    Soup, Cold, 36–37
Celery, Braised, 139–140
Chalet Froscati (Santa Monica, Calif.), 8
Charcoal Broiling. See Broiling; Broiled
    Foods
Charcoal Grills, 53, 54
Charpentier, Henry, 126
Cheese Dressing, Roquefort, 51
Cheese Ramekins à la Crème, 94–95
Chestnut Stuffing, 66
Chestnuts with Red Cabbage, 139
Chevillot, Charles, 179
Chevillot Salad, 179
Chicken,
    Boiled, 156–157
        Discussed, 145
    Braising, Discussed, 129
    Broiled, 59
        Discussed, 53
    Broth, Consommé Bellevue with, 34–35
    Coq au Vin, 113–114
    à la Crème Tarragon, 131

Deep-Fat Fried, Discussed, 101
    Liver Pâté Truffles, 114–115
    Roast, 65
        Discussed, 64
    Selecting, 17
    Soup, Cream of, 33
    Stock,
        Bones for, 30
        for White, 31–32
    for Veal Breast Stuffing, 77–78
    Veal Paupiettes with, 134
Chowder,
    Clam, 35–36
    Scallop, Bay, 35
Clam Chowder, 35–36
Clam Juice, Consommé Bellevue with, 34–
    35
Clams with Escargot Butter, 89
Clarification, 33
Cod, Poached Fillets of, 152–153
Colanders, 26
Color, 12
Consistency, the Menu and, 13
Consommé, 33
    Bellevue, 34–35
Cookies, Baking of, 87
Cooking, Defined, 11
Coq au Vin, 113–114
Corkscrews, 26
Cornstarch, 42
Counters, 21, 23
Court Bouillon for Poaching Fish, 148–149
Crab Meat Norfolk, 88
Cream, 14
    Sour, 21
Creole Sauce, 49
Crêpes au Confiture, 125
Crêpes Suzette, 126–127
Croutons, 42
Cups,
    Custard, 27
    Measuring, 26
Custard,
    Cups, 27
    Quiche Lorraine, 93–94
    Tart, Pears in, 96

Dandelion Salad, 179–180
    with Bacon, 180
Deep-Fat Frying; Fried Foods, 11, 101–107
    Apple Beignet, 107
    Beignets, 106–107
        Apple, 107

Beignets (*continued*)
  Batter, 106–107
  Eggplant, 106
  Eggplant Beignet, 106
  Potato Chips, 103–104
  Potatoes,
    Dauphine, 104
    French-Fried, 105–106
    Souffléed, 104–105
  Whitebait, 103
  Whiting en Colère, 103
Deer. *See also* Venison
  Bones for Stock, 30
Délice Lyonnaise, 95–96
Demi-Glaze, 32
Desserts,
  Baked Alaska, 99
  Crêpes Suzette, 126–127
  Délice Lyonnaise, 95–96
  Fruit, Baked Mixed, 97
  Fruit with Four Liqueurs, 20
  Fruit, Selecting, 20
  Genoise, 95
  Orange à l'Arabe, 172
  Orange Mousse, 174
  Pears,
    Baked, 97–99
    in Custard Tart, 96
    Poached in Red or White Wine, 174
  Pineapple Sherbet, 175
  Strawberries, Fresh, 20
Dippers, 26
Drainboards, 23
Duck,
  Frozen, 17
  Grandmère, 74–75
  à l'Orange, 71–74
  Roasting, Discussed, 64

Egg and Lemon Soup, Greek, Discussed, 33
Egg Yolks, 21
Eggplant,
  Baked, 91
  Beignet, 106
  Ratatouille with, 141–143
  Sautéed, 120
Eggs,
  with Black Butter, Fried, 119
  Poached, 162
Endive Meunière, 119–120
Endive Salad, 179
Equipment, Kitchen, 23–27

Escargot Butter, 88
  Clams with, 89
  Mussels with, 89
Escargots, 88

Finnan Haddie, Broiled, 58
  Discussed, 54
Fish and Shellfish. *See also* specific fish, etc.
  Boiling Seafood, 145
  Bouillabaisse, Discussed, 145
  Braising of, 129–130
  Broiling of, 54
  Poached, 11, 148–149
    Cold, 149–150
    Cold, Aspic Coating for, 150–151
    Cold, Decorating Whole, 150
    Cold, Green Sauce for, 48
    Court Bouillon for, 148–149
    Fillet of Sole Bonne Femme, 155
    Fillets, 152–153
    Whole, 148–149
    Whole, Decorating, 150
  Poachers, 27
  Sautéing, 109, 110
  Selecting, 17
  Soup, Cream of, 33
  Stock, 31
    Discussed, 30
Floors, Kitchen, 23
Flounder,
  Meunière, Fillet of, 112
  Mousse of Fillets of, 155
  Poached Fillets, 152–153
  Stock, 31
Flour, 21
Fluke,
  Meunière, Fillet of, 112
  Stock, 31
Food Mills, 26
Forks, Two-Pronged, 26
Formica, 23
France, 5–8
Freezing; Frozen Meat, 17
French-Fryers, 27
French Frying. *See* Deep-Fat Frying
French Pie Crust, 92–93
Frogs' Legs Provençal, 112–113
Fruit. *See also* Pears; etc.
  Baked Mixed, 97
  with Four Liqueurs, 20
  Selecting, 20
Frying. *See* Deep-Fat Frying; Sautéing

Frying Pans, 26
Fun, the Menu and, 13

Gadgets, 26
Gage and Tollner's (Brooklyn), 53
Garbage Disposals, 23
Garnishes, 13–14
  for Duck Grandmère, 75
  for Sauces,
Gazpacho, 37
Gelatin,
  Aspic Coating for Cold Poached Fish,
    150–151
  Parslied Ham, 161
  and Stocks, 29, 30
Generosity, 14
Genoise, 95
Giblet Sauce, 67
Glazed Foods. *See* specific Foods
Glazes,
  Apple, 138
  Meat, 33
Goosefat, 64
Granny's Spaghetti, 172
Grapefruit Knives, 26
Graters, 26
Gravy. *See* specific Meats
Green Sauce for Cold Poached Fish, 48

Halibut,
  Poached Fillets, 152–153
  Stock, 31
Ham, Parslied, 161
Herbs, 21
Hibachi Stoves, 54
Hollandaise Sauce, 46–47
  Discussed, 43
Horseradish Sauce,
  for Boiled Beef, 158
  Cold, 48
Hotel Raleigh (Washington, D. C.), 2–3
Hotel Statler (New York), 5

Ice Cream, Baked Alaska, 99
Irish Stew, 158–159

Japan, 4
Jupiter Island Golf Club Restaurant (Hobe
  Sound, Fla.), 8

Kidneys,
    Broiled (Veal or Lamb), 60
        Discussed, 53
    and Veal Cinzano, 133–134
    Veal Kidneys Bordelaise, 116
Kirschwasser, 20
Kitchen, the, 23–27
Knives, 26
Kohlrabi, 169
Korea, 4
Kosher Salt, 21

Lamb,
    Broiled,
        Chops, Discussed, 53
        Kidneys, 60
        Rack of, 59–60
    Gravy, 60
    Kidneys, Broiled, 60
    Navarin, 135
    Roast,
        Leg of, 78–79
        Sauce for, 42
        Saddle of, 79–82
    Selecting, 17
    Stew,
        Irish, 158–159
        Navarin, 135
    Stock, 29, 30
Leek and Potato Soup, 37–38
    Vichyssoise, 40
Lemon Butter,
    Dip, 147
    Sole Mousse with, 155
Lemons, 20
Lettuce,
    Braised, 140
    Salad, 177
Liver,
    with Black Butter, Calves', 116–117
    Pâté Truffles, Chicken, 114–115
Lobster,
    Bisque, 34
    Boiling, Discussed, 26
    Broiled, 55
        Discussed, 54
    Stock, 31

Mama's Peas, 170
Marrow on Toast, 160
Martha's Vineyard, 1–2

Mayonnaise, 47–48
    Described, 44
Meat. See also Beef; etc.
    Boiling, 145–146
    Braising, 129–130
    Broiling, 53–54
    General Information, 17
    Glaze, 33
    Roasting, 11–12, 63–85
    Salting, 30
    Sautéing, 12, 109, 110
    Stocks, 29, 30
Melon, Selecting, 20
Menus, Simple, 13
Mercies, Paul, 7
Meringue Desserts,
    Baked Alaska, 99
    Délice Lyonnaise, 95–96
Mirepoix, 64, 67
Misqamicut Club (Watch Hill, R. I.), 8
Mores, Jean, 3
Mousse of Fillets of Sole, 155
Mushroom Soup, Cream of, 33
Mushrooms,
    Garnish for Duck Grandmère, 74–75
    à la Grecque, 162
    Sautéed, 119
    Stuffed Caps, 90
Mussels,
    with Escargot Butter, 89
    Marinière, 147–148
Mustard, 161

Newburg Sauce, 50

Onions, as Garnish for Duck Grandmère, 75
Orange à l'Arabe, 172
Orange Mousse, 174
Orange Sauce for Duck, 71
Ovens, 23–24
Oyster Stew, 36

Palisade, N. Y., 9
Pancakes. See Crêpes
Pans, 26–27
Parsley, 13–14
    Deep-Fat Fried, 102
    in Stock, 29
Parslied Ham, 161
Parsnips, 169
Partridges, Roast, 75–76

Pastry Brushes, 26
Pâté, Chicken Liver, Truffles, 114–115
Pâté à Choux, 104
Pea Soup Saint Germain, 40–41
Peaches, Sauce for, 20
Pears,
    Baked, 97–99
    in Custard Tart, 96
    Poached in Red or White Wine, 174
Peas, Mama's, 170
Pepper, 21
Peppers, Ratatouille with, 141–143
Periwinkles, 147
Pie,
    Apple, Tatin, 96–97
    Crust, French, 92–93
    Quiche Lorraine, 93–94
Pike,
    Poached Fillets, 152–153
    Poached Whole, 148
Pigeons,
    Roast, 75–76
    Selecting, 17
Pineapple Sherbet, Fresh, 175
Platters, 14
Poaching. See Boiling; Boiled Foods
Point, Fernand, 7, 8, 9
Polish Sausage, 161–162
Porgy au Gratin, 89–90
Pork,
    Braised, with Baked Apples, Glazed, 137–138
    Broiled Chops, 61
        Discussed, 53
    Roast, 84–85
        Discussed, 64
    Selecting, 17
    for Veal Breast Stuffing, 77–78
Potato Chips, 103–104
Potato Peelers, 26
Potato Salad, 180
Potato Soup, Leek and, 37–38
    Vichyssoise, 40
Potatoes,
    Baked, 91
    Boiled, 170
    Boulangère, 91
    Dauphine, 104
    Deep-Fat Fried, 101–102, 103–106
    Fondantes, 141
    French-Fried, 105–106
    Gratin Dauphinoise, 92
    Hashed Brown, 120–121
    Mashed, 170–171

Potatoes (*continued*)
    Paillasson, 121
    Parisienne, 124
    Riced, 171
    Rissolé, 124
    Sablés, 124–125
    Sautéed, 120–125
    Souffléed, 104–105
Pots, 26, 27

Quiche Lorraine, 93–94

Ramekins, 27
Ratatouille Niçoise, 141–143
Ray with Black Butter, 156
Red Cabbage, Chestnuts with, 139
Red Snapper,
    Poached Fillets, 152–153
    Poached Whole, 148
Refrigerators, 23
Restaurant Chez Nandron (Lyons), 5–7
Restaurant de la Pyramid Chez Point
    (Lyons), 7–8
Rice, Boiled, 171
Ring Molds, 27
Rissolé Potatoes, 124
Roasting; Roasted Meats, 63–85
    Beef, Ribs of, 83–84
    Chicken, 65
    Duck Grandmère, 74–75
    Duck à l'Orange, 71–74
    Lamb,
        Leg of, 78–79
        Saddle of, 79–82
    Pigeons, 75–76
    Pork, 84–85
    Turkey, with Chestnut Dressing, 65–67
    Veal,
        Breast, Stuffed, 77–78
        Leg of, 76–77
Roe, Broiled Shad,
    with Bacon, 56–57
    Canapé, 57
Rolling Pins, 26
Roquefort Dressing, 51
Russian Dressing, 51

Salade Niçoise, 181
Salads and Salad Dressings, 177–182
    Chevillot, 179
    Dandelion, 179–180
        with Bacon, 180

Endive, 179
    Niçoise, 181
    on Menu, 13
    Potato, 180
    Roquefort Dressing, 51
    Russian Dressing, 51
    Tomato, 180–181
    Vegetable, 182
        Suggestions for, 177–178
    Vinaigrette Dressing, 49–50
Salmon, Poached Whole, 148
Salt, 21
Sauces, 29, 42–51
    Amandine, 45
    Béarnaise, 47
    Beurre Blanc, 45–46
    Beurre Mâitre d'Hôtel, 45
    Beurre Manié, 44
    Braising and, 129–130
    Butter. *See* Butters; Butter Sauces
    Coq au Vin, 113
    Creole, 49
    for Délice Lyonnaise, 96
    for Duck,
        Grandmère, 75
        Orange, 71
    Fruit, 20
    Green, for Cold Poached Fish, 48
    Hollandaise, 46–47
        Described, 43
    Horseradish,
        for Boiled Beef, 158
        Cold, 48
    Lemon Butter,
        Dip, 147
        for Sole Mousse, 155
    Mayonnaise, 47–48
        Discussed, 44
    Mousseline, 47
    Newburg, 50
    Niçoise, 181
    Orange, for Duck, 71
    Reducing, for Flavor, 43
    Roquefort Dressing, 51
    Russian Dressing, 51
    Shallot, for Beef, 44–45
    Strawberry, 20
    Thickening, 42
    for Turkey, 67
    Vinaigrette, 49–50
        for Artichokes, 50
Sausage,
    Chestnut Stuffing with, 66
    Polish, 161–162

Sautéing; Sautéed Foods, 11, 12, 109–127
    Beef Steak, 117–118
    Brains in Black Butter, Calves', 117
    Chicken,
        Coq au Vin, 113–114
        Liver Pâté Truffles, 114–115
    Coq au Vin, 113–114
    Crêpes au Confiture, 125
    Crêpes Suzette, 126–127
    Eggplant, 120
    Eggs with Black Butter, 119
    Endive Meunière, 119–120
    Frogs' Legs Provençal, 112–113
    Kidneys Bordelaise, Veal, 115
    Liver,
        with Black Butter, Calves', 116–117
        Pâté Truffles, Chicken, 114–115
    Mushrooms, 119
    Potatoes,
        Hashed Brown, 120–121
        Paillasson, 121
        Parisienne, 124
        Rissolé, 124
        Sablés, 124–125
    Scallops Meunière, 111
    Sole,
        Bonne Femme, Fillet of, 155
        Meunière, Fillet of, 112
    Steak, 117–118
        Time Chart for, 118
    Tomatoes, Cherry, 125
    Veal, 115–117
        Brains in Black Butter, 117
        Kidneys Bordelaise, 116
        Liver in Black Butter, 116–117
        Scallops à la Crème, 115
    Zucchini, 120
Savin, Gilles, 5, 7
Scallop Chowder, Bay, 35
Scallops Sauté Meunière, Bay, 111
Schifeler, Kurt, 2
Scoops, 26
Scrapers, Rubber, 26
Scup au Gratin, 89–90
Shad, Broiled, 57
    with Bacon and Shad Roe, 56–57
Shad Roe, Broiled,
    with Bacon, 56–57
    Canapé, 57
Shallot Sauce for Beef, 44–45
Shapes, Menu and, 12–13
Sherbet, Pineapple, 175
Shiners. *See* Whitebait
Sieves, 26

Simmering, 30
Sinks, 23
Snails, 88
Snapper,
    Poached Fillets of Red, 152–153
    Poached Whole Red, 148–149
    Stock, 31
Sole,
    Bonne Femme, Fillet of, 155
    Meunière, Fillet of, 112
    Mousse of Fillets of, 155
    Poached Fillets, 152–153
    Stock, 31
Soltaer, André, 96
Souffléed Potatoes, 104–105
Soups, 33–42
    Cauliflower, Cold, 36–37
    Clam Chowder, 35–36
    Consommé Bellevue, 34–35
    Croutons for, 42
    Gazpacho, 37
    Leek and Potato, 37–38
        Vichyssoise, 40
    Lobster Bisque, 34
    Oyster Stew, 36
    Pea, Saint Germain, 40–41
    Potato and Leek, 37–38
        Vichyssoise, 40
    Scallop Chowder, 35
    Vichyssoise, 40
Squabs, Roast, 75–76
Squash. See also Zucchini
    Braised Butternut, 141
Spaghetti, Granny's, 172
Spatulas, 26
Spinach, 14
    Timbale, 90
Spoons, 26
Steam, Braising and, 146
Steaming, 29–30
Stewing. See Braising; Braised Foods
Stocks, 29–30
    Brown, 32
    Demi-Glaze, 32
    Fish, 31
    Lobster, 31
    Meat Glaze, 33
    Turkey, 65–66
    White, 31–32
Stoves, 23–24
    Baking and, 87
Strainers, 26
Strawberries, 20
    Sauce, 20

Striped Bass,
    Poached Fillets, 152–153
    Poached Whole, 148
Stuffing, Chestnut, 66
Sugar, 21
Sweetbreads,
    Braising, Discussed, 129
    Broiled, 60–61
Swordfish,
    Amandine, 58
    Broiled Thick Steak, Charcoal-, 58–59
    Broiling, Discussed, 53, 54

Tables, 21
Tarts,
    Apple, Flambé aux Calvados, 94
    Pears in Custard, 96
Taste, 14
Tempesti, Dino, 6
Timbale, Spinach, 90
Time Charts,
    for Beef,
    for Roasting,
        Beef Ribs, 84
        Chicken, 65
        Duck, 74
        Lamb, Leg of, 79
        Lamb, Saddle of, 82
        Pork, 85
        Turkey, 67
        Veal, Leg of, 77
        Veal, Stuffed Breast of, 78
    for Sautéing, 118
Toasters, 23
Tomato Salad, 180–181
Tomatoes,
    Broiled, 61
    Ratatouille with, 141–143
    Sautéed Cherry, 125
Tongs, 26
Tongue,
    Boiled Beef, 158
    with Creole Sauce, Smoked, 159–160
Tools, Kitchen, 23–27
Tripe Lyonnaise, 160–161
Trout, Poached Whole, 148–149
Turkey,
    Braising, Discussed, 129
    Roast, with Chestnut Dressing, 65–67
    Roasting, Discussed, 64
    Stock, 65–66

Utensils, 26–27

Veal,
    Blanquette de Veau, 157–158
    Brains in Black Butter, Calves', 117
    Braised Rolled Shoulder of, 132–133
    Braising, Discussed, 129
    Kidneys,
        Bordelaise, 116
        Broiled, 60
        Cinzano, 133–134
    Liver with Black Butter, Calves', 116–117
    Paupiettes of, 134
    Roast Leg of, 76–77
    Roast Stuffed Breast of, 77–78
    Roasting, Discussed, 64
    Sautéed, 115
    Scallops à la Crème, 115
    Selecting, 17
    Stew, Blanquette de Veau, 157–158
    for Stock, 30
        Brown, 32
        White, 31–32
Vegetable Salad, 182
    Suggestions for, 177–178
Vegetable Soup, Gazpacho, 37
Vegetables. See also Broccoli; Cabbage; etc.
    Boiling, 29, 145, 146
    Braising, 129, 130
    Garnish for Duck Grandmère, 74–75
    Mirepoix, 64, 67
    Ratatouille Niçoise, 141–143
    Sautéed, 109, 110
    Selecting, 17–19
    in Stocks, 29
Velouté, 33
Venison, Braising Discussed, 129
Vichyssoise, 40
Vinaigrette, 49–50
    for Artichokes, 50
    Dip, 147

Watercress, 13–14
Whisks, 26
White Stock, 31–32
    Discussed, 29–30
Whitebait, 11
    Deep-Fat Fried, 103
Whitefish, Mousse of Fillets of, 155
Whiting en Colère, 103
Wine, 21

Zucchini,
    Ratatouille with, 141–143
    Sautéed, 120